Down Memory Lane

Volume I
July 24, 1927 to 1948

by
Shri Parthasarathi Rajagopalachari

President
Shri Ram Chandra Mission

First Edition: July 24, 1993, 1000 Copies

All rights reserved

© Shri Ram Chandra Mission
North American Publishing Committee
Pacific Grove, CA, USA, 1993

No part of this book may be reproduced in any form or by any means without permission in writing from Shri Ram Chandra Mission.

Printed in U.S.A.

ISBN 0-945242-23-9

Bill Lahics

Down Memory Lane

Volume I

July 24, 1927 to 1948

Parthasarathi Rajagopalachari - 1948

Contents

Down Memory Lane

I	My Mother	1
II	My Grandparents	17
III	My Elder Generation	55
IV	Appa	97
V	The Early Years	179
VI	The Pleasures of School Education	253
VII	Growing Up in Calcutta	279
VIII	Life Besides the Ganges at Benares	309

Family Trees
of
Parthasarathi Rajagopalachari

Descendants of Viraraghava Iyengar (Father's Family)

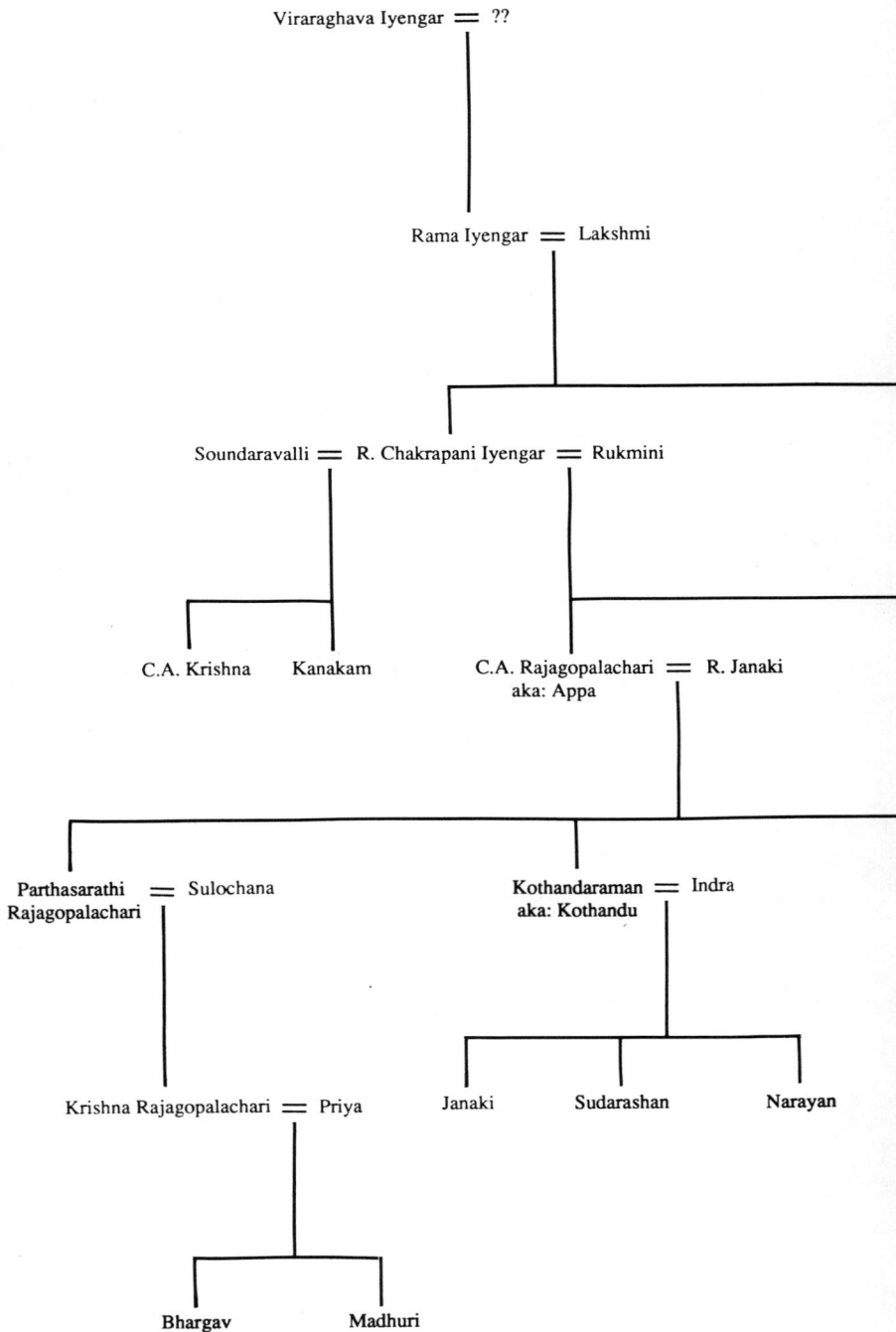

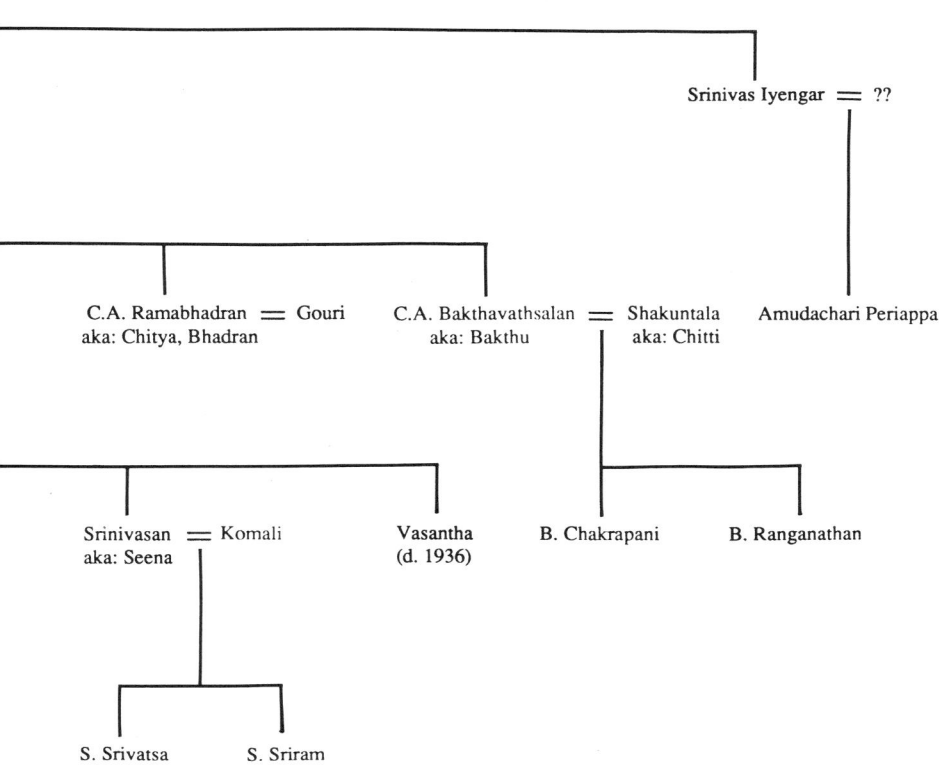

Descendants of T. Ramanuja Iyengar (Mother's Family)

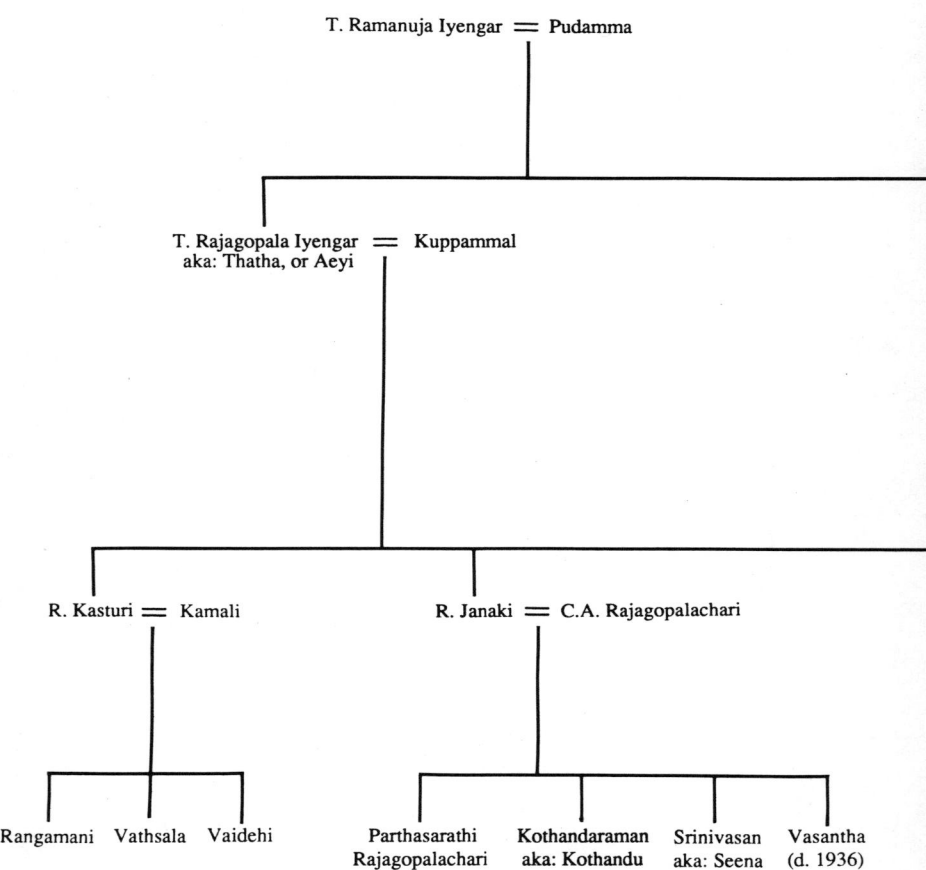

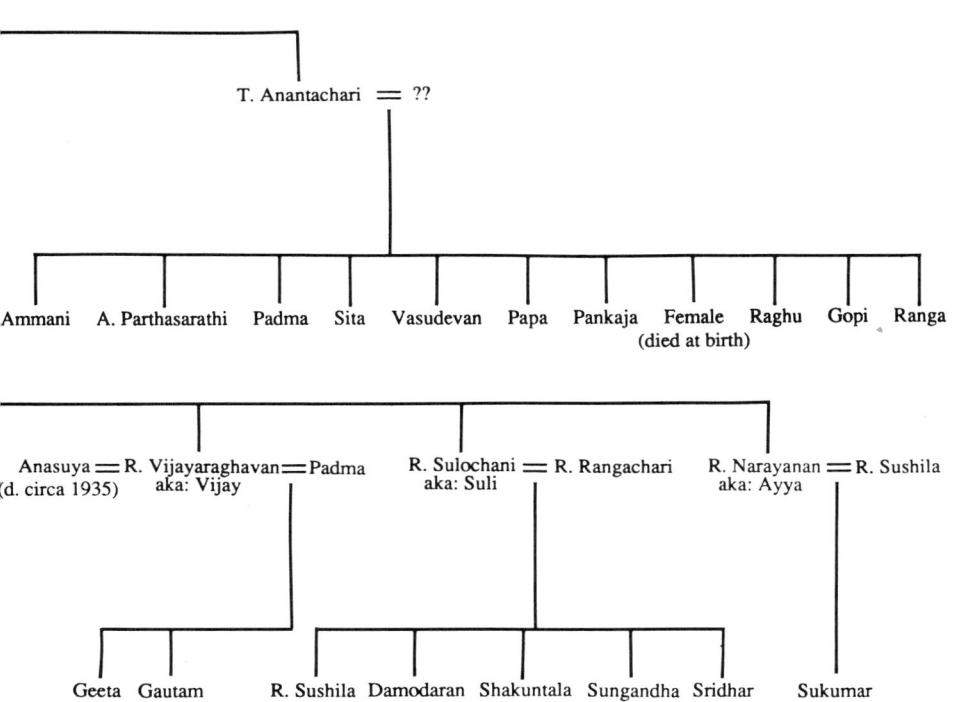

Janaki - 1925

I

My Mother

My Mother

As I look back upon my life from the lofty eminence of sixty-five years, geriatrically speaking of course, the earliest memory that I am able to draw out of my inner self is that of my beloved mother, Janaki. I see her lying stiff and motionless in a long, rectangular receptacle, packed with ice, surrounded by a large number of weeping adults of all ages. I was sorry for her, thinking how cold she must feel, packed in that fashion with all that ice around her, and this made me weep too. I naturally assumed that all the others were weeping for the same reason. Since I was only five years old, I had no knowledge of death.

My mother had been delivered of her fourth child less than a fortnight earlier. My only sister had been born, and all had been well with the mother and the new born baby. The delivery was conducted by a local midwife and there had been no difficulty at all. Everyone was happy that a female child had arrived, since her first three children were all boys. On the 10th day after her delivery, my mother was given a ritual purificatory bath in cold water, out in the open yard. This was the custom, because the act of child birth was considered to create some sort of religious pollution, called *theetu* in Tamil, and this required ritual purification as specified in the *shastras*. Among the Brahmins of south India, most of the natural occurrences involving life and death require such ritual purification, and a bath is the preparation for the first of those rituals to follow. The rituals are differentiated by calling them as 'growth' in the case of birth, and 'decay' where death rudely intrudes. It was therefore perfectly natural for my mother to be subjected to this ritual.

However, since she had her bath out in the open, my mother immediately caught a cold. This seems to have been neglected as a 'mere cold' and before anyone was even aware of it, it had developed into the dreaded pneumonia. In those days — and we are now in the thirties, let it be remembered — there were no antibiotics or such remedies. She must have been treated with domestic medication like hot fomentation, herbal decoctions and the like, but these were powerless to stem the course of the disease. My dear mother was gone a few days later, before anyone even realised that there was something serious, and that death had been knocking at her door for some time. Poor, dear girl — for she was hardly more than a girl — she was the victim of crass superstition, and her young life was snuffed out like a candle. According to my reckoning, she could certainly not have been more than twenty-two or twenty-three years old at the time, and she already a mother of four children! My father himself was only twenty-eight years old when he became a widower. I was the eldest of her four children, and this last baby, this unfortunate girl who grew up motherless, was later named Vasantha. This tragedy occurred on the 25th day of May 1933, a few months before my seventh birthday.

I have heard a second version of her death. This version says that she ate some rice preparation which went into the making of *vatthals* and was called *koozhu*. As a result of this she had a stomach upset, and developed fever a day or so later. This fever was perhaps not taken seriously, and it developed into the much feared pneumonia. Then followed the sad and miserable sequence of events culminating in her departure from her mortal existence. Since the first version was related to me by none other than my own father, I believe it to be the

My Mother

more accurate version. I do not doubt that the other version has at least partial veracity, and that perhaps something my mother ate did disagree with her. Whatever is the truth, the end was tragic beyond imagination, for it left four children between the age of less than six years to a baby of a few days only, all motherless.

My mother had gone to her parents' home in Tuticorin, deep down in the south of India, in the then Madras Presidency. My father was in Bombay, where he was a clerk in the accounts department of the Great Indian Peninsula Railway which, much later, became the Central Railway. My mother's death being sudden and unforeseen, my father was informed by telegram. He left Bombay at once, but train travel in India has always been long and time-consuming, and he reached Tuticorin only three days after my mother had expired. The body had to be preserved to await his arrival — hence the wooden, lead-lined coffin packed with ice. I can remember seeing my father break down completely as he staggered into the room where my mother was. He was always a strong man, but the loss of his own mother on the 11th of July 1932 had already deeply affected him. The loss of his wife when he was just twenty-eight years old himself, could not have been anything but crippling.

This is not only the earliest memory of my life, but the saddest too. Strangely, it is also the only memory that I have of my beloved mother. I can remember nothing else about her. Nevertheless I have been deeply attached to her in my inner self, and have wept many a bitter hour through the long and lonely nights that have followed me all the fifty-eight years that have elapsed since she left this world. The sister that was born under such tragic circumstances died a few years later. I do not remember ever seeing her, for she was brought up in my grandparents' household in Agaravallam, a village in Tanjore district, where they had a large house and extensive landed properties. I can remember only one photograph of that short-lived sister, where she is shown held in the arms of my father's youngest brother, Bakthu. Poor child, she was blamed as the person responsible for sending my mother out of this world!

We three brothers were largely brought up by my father. My youngest brother, Seena, as he was affectionately called, stayed with my grandparents till 1937, but my brother Kothandaraman and I were with my father. My father held the opinion that our grandparents would spoil us! True, of course, for grandparents do tend to pamper their grandchildren; but I have always felt, and still feel, that such pampering balances the disciplinary efforts of the often youthful and inexperienced parents. In India marriages are performed quite early, and my parents must have been married when my father was barely eighteen years old, and my mother perhaps just fourteen or fifteen!

My mother was the darling of the household into which she had been born, and my grandfather, especially, doted upon her. My maternal grandparents had five children, and she was the second. She was considered to have brought my grandfather a great deal of luck, because all his prosperity began as soon as she was born. He had joined as a camp clerk in the Salt and Customs Department of the Madras Government, in British India, on a salary of eight rupees a month. His duties, as camp clerk, even included running behind the horse of his superior officers, who were all, needless to say, British. From that lowly beginning he eventually rose to the position of Assistant Commissioner in the same department. As I have said, his fantastic rise began with my mother's birth. She was therefore not only the darling of the family but also some sort of mascot — the bringer of luck! — and her every word was law in their home. Very sadly, my grandfather's fortunes began

My Mother

to decline steeply after my mother passed away, and in just a few years, by 1937, he was in desperate straits, having been accused of various misdeeds by jealous colleagues, since he was the only Indian to have become Assistant Commissioner over the heads of many colleagues whom he had superseded. He was never the same after her passing, and always attributed his fall to her demise.

My mother was always deeply concerned about me. She had the feeling that I was weak, and would not be able to look after myself. My grandmother has told me several times that just before she died, my mother had called both of them to herself, and told them, "My two younger sons are strong, and will manage well, but my eldest, Pachu, is weak and dependent, and I am worried about him. Please look after him carefully." After her passing my father did not remarry, though he was indeed a very eligible widower. This was because of his strong conviction that a step mother would not look after his children as they should be looked after. So we grew up in an all-male environment. One of my father's close friends, Shri G. Vanmikanathan, has written a book about his very close friends, in which there is a whole chapter devoted to my father. There Shri Vanmikanathan has referred to my father as a modern Bhishma, a very flattering comparison with the Bhishma of the Kaurava dynasty who features so largely in the *Mahabharata.* The young Prince Devavrata took the awesome vow of total celibacy, and was thereafter addressed as Bhishma — he who took the terrible vow!

My mother Janaki, affectionately known as Jana, was a tall woman, far above the average height for a south Indian Brahmin lady. She was five feet seven inches tall, exactly the same as my father. She was slim and very beautiful, though rather dark complexioned. She had a warm and affectionate personality, and was very generous. She was adored by all who knew her. My grandfather told me that she would cajole him into giving gifts to the servants of the household all the time, and if her cajoling didn't work, she would fight with him till he acceded to her demands. My grandfather told me that he was never able to cow her spirit. He had tremendous admiration for her sense of fairness, and for her love for all, without the least trace of bias or thought about their social or religious station in life. She was the champion of all the oppressed in the neighbourhood, and would fight with an indomitable spirit wherever she felt that someone had been wronged, or unreasonably treated. It is no wonder, then, that she was not only the adored daughter of her father's household, but that even those who knew her but briefly came to love her.

My mother had exceedingly poor eyesight. I remember that her last pair of spectacles were with us till the year 1966 or so, and then they just disappeared. Her myopia was awful, and she wore spectacles of the power of -13 or so! The pair of spectacles that she left behind was one of the few things of hers that we had. There was also a diamond nose ring which too mysteriously disappeared around the same time as her glasses. The nose ring had several diamonds in it, and it had been the generally accepted idea that my father's three daughters-in-law would inherit the stones. It was as if we were not supposed to have any material possession which had belonged to my mother. However, one thing has remained with me. It is a greetings card, a tiny one measuring hardly three by four inches, featuring a pair of rather benevolent looking bull dogs on the cover. Inside is a printed message reading, "With the seasons greetings and all good wishes for a Happy New Year from," and there my mother has written in her rather unschooled hand, "his loving wife R.Janaki to her dear husband," and below it is the date, 31-12-23. This is the only thing that I have. Perhaps they were married in 1923!

My Mother

I had known that there was a small bundle of letters tied up with a piece of coloured ribbon in my father's wardrobe, and I knew that they were letters that my mother had written to him. One day that small bundle too had disappeared. I was left with the vague suspicion that my father had done away with all that reminded him of his wife. One cannot blame him for that. He had lived a lonely life for well nigh fifty-five years!

Strangely enough, my son Krishna read the first draft of this narrative, and brought to me the missing bundle of letters. He had found them in my father's *almirah* after my father had passed away, and kept them with him. Her first letter to my father is written from a place called Adhirampattinam, and has no date. I would like to translate it here into English, for of course she wrote to my father only in Tamil. It will be noted that there are no terms of endearment either at the beginning or at the end of the letter.

Adhirampattinam

"All well!

My respects to you. I have received the letter written by you. I am now feeling better after the bout of fever. My father is having fever since the past four or five days. That is why I couldn't reply to your letter earlier. I am taking only home remedies. As soon as father is better, he will write to you, I hope you are well and in good health. For the rest all are well here. There is nothing else to add."

Janaki

The second letter is dated the 24th July 1922, and is written from Surla. Of the twenty-seven letters that she wrote my father in 1922, only this one single letter is from Surla. All the others are from Adhirampattinam. Eight of her nine letters written during 1923 are from Surla. This is a clear indication that my grandfather had been transferred from Adhirampattinam to that place. My grandfather obviously had a touring job, for her first letter in 1923 is from Icchapuram. This is confirmed by the fact that her first letter in 1924 is written from Chinnaganjam, whereas all the other nine are from Surla. This also shows that she accompanied her father on his travels, which must have been for a long enough period of stay to justify his taking her with him. My grandmother no doubt accompanied them too.

During 1924, 1925 and 1926, the family seems to have lived in Chinnaganjam, Anaparthi and Naupada. The letters of 1927 are written from Vayalur, where I was born. Of the five letters that she wrote to my father from Vayalur, the first reference to myself is in her letter dated the 18th of August. She writes, "I want to leave the baby here for a day so that I can go to see Sulochani. What do you think of this? The baby is healthy and well." The Sulochani referred to here is my mother's younger sister, Suli, who had apparently been unwell for some time. In 1928 my mother has written only one letter to my father. I surmise that by the end of 1928 the family had moved to Agaravallam, for all her six letters to my father that year are from there. In her letter of the 5th December, 1929, she writes, "Pachu is well. The baby is having a cold since the past two days. The child is otherwise healthy and well." The child referred to in this letter is my brother, Kothandaraman, popularly addressed as Kothandu. The second child of the family has entered this world!

After Kothandu's birth, the family has obviously moved to a place called Tada, some seventy miles to the north of Madras, on the road to Calcutta. My Thatha must have been actually serving in Tada, leaving the family to stay on in Agaravallam to help with my mother's confinement. My father has received only two letters from her during 1930. The family continued to stay in Tada during 1931, as is evident from her

My Mother

six letters, all written from there. She seems to have been very lonely and dispirited, for there are plaintive appeals to my father to visit her, and to stay long with her.

It is very obvious from a reading of her letters that she felt neglected by him. In her letter to him dated the 19th October of that year, she writes, "To help me Seena has come." I don't think she was being sarcastic, for the general tone of the letter is so much one of utter loneliness and suffering. That brings the third of her sons into the picture too! I wonder if she dated the letter wrongly, though, because Seena was born later than that, if the date of birth as recorded is correct.

During 1932 there are just two letters to my father, and in 1933 only four. All those six letters are written from Tuticorin, a harbour in the south of India, where my grandfather was then serving, tending the salt pans of the Government. Altogether she has written seventy-six letters to him — seventy-seven if one counts the greetings card too — during the eleven years of their marriage. Of this total, as many as twenty-seven were written in the first year of her marriage! From a reading of her letters to him, it is quite obvious that they were married in the early part of 1922, and equally obvious that she and my father lived together only for short spells. She very obviously hated that, and longed to be with him. She was however compelled to mostly live with her parents at the various places that my grandfather was posted to. She died on the 25th of May 1933. My father has written on the letter that she passed away that day at 11:30 A.M.

I now give the translation of her last letter to her husband written from Tuticorin. It is dated the 21st May — just four days before her end came. A perusal of the contents shows that she wrote it eight days after her daughter, her fourth child, was born. The baby would not have been even given a name as yet, for this was rarely done before the ritual purification — the *punyaahavachanam* — had been performed!

Tuticorin

21-5-33

"All well!

I have received your letter. I am sure that you would have received the letter written by my father to you. Even though eight days have passed, I am still unable to get up from my bed. I am extremely weak. You have written that you intend to take Pachu away with you, and have asked for my opinion in the matter. I feel that you want to dump me here for four months more and go away. That cannot be done. I shall accompany you. Please write to my father accordingly before the tenth or the fifteenth of the next month. Even before you come here, the period of my impurities will be over.

I am not afraid of doing any work. You need not worry about me on that score. If you can employ someone to wash the clothes, I can manage all the rest of the work. If I do not accompany you now, then according to the *shastras*, I can come to you only after the middle of July. Please do not think ill of my father and mother because I wish to go back with you so soon. Their only fault is in not writing letters. On Friday they have bought me a bangle studded alternately with pearls and rubies, costing Rs. 125.00. Initially I refused it. My father said, 'If you refuse anything from me as long as I am alive, it will cause me the greatest sorrow.' After that I could say nothing. When you come please bring some spoons and ladles similar to the ones Kasturi has brought, as a special gift."

The letter ends here abruptly, and does not even have her signature. Obviously the effort required to write it had fatigued her, and she was unable to finish it. It was posted just like that. There can be no doubt that my father read it only after he had

My Mother

returned as a widower to Bombay. Strange are the ways of destiny. She wanted to go back with him, and he had to go back without her, having lost her forever!

Even though I have practically no memory of any personal interaction with my mother, I have always had a deep and abiding love for her. How much I loved her, and how tremendously I missed her, no one can ever know or understand. My longing for her was very deep, and a secret thing. I have wept many a long and bitter hour during all the awfully lonely nights of my childhood and youth, when desolation that I had no mother to look after me and love me would flood me with a sorrow and bitterness that I could hardly endure. I don't think that even my father ever suspected this aspect of my inner life. Many mystical persons have told me that her dear departed soul was always hovering around me, protecting me, and this only deepened my desolation and despair, for the one thing that a person cannot ever acquire a second time is a mother. One consequence of all this deeply hidden trauma associated with the early loss of my mother, and the horrible memory of her last presence, is that I have always had difficulty sleeping alone. My father's stoicism demanded that he be very stern with us, and he made us sleep separately from our early years. This only tended to deepen our loneliness, and our sense of separation from human warmth and company, and strengthened our sense of isolation. I still have this problem of being quite uncomfortable when I have to sleep alone.

I have inherited all my physical traits from my mother — my height, the poor eyesight (though mercifully my eyesight is not that bad), in fact everything. I am supposed to have inherited such mental capabilities as I possess from my father. But the greatest gift that I have received from my beloved mother was revealed to me very many years later by my Revered Master, Shri Ram Chandraji Maharaj. We were seated together in my Master's bedroom in Shahjahanpur one bitter winter night. It was 1:00 A.M. in the morning. My Master was in a reminiscent mood, as if he was nostalgically looking into the past. We had been speaking about my father and his tremendous personal qualities. My Master was praising my father for the qualities of his heart, and said, "He has the heart of a lion. His heart is like the heart of my Master, Lalaji Sahib. He has great courage and strength of heart. But your heart is tender and soft like mine. You have inherited your heart from your mother. I am happy about this!" So that was the divine gift that my mother bestowed upon me — her soft and loving heart — as was confirmed to me by my Master himself. I must admit that I have never felt, or thought, that I had a soft heart! But there it is, and for that most noble and loving gift, I shall be eternally grateful to my beloved mother. There is no doubt that it has been an important contribution to my spiritual life. I think of it as my spiritual capital gifted to me by my beloved mother.

After I came to the feet of my Divine Master, Babuji Maharaj, I once wrote to him about her, praying to him to benevolently shower his grace upon her. I wrote to him about her twice from my office, because a tremendous feeling of gratitude and love for her overpowered my being. Even though I was reluctant to bother my Master, I was compelled to write to him about her to request him to assist her soul on its onward path towards the Goal. Rather typically, my Master did not answer those letters. A month or so after I had written my second letter to him he came to Madras. As soon as he came to our house *Gayathri*, one of the first things he asked me was, "Can you show me a photograph of your mother?" I wondered why he wanted to see her photograph. I am quite ashamed to say that I had forgotten the entire matter of my having written two letters to him about her! However, I brought down from

My Mother

the wall the only photograph of my mother that we had, and gave it to him. He put on his glasses and studied the photograph keenly for a few minutes. Then he looked at me with a deep love shining from his eyes, and said, "Your mother was a very good lady, and she loved you very much. She has not yet taken rebirth. I shall pray to Lalaji Sahib for her."

A few days later, we had gone to Shri Vira Raghavan's place for Sunday *satsangh*. Master was staying with us at *Gayathri*. As soon as we returned home, Master asked me, "Are you free for a few moments?" I said I of course had all the time in the world for him. He took me upstairs to the room which we rather pretentiously called our library, from which my Master did all the important spiritual work that he did when he was with us. There he said, "Today by the grace of Lalaji Maharaj your mother has been granted her liberation. It was done during the *satsangh*. Now I shall give you the proof of it. Please sit in meditation." I protested that I needed no proof, but he insisted. Rather unusually, he did not sit in his usual seat, but put on his cap — which he does only when Lalaji Sahib pays a visit — and sat next to me, facing the empty seat in front of us — the seat of the Master! He said, "Now your mother will transmit to you. Please meditate." I sat in meditation. I immediately felt as if my mother had taken me on her lap, and was lovingly caressing me, crooning to me. I had tears in my eyes. Master terminated the sitting after some ten minutes, and asked me what I had felt. I related the experience to him. He said, "Yes! That was exactly what happened. Now see, that is the mother's love which you experienced. But now she wants to go. Who will stay in this unfortunate and ill-destined world after liberation! She is in a hurry to go. She is blessing the Mission, and blessing it to grow and grow!"

This event deepened my loneliness and desolation even more. I felt that after her liberation I had lost her forever, since she would never be reborn again, and any chance of our coming together in some future life was destroyed once and for all. After that sitting from my mother I went into my bathroom and locked myself in, and wept bitterly for half an hour in utter loneliness and despair. Such is human ignorance!

    I had been performing the annual rituals for the departed souls, as prescribed in the Hindu *Shastras*, ever since I was invested with the sacred thread. I did it with full faith, and with scrupulous regard to strict performance of the rituals, and to personal purity. No doubt all that had played a part in leading me to the Divine feet of my beloved Master, who finally granted to my mother the spiritual gift of Liberation, relieving me from the duties that I had towards her as her eldest son. In this mysterious manner my duty towards her was fulfilled by my Master, for which act of gracious love and mercy I shall be eternally indebted to him.

Janaki - 1928

From left: Srinivasan, Parthasarathi, T. Rajagopala Iyengar (Thatha) with Vasantha, Kothandaraman, Rangamani - 1939

II

My Grandparents

My Grandparents

It was not possible for me to have any personal knowledge of my paternal grandfather, Shri R. Chakrapani Iyengar. He passed away in the year 1914, and whatever I know of him is only what I have heard about him from my father. My grandfather was a very pious and orthodox Brahmin of the Vaishnavite tradition. The Vaishnavite Brahmins worship Lord Vishnu, and often have the suffix 'Iyengar' after their names. The Shaivites worship Lord Shiva, and can be identified by the suffix 'Iyer'. The Vaishnava Brahmins adorn their foreheads with a caste mark, consisting of a vertical 'U' in white, inside which is a single line in red. This is said to represent the sacred foot of their Lord, Lord Vishnu. On the other hand the worshippers of Lord Shiva are to be recognized by the three horizontal stripes of *vibhuti* or sacred ash smeared across their foreheads.

My grandfather did the daily prayers — the *sandhyavandanah* thrice daily, at dawn, at midday, and finally at sunset, with meticulous regard to personal purity of body and mind. He also performed the ritual *puja* of the deities maintained in the holy shrine at home, with great faith and ardour. The daily bath was mandatory, and no food could be taken until the *puja* had been completed. The *puja* generally took several hours, so that starting with a bath in the river, or at the well at home when the river ran dry, the first meal of the day — lunch — was generally eaten well beyond noon. Only the children of the household were permitted to have something before the *puja* was completed. The woman who cooked the meal — in this instance my grandmother — had of course to have her own bath well before my grandfather had his, so that she was ready to help him with all the paraphernalia that went into the preparation for their performance.

The Brahmin wife has traditionally been considered to be a part of the husband, and she is called the *ardhangini* — one who is half of the whole! The wife is also known as the *dharmapathni*. No rituals were permitted to be performed without the *dharmapathni* by the side of the husband. The ladies therefore had a really demanding schedule to maintain — and young girls had to learn from a very young age that they had to sleep last and to wake up first, if they were to be called good women! There was of course much to be done by the women — such as for instance lighting the ritual fire, cooking the sacred *prasad* to be offered to the Lord at the end of the *puja*, and so on.

The lot of women has never been an easy one in India, and the Brahmin woman in orthodox households had to be trained from a very early age to bear the life of a *dharmapathni*, which term means, "A wife who keeps her husband's feet firmly on the path of *dharma*." The general or common meaning ascribed to this ancient Sanskrit term is 'scriptural wife' — but I think that it is too superficial a meaning of this sacred word. It is far too sacred a word. It casts upon the wife the duty and the responsibility of keeping her husband on the path of righteousness in all spheres of life, and that is by no means an easy assignment.

My grandfather had the ideal wife in my grandmother who was named Rukmini. According to my father, and more especially according to my father's younger brother, Shri C. A. Ramabhadran, my grandmother was the perfect woman who helped her husband in all possible ways. According to my uncle, the orthodox man of those days rarely had any opportunity to wander from the 'straight and narrow path' of virtue. Further, the inclination to wander from the path of virtue was lacking, for the idea of a virtuous life, firmly treading the path of *dharma*, was deeply ingrained in the Brahmin psyche. Social and religious conditioning began virtually from the baby's life in the cradle, with the ladies singing from the ancient epics such as the *Ramayana* and the *Mahabharata*. As the children grew up, they were told stories from the great epics, and the life that the heroes of the past had lived. Their courage in the face of the severest adversity, their resistance to temptation, their spirit of sacrifice, were all extolled as values to be emulated by the growing youngsters. Women of orthodox families perhaps had fewer problems than their modern counterparts, as far as keeping their husbands morally pure was concerned. But their duties within the house were enormous, and if it is remembered that water had to be drawn by hand from the well at the back of the house, that firewood had to be chopped by hand daily for the fires, which were laboriously lit, as no man could be allowed into the kitchen to do these jobs, and that all the cooking had to be done after the lady had her bath in cold water, well, the situation of the women of those days becomes quite obvious. It was no easy matter for them. In addition they had to maintain the purity of the household, and especially that of the kitchen, all day.

I remember that we children had to wait outside the kitchen whenever we wanted a drink of water. A lady of the house would ladle out the water from a pot into a tumbler — as the silver glasses are called in India — and hand it to us, taking care to see that we did not even inadvertently touch her. If, God forbid, she was touched, then she would have to bathe again at the well! Such were the stringent requirements of personal purity in those days! We were also fed outside the kitchen, all seated together, all of us eating on banana leaves.

Only the very small children who were below the age of initiation — that is children not yet invested with the sacred thread — were allowed into the kitchen freely, but they had to be naked!

The day of the women therefore dawned well before dawn, and ended only after the vessels had all been washed and put away after dinner. Only then could they sigh with relief and go to bed. By then the rest of the household had perhaps been asleep for an hour or more. Such was the life that my grandmother Rukmini led. It is a matter for introspection how, amidst all these demands, women found any happiness at all. Those were days without any labour saving devices or appliances, when literally everything had to be done by hand. There was of course no electricity. Electricity came to the villages of India only long after India had gained her independence. The rice, for instance, was pounded by hand. The vegetables were of course prepared by hand. Fires were laboriously lit using badly made matches, and involved much puffing and blowing to get the firewood to burn. There were generally wet and red eyes in the mornings because of the problem of getting the kitchen fires going. The fires burned all day, as during those days of joint family existence, it was not unusual for a family to have, on an average, ten to fifteen members to feed — at the rate of three meals a day!

The day began with coffee for the elders, followed by tiffin as the breakfast was called. Then the males went out to work and came back around 1:00 P.M., and lunch was therefore quite late. This was followed by another tiffin around 5:00 P.M., and therefore the last meal of the day, dinner, was taken rather late, at around 9:00 P.M. My grandfather is said to have been very austere in his food habits, and did not eat two meals a day, nor did he drink coffee, the national drink of the south. Of course much use was made of prepared materials, so that everything had not to be cooked every time, but nevertheless there was an enormous amount of work to be done. And when the annual preparations, such as pickles, and things to be fried such as *vatthals* came around, there was tremendous acceleration of the day's activities. Generally even children were allowed to participate in certain activities after they had their baths, and had been admonished to remain pure by not sucking their thumbs!

This was a time of joy for us children, for a holiday atmosphere prevailed, and there was a general relaxation of the usual rules. We were permitted to handle those delectable foodstuffs, in the course of preparation, which came around only once a year, and were all the more desirable for that. I remember that when *appalam* (called *papad* in the north) was made, the black gram dal had to be prepared in several stages, and the penultimate stage was the wet dough, which had to be made into small balls, convenient for the ladies to roll out into the flat, circular shape of the *papad*. These dough balls were astonishingly tasty, and we children would demand payment for our work, which usually amounted to two balls per hundred that we made. Of course there was quite a deal of innocent filching as the work went on. The consequences followed later, when the children had loose motions, since castor oil was used in preparing the dough!

As for the preparation of *vatthals*, it was a more tedious affair, beginning with the soaking of rice overnight. This soaked stuff was ground into a viscous dough the next morning in very heavy stone vessels, requiring a great deal of physical exertion. Barley was soaked separately and similarly ground. The doughs were left to ferment a bit, and the next morning the rice dough was put on a blazing wood fire in an enormous copper vessel and slowly brought to a boil, while a paste of green chillies and salt was added to the required taste. As the dough neared boiling point, the dough of barley had to be very very slowly added in a thin stream to the boiling rice dough, all the while stirring the viscous and increasingly thickening mass, until all the barley dough had been added. The whole thing continued on the fire until the dough reached a consistency where, if touched with a wet palm, it would not stick to one's fingers. The vessel was then lifted off the fire and set down to cool.

When sufficiently cool, the ladies squeezed the dough out through special vessels, producing a spaghetti-like mass, which was laid on beds of knitted coconut palm fronds, and laid out in the sun to dry. That was when our fun and enjoyment commenced, for the half dry *vatthal* was perhaps the most delicious thing I have ever tasted — and we robbed the drying beds mercilessly, much to the annoyance of the ladies. This work would go on for several days, and then all the prepared stuffs had to be carefully put away in specially purified containers — generally large baked clay pots — to be used when necessary. It was all very exciting to us younger folk, and was a change from the daily routine, though for the women it was another concentrated dose of hard work.

A concomitant of all this daily load was that women did not have much time to be with their husbands. Intimacy during the day was neither possible, nor did social convention permit it. Women were expected to be very reserved, and the general means of communication between husband and wife was by means of glances pregnant with meaning. A wife was not permitted to address her husband by name under any circumstance! Romance was unthought of in those days of arranged marriages, and this custom still prevails. But there was always the odd couple that fell in love, even in such small and closed communities as those tiny villages represented. Lovers ran great risks, for society was terribly intolerant. Such romance as existed was therefore confined to girls and boys of the same religious caste or community. An inter-caste marriage could set up awful feuds between the communities concerned, in comparison with which the feud between the Montagues and the Capulets, the families of Romeo and Juliet, would pale into insignificance! One of the recurring themes in India cinema is this very same aspect of an intolerant society.

I remember that my youngest maternal uncle, Ayya, was involved in a romantic affair. It was a sanctioned romance since it involved Ayya and his own sister's daughter, Sushila. It has been the custom in south India for a man to have a 'right' over his sister's daughter — she is called *moraipennu* in Tamil. This right is especially respected among non-Brahmins, and is considered to be inviolable. If the one who has this right is denied marriage with the *moraipennu* in the family, it can result in violence even leading up to bloodshed! This concept of the *moraipennu* is not prevalent among the Brahmins. However, it is quite common for a man to marry his sister's daughter. Ayya's romance ended with his marriage with Sushila. The entire family heaved a sigh of relief, and was happy. It had been expected to happen, and it had happened.

Some years later, after they had a couple of children, Ayya was involved in a second romance, this time with a married woman, a Brahmin woman to boot! Everyone knew of the extraordinary ingenuity with which he went about the job of finding a new location for his daily meetings with his girl. Being children, we were privy to most of the so-called confidential or secret things that were going on, and so children were the first source for such information! This second romance ended in his second marriage, and this caused much sorrow to the entire family, and especially to his first wife who was of course my cousin.

Down Memory Lane

My eldest uncle, Kasturi, also had a love marriage. He too married within the family, his wife, Kamali, being his paternal aunt's daughter. This perhaps shows that proximity and availability were the cause of love in both these romantic marriages. Sad to say, neither Kasturi nor Ayya had happy marriages. Ayya died many years ago in a tuberculosis sanatorium near Mayavaram, leaving both his wives behind. Kasturi died several years ago, much before Ayya passed away, and his widow, my aunt Kamali, has lived long enough to see the death of her only son, Rangamani, who passed away just a few months ago in August 1990, suddenly of heart attack. Poor Kamali! She too has suffered all her life, her marriage by no means having been a happy one. So much for love marriages! And to lose a son at her advanced age of seventy-five years! Her life has been one of continuous and unmitigated misery, first suffering under the harsh rule of her husband Kasturi and, after his death, continuing to suffer, perhaps even more, under her son. I pray that she may find at least a modicum of peace in her remaining years. Strangely enough, my middle maternal uncle, Vijay, too got involved in a love marriage after his first wife, Anasuya, died many years ago. I am happy to say that both he and his second wife Padma are well, and have migrated to Canada where they are living close to their only son, Gautam Tupil.

There was hardly any privacy in the houses of those days, no separate bedrooms being available. All slept on the floor on mats wherever they could find space, with a block of wood for a pillow. The men generally slept out in the open in front of the house, the women sleeping indoors. Any privacy that a married couple needed had therefore to be engineered with considerable acumen and foresight! It was not always possible of course, and tempers were generally frayed in the mornings. The younger children always slept with the women, and that of course posed more problems, but there must have been

My Grandparents

ways, often very ingenious, of overcoming all those hurdles to romance, judging by the number of children that were born in those days. It was normal for a couple to have three or four children. Where the first wife died and the man married a second time, there would be more children. As a matter of fact infant mortality and the death of women during delivery were the main causes for second marriages, as well as for the lack of contraception — for who could say how many of the children born would survive to see adulthood?

My grandmother, Rukmini, for instance had at least six children, for I have heard my father say that two of his brothers had died at an early age. The remaining family consisted of my father, who was the eldest surviving son, followed by Shri C.A. Ramabhadran, two years junior to him. Then came Shri C.A. Bakthavathsalan, who was ten years or so younger. As a matter of fact, my grandfather had been married twice, and he had two children by his first wife, Soundaravalli: Shri C.A. Krishnan, and a daughter Kanakam. My grandmother Rukmini was the second wife. Therefore my grandfather sired eight children in all, according to the information available to me.

My grandfather was a professor of chemistry at the Maharaja's college in Pudukottai, some thirty-five miles to the east of Tiruchirapalli in what was then the Madras Presidency. He seems to have left Pudukottai and moved to Madras towards the end of the first decade of the present century. In Madras, he again took up service as a teacher, and they all lived in Triplicane. My grandfather suffered from polio in his young age, and therefore he had one leg shorter than the other. But even with this impediment, which made walking very difficult for him, my grandfather used to trudge more than a mile daily to his college, as he could not afford the meagre tram fare. They were always on the brink of absolute poverty, and led a very difficult life. Their's was a life of severe austerity, and most of their meals consisted of nothing more than cooked rice mixed with weak buttermilk. The occasional day on which they had some sort of tiffin was a day of rejoicing, and this was generally engineered by my uncle, Ramabhadran, who seems to have rebelled against their low standard of living even from his early years.

The children were taught in Tamil, which was their mother tongue. Vedic education was an indispensable part of the curriculum, as befitting Brahmin children. Some knowledge of Sanskrit was garnered by most children through such Vedic instruction. Both my father and my uncle, Ramabhadran, were well versed in the basic texts, and could chant them with ease, with scrupulous regard to the metrical and other rigid requirements of Vedic chanting. All this was made possible by the tremendous sacrifices that my grandfather and my grandmother made, as I am told that the monthly income was less than thirty rupees! And a family of five had to exist on that income somehow.

Nowadays it has become the fashion to speak of standards of living, as if the standard is a sacred cow. But when one looks to the life of those brave and simple souls of the past, who eked out a meagre, but nevertheless self-elevating, life, then we are put to shame. To understand how much can be achieved on very little, one must study, with devotion and love, the lives of these unrecognized warriors of the soul. Their's was a courage which can only rarely be paralleled, for it was a courage of the soul for which no honours were accorded, nor any recognition given — nor did they expect any for they were satisfied with the faith that God in heaven would reward their austerity, and their sacrifices made for the welfare of the family, and thus for the community. The women naturally suffered under the terrible austerities for they had to sacrifice far more than the men folk did.

My Grandparents

Under British rule English was taught as a second language. As a matter of fact, English has become so important in the daily life of the people of India that it has assumed the importance of the first language. Almost every educated person mixes English words in his speech, even when speaking in his own mother tongue! I believe that the development of the ability to speak English has contributed a great deal to the development of this country, since it made international intermingling possible. Both my father and my Chitya were masters of the English language, though my father retained the delightful accent peculiar to Indian-English, as it is called! My Chitya had a more polished accent, having acquired it from the British officers under whom he was trained for the elite Indian Forest Service.

The life of women in India has always been one of extraordinary sacrifice, and faith in the intangible Being we call God. If men took the trouble of looking at the lives that their women lead, and the pressures under which they run their households, the men would be put to shame. The women of India are India's greatest asset. They have always been so and, God willing, it shall always be so, if this great land of India is to thrive in the spiritual field. The women of this country have a special destiny to fulfill. They are the queens of their homes. They are the very soul of India, and this has been justly accorded due recognition in the sacred literature of this country. Swami Vivekananda was very vocal in his praise for the women and extolled them as perhaps no other has done. In India we have this peculiar and inexplicable phenomenon that on the one hand the women are worshipped as the Mother, and on the other hand they have been shamelessly exploited, to the everlasting disgrace of the men of this land. It is not possible to explain this ridiculous, absurd, and sometimes tragic duality of the male mind, but there it is. If the saints of India are to be believed, much of the suffering that this country has undergone, and is undergoing, is because of the shameless treatment meted out to women.

My grandmother was bereaved in 1918, when my grandfather passed away. She had three sons to bring up aged thirteen, eleven and four respectively. After the death of my grandfather her life was made enormously more difficult, for they had now an unbelievably low monthly income of eight rupees! It is impossible to even try to understand how they managed, but some glimpse of their willingness to progress against adversity can be had from the fact that my father and my uncle Ramabhadran did their homework under the street lamps outside their residence as there was no money to buy kerosene for the lamps at home!

They possessed indomitable courage and fortitude, such as is difficult to see in these pampered times of luxurious living, when people cannot think of walking to the next bus stop even when it is a few hundred yards away. My grandmother suffered unimaginably till she died in 1932. But whenever my uncle spoke about her to me — and it was rare for him to do so because he would become extremely emotional and weep — he always spoke of her cheerfulness and her smiling countenance. He had tears in his eyes when he spoke of her missing her own meagre meals to feed her children, for she often subsisted on just one meal a day, while they, as school-going children, had to have their bellies filled to the extent possible.

My youngest uncle, Bakthavathsalan, seems to have escaped much of the misery that the others had to face, because he was not only too young to feel or know what was going on, but he was also shielded by his elder brothers who protected him from exposure to the general suffering. His was a cher-

My Grandparents

ished life, and his elder brothers saw to it that the youngest lived happily. I wonder if Bakthu ever realised how many sacrifices his elder brothers had made for him. Somehow I have the feeling that not only was he not grateful, but he perhaps also resented what he thought to be unnecessary interference by them in his life. I know that my father realised this too, but instead of leaving Bakthu to himself, he made the mistake of getting even more deeply attentive. Bhadran also realised it, and he adopted the wiser approach of leaving Bakthu to himself, offering unobtrusive financial help from time to time.

Towards the end of her life, my grandmother, Rukmini, had better living conditions as two of her children had already secured employment. My father was employed by the Great Indian Peninsula Railway as a clerk, and my uncle had succeeded in joining the Indian Forest Service as a gazetted officer, on a truly magnificent salary of a couple of hundred rupees a month. My grandmother lived in the village of Kuttalam in the Thanjavur district with her brother, and there her end came. Only my youngest uncle, Bakthavathsalan, was with her when she passed away. My father was in Madras while my uncle Bhadran was in Assam. There is a tragi-comic story connected with her death. When she died, a telegram was sent to Assam to inform my uncle, because Assam was very far away, and therefore a telegram was necessary, while only a post card was sent to my father, because he was in Madras, and that was nearby! The result was that neither of them received the message of her passing away in time for them to reach Kuttalam before the cremation. If anything this serves to highlight the danger of logic, and its application to life in certain contexts.

My uncle's greatest regret was that she died just when the family fortunes were beginning to look up. He always had tears in his eyes when he spoke of the cruelty of destiny which made it impossible for her to live a relaxed and trouble-free life, happy in the company of her sons. But such is destiny, and who can overcome its stranglehold! For my father it was a double tragedy for he lost his mother and his wife within the period of a year. He was already the father of four children, and there was also my uncle, Bakthu, who was as yet unsettled in life, being just around eighteen or nineteen years old. So though monetary problems did not loom as large as in the past, his responsibilities increased manifold. After her death, it was once again a troubled life for my father and uncles.

Just for the record, I would like to name the progenitors whom I can remember, because the fact of having performed the annual ceremonies for the dead forefathers, called the *shradh* in Sanskrit, makes it possible to remember the names of the three preceding generations. Since my father was alive all those years, I am able to go back three generations before him. Actually it is appropriate that I begin the record of my family from the original progenitor believed to have been the great *rishi*, Bhargava. In reality, the traditions of my family, the spiritual tradition as well as the blood-line, if it may be rather inappropriately called so, is a result of the blending of five great streams of tradition derived from the great *rishis* of the hoary and ancient past, named Bhargava, Chyavana, Aapnavaana, Aurva and Jamadagni.

When we meet our elders, we have the tradition of paying our respects to them by prostrating ourselves before them, and then introducing ourselves by reciting the introductory recital in which all the names of the *rishis* who are our progenitors are given. This enables all boys — for only boys who have been invested with the sacred thread are required to do this — to remember their forefathers. This is how the knowledge of one's *parampara* or genealogy is handed on from generation to generation.

My Grandparents

It is of course impossible to name any of the subsequent descendants of those *rishis*, and so I am compelled to jump several millennia to my great-great-grandfather, Shri Viraraghava Iyengar. It is unfortunate that there is no record of his wife's name. Nor are any details of his family available. My father has told me a fascinating story connected with his end. One Friday morning my great-great-grandfather called my great-great-grandmother to him early in the morning, and told her that the next day all the family should bathe early in the morning, and that all of them should also have eaten before eight o'clock. He also ordered that no one was to leave the house the following day. Naturally my great-great-grandmother asked him why these things had to be done. He told her, "Tomorrow is my last day on earth. Soon after eight o'clock in the morning, a coldness will appear in my feet. This will spread to the knees later, and by three in the afternoon the cold will have spread to my chest. Around five o'clock in the evening the cold will assail my neck region, and after that I will not be able to speak. Thereafter I will only be able to make signs with my eyes, but that will be barely for an hour, for by then death will have come for me. That is why I want everyone to stay at home tomorrow the whole day." My father related that it had all happened exactly as my great-great-grandfather had said it would. Great men of those days that they were, he had been able to 'see' exactly what would happen to him at the end!

The next was his son, Shri Rama Iyengar, my great-grandfather, and his wife Lakshmi. The mists of time obscure all details of that family too. He was followed by my grandfather, Shri Chakrapani Iyengar who, as I have already stated, married twice, my grandmother Rukmini being the second wife. Then of course followed my father's generation, consisting of three sons and a daughter.

From left, standing: Lakshmi, Rama Iyengar, Kanakam; C.A. Krishna, seated - 1899

From left, standing: Amudachari Periappa, C.A. Ramabhadran (Chitya), C.A. Rajagopalachari (Appa); R. Chakrapani Iyengar, seated - 1915

Down Memory Lane

All the progenitors of my family were extremely orthodox and religious. They were all regular in their practice of the daily Vedic discipline, with total regard to bodily and mental purity. This often made them intolerant of lesser mortals, and gave the wives considerable trouble. It is related, for instance, that my great-grandfather was so easily irritated that when he found fault with his wife, he would lean back against a window, because he had an impediment in his legs, hold on to the bars, and order his wife to stand in front of him, and administer a kick or two just for the sake of discipline! Tough times they were for the women of such orthodox Brahmin households! But with all that there was greater harmony, peace and contentment than one finds these days, with all the so-called freedom, personal and social. Such a freedom only seems to have made it more difficult for the younger generation because the onus of responsibility for personal choice is often intolerable for the young, inexperienced shoulders to bear. There is always the need for a guiding hand in one's formative years, and blessed were those times when such wise guidance was available within the family. One regrets that changed modes of living have made each individual today more or less an island upon the surface of a barren and forbidding ocean. This has generated a sense of isolation and loneliness, to overcome which there is a great deal of time spent outside the home, seeking company and entertainment to beguile such lonely hours.

My father has told me many times that the family discipline called for stringent patterns of behaviour. For instance young persons were not expected to be seated when elders were present in the room. Chairs were virtually unknown, and it was only the occasional family that had one, and then it was always reserved for the eldest member of the family. Even in his absence no one else would have the temerity to occupy it. My

My Grandparents

father used to say that it was rare for him to be present in the same room as his father. This was not merely an expression of discipline, but it was part of a larger pattern of culture and tradition handed down through the generations. It was a mixture of love, regard, veneration and many things more. It was generally not resented, and the children of those days felt a freedom that the pampered ones of today, mollycoddled out of their wits, can ever appreciate or understand. The members of the younger generation appeared before the elders only when called, or on special family occasions.

I have intimate knowledge of my maternal grandparents because, after the passing away of my mother, they brought us up. I do not remember whether my younger brother, Kothandaraman, and I stayed there in Tuticorin very long after my mother passed away. My memory says that my father took us away with him to Bombay — and my memory could very well be wrong. My youngest brother Srinivasan, and my sister Vasantha were both with my grandparents, T. Rajagopala Iyengar, and his wife, Kuppammal, going with them wherever they moved. We always went to them for our holidays, and those were times of great happiness for all of us, for our grandparents loved to have us, and fussed over us and spoilt us because we were motherless children. This was something of which my father was afraid — I mean the being spoilt part of it — and he warned us about the danger of picking up undisciplined patterns of behaviour etc., which well-meant warning we left behind us as our train steamed out of the station.

My grandfather belonged to a well-known Sree Vaishnava family called the Tupil *parampara*. His father, Sri T. Ramanuja Iyengar, had married twice, and my grandfather was the elder son of the first wife whom I have never seen — she having passed away many years before I was born. He had a younger brother, Shri T. Anantachari, and a sister, Kanakam. The second wife of his father was addressed by all of us as *pudamma* which meant nothing more than 'new mother'. I never knew her name. In those days names were unimportant. Relationship was all. In any case there was not much mixing between the two families. My great-grandfather was nearly seventy years old even then, and lived with his second wife. They had some six or seven children. We were quite friendly with them, but later on in life I lost track of them completely.

It was quite usual for men in those days to marry twice. I know of a colleague of my father who had married thrice! A record in my personal experience. The reason was that men were married by the time they were ten or twelve years of age. Their brides were generally eight or ten years old, if that. They became mothers by the time they were fourteen or fifteen, and as family planning was unknown, children came regularly. Given the appalling ignorance and superstition, such as prevailed in the days of *Semmelweis* in Austria, infant mortality was very high, and often claimed the life of the mother too. Whenever this happened the young husband was left with very young children to bring up, and came under pressure to marry again — which was generally what happened.

Such second marriages were under the pressure of need. The couple being young, more children inexorably followed one after another, and the result was large families as are unknown today. There were formidable problems, especially when there were daughters, for the marriage of a daughter, necessitating the payment of dowry, was a very heavy burden on the average Brahmin family. If there were many daughters, then the result was generally ruin, for few Brahmin families were wealthy. Brahmins depended mostly on small incomes from teaching, or from working as priests. By Vedic tradition these were the occupations that a Brahmin could accept. Busi-

My Grandparents

ness, animal husbandry and farming were all forbidden. They could be ministers of kings, and many were ministers till the royal houses of India were abolished when the states were integrated after India attained its freedom from British rule.

My grandfather was a most lovable person, though he had a very short temper indeed. When enraged he would dance on the floor, shouting away at his loudest, and all were impressed. Some were even frightened by it, except of course my grandmother, and this enraged him even more. My grandmother was a patient and loving woman who governed the large family of more than thirty members with an iron hand. Her word was law, and even my angry grandfather rarely had the temerity to interfere in household matters.

She, poor lady, was a severe diabetic. Those were the days before Insulin. She had a fondness for sweets, and could never control herself. The result was acute suffering. She had carbuncles at least thrice to my knowledge, and had to be operated upon. Those operations left her back covered with huge cross-shaped scars. She suffered enormously, but patiently bore everything, and always had a sweet smile for everyone. It was when she went to bed at night that all her physical suffering surfaced. She often spent sleepless nights, with one grandchild or the other massaging her back. Her leg pains were so bad that we often had to walk up and down her legs, and this for several hours, before she could sleep. She had a long day of more than 18 hours, but never complained about it. She was rarely angry, and on those rare occasions only with my grandfather. He was always to blame, but we all loved him so much that we generally sympathized with him, but my grandmother didn't mind this.

Thatha had a special fondness for us three, as we were not only the sons of his beloved, favourite and long-mourned daughter Jana, but we were also motherless. He always had his pockets full of sweets, having a sweet tooth himself. So there were always sweets to be had. Later on when he became virtually destitute, we had to buy the sweets for him. For all the gross mistakes that he committed, which condemned him to a miserable end, we loved him with all our hearts, and could not bear it if others criticized him in our presence. I even resented it when my father had blistering criticism for him. With all the rambunctious life, there was yet peace and harmony, and I have nothing but the most pleasant memories of my life with them.

My grandfather was a government servant, and served in the Salt & Customs Department, a revenue department of the Government of the then Madras Presidency, under the British rule of those days. All the senior officers were of course Britishers. But even though he joined the department as a camp clerk on a salary of perhaps eight rupees per month, his prestige was very high, since being a government servant was considered to be the thing, as it provided a life-long source of steady income, and security of service too. And to cap it all, he had an authentic uniform to parade in! We children loved to have him dress up for us, and he never failed to oblige, since he was himself extremely proud of it. The days of the freedom struggle were still far away, as far as the people in the south of India were concerned, and in any case politics hardly interested anyone. Newspapers were relatively unknown, and so each village led its own insular existence, and all that passed for news was generally village gossip.

He was a man of remarkable courage, capable of enormous physical effort. His duties included conducting raids on those who did not pay the taxes, and this could often be dangerous, as smugglers were armed. But he had a great record, and it is not surprising that he rose to the position of Assistant

My Grandparents

Commissioner of Salt & Customs, a position held only by the British before him. I remember that in the mid-thirties, he had a Willys car, and was known to be one of only two persons in the whole of the Tanjore District to own a car. There being few petrol bunks, he used to store petrol in huge quantities in a dump within our compound. I think there was often as much as 500 gallons of it stored in one gallon cans. There were of course no regulations at all in those days, such as the Explosives Act etc., of the present day. The danger was appalling. And to cap it all, there was no insurance cover, insurance being literally unknown in the villages. But everything was done with a nonchalance that only total ignorance of the consequences could have made possible. As a matter of fact the children were always playing hide and seek around the petrol dump, occasionally even knocking down a few cans.

My grandfather started life on a salary of eight rupees a month, and went on to earn the really enormous salary of about one thousand and two hundred rupees a month, and that before the year 1937! In those days we had rupee coins minted from solid silver, and a rupee was worth a lot of money. The exchange rate with the English pound sterling was thirteen rupees to the pound. There were even gold sovereigns in circulation! Thatha of course became a very wealthy man, and had vast agricultural lands in the best areas of Tanjore district. There were also orchards, and the proximity of the Veeracholan river, which flowed just a mile away from our home, made agriculture there not only comparatively easy, but very profitable too. He had something like a hundred acres of prime land, and those being the days of total manual labour, farm machines not yet having been developed, he employed a labour force of between sixty and one hundred men and women.

They were all paid with grain. Only on Saturdays did they receive one quarter of a rupee each, which was sufficient for every man Jack of them to get drunk upon. They generally came for work the following Monday morning with considerable hangovers, meriting the use of a bull whip which my grandfather used freely to help them to restore themselves to comparative sobriety. It was a time of feudalism, and such things were not resented by the workers, as they knew they were in the wrong. My grandfather treated them extremely fairly, and they would not have liked to lose employment with him since apart from wages, they all lived in rent-free thatched huts on the estate, and this gave them a sense of belonging. I have rarely seen a more merry or happy group of farm hands. Most of them were life-time employees, and liked the security this afforded. They generally found wives or husbands from similar labour forces in and around our village, and their lives were steady, certain and peaceful. They had no worries for the future, for whatever the fate of the land owner's personal circumstances, they were looked after as always. I feel that there was generally more happiness and contentment all round, and it did not really matter whether one was rich or poor.

Those farm hands of course adopted the children, and fussed over us all day, playing pranks in their own ways, and helping us to devise ever new escapades, which often got us into trouble. I remember on one such occasion one of my cousins was nearly drowned in the river, though the river ran only three feet deep. The trouble arose because one of the farm boys, who couldn't swim for his life, led my cousin into the deeps on the curve, and both nearly drowned! Jolly and happy days those were, such as will perhaps never recur again. One can never be a child again of course, but it is a terrible pity that one cannot recapture those days of sunshine and laughter, and all that is left to humanity at large is the sense of nostalgia, coupled with an often aching longing for the innocence and sheer joy of it all. It is no wonder that childhood is called the age of innocence!

The workers all belonged to the class known as untouchables. We were not expected to touch them, and they generally kept a respectable distance from all of us. It was also forbidden to go through the street in which they had their huts, as it was considered unclean. I once came home from the fields on one of the bullock carts which, for some strange reason, blundered laboriously through that particular street. When my grandmother came to know of it, she sent me to the well at the back of the house where I had to have a couple of buckets of water drawn by another person and poured over me, before I was permitted to draw water myself to complete my purificatory bath. Otherwise I would have polluted the well! We had separate servants belonging to the Sudra class who were permitted into the house as house servants. They were not untouchables, but belonged to the fourth class. The untouchables were called *panchamas*, or the fifth caste! Later on, after Mahatma Gandhi entered the scene, the people of the fifth class were labelled *harijan*, meaning God's people.

Under the caste system the *Brahmins* headed the list, followed by the *Kshatriyas*. Then came the *Vaishyas*, with the *Sudras* forming the tail. The so-called untouchables did not have a place in this scheme. I must say that whatever may have been the merits or the demerits of the caste system, the workers were generally treated very well, and my grandmother especially took maternal care of them. They were well fed, decently housed, and even medical aid, such as was available to all of us, was rendered to them without any thought that they belonged to a low class or anything like that.

This is not the case after the class barriers were broken down by political machinery, which seems to have only aggravated class hatred at all levels. As a matter of fact I can say that today there are more and more castes and sub-castes, whereas in those days I was aware only of the four or five castes mentioned earlier. Modern India seethes with class hatred, and the future of the country might very well depend on how this vital issue is resolved. It is really an unfortunate reality that very little is being done to at least try to ameliorate this hatred. On the contrary there is a general feeling that the powers-that-be are interested not only in prolonging the class differences, and fueling class-consciousness, but are perhaps adding fuel to the fire of class bitterness and hatred.

My grandfather must have been born around the year 1885 or so. He was an extraordinarily handsome person, exceptionally fair, very tall and slim, and always well groomed. His younger brother Shri Anantachari was similar in all respects. Both were brave and courageous, but terribly short-tempered, intolerant, and always prepared for a fight. This was one failing in them, and they never changed in this respect. I can say that my grandfather mellowed with age, and with a great deal of personal suffering that came upon him around the time of his retirement from service. In his later days he became very soft and quite lovable, but the mean streak never quite disappeared.

In contrast, my grandmother was quite short, and quite dark complexioned too. But she had qualities of the heart that more than made up for her lack of beauty, and that is what, in the final analysis, really matters. They seem to have led a reasonably happy married life, according to the standards of those days. But I don't think that there was ever any real intimacy between them. She suffered so much in her own health that perhaps she had no time for fanciful ideas about how her husband treated her! While he was robust, and enjoyed exuberant health all his life, she was never really free from the pains and aches and all the attendant problems of a severe diabetic condition. All my life I have seen her suffer day and night without a murmur, her iron control relaxing somewhat only when she went to bed late at night.

My grandfather, Shri T. Rajagopala Iyengar, was popularly known in the senior circles of our family as 'Aeyi' — easy to say, but very difficult to write out in English. To us, of course, he was 'Thatha', the Tamil term for grandfather. The paternal grandfather was unknown to me, he having died a decade before my birth. As I have remarked, my Thatha was a tall and slim person, very fair complexioned and very handsome. He was perhaps around five feet ten inches in height. He enjoyed exuberant health, but was cursed with what used to be called a sick headache, arising out of a bilious nature. In those days a cup of strong coffee, freshly brewed, was the household remedy for it and, on his sick days, he consumed several tumblers of it. South Indians consume coffee the first thing in the morning, and coffee brewing has been treated as something of an art. The only other remedy for the headache was aspirin. Medication was simple, easy and generally effective too. There were not all the complications that we face in modern times to maintain even a moderate degree of health.

There were many household remedies concocted out of herbs, condiments and such other easily available things. They had the advantage that no money was required, and almost every elderly lady in the house knew what to do to prepare them. The third advantage was that they were prepared very easily and quickly; but the greatest benefit was that they had absolutely no side effects — the bane and the curse of modern allopathic medicine. My grandmother, and more especially her younger widowed sister Rajamma, were masters of this form of basic therapy, and so there was very little suffering in those days. Diseases too seem to have been simple ones. Perhaps this is the feeling of a child, but then I was witness to the life of a family through several decades.

It was wonderful to have those domestic remedies, as doctors were few, and not easily available except in the larger towns. I also have the feeling that we had less of sickness, and the diseases were milder. The exceptions were the two scourges, smallpox and cholera, which periodically decimated the population. There were of course no remedies for them, but here too domestic medical wisdom came to help sufferers, and managed to save many who would have otherwise fallen prey to them. This was possible only when early medication was possible. The leaves of the Neem tree (Margosa) played a very large part in such cases.

It has always been my feeling that as deadlier forms of medicines are developed, the germs and microbes, in their struggle for their own survival, become stronger and stronger. One has only to look at the modern syndrome where medicines are getting more and more potent and strong, and the diseases are also growing more and more menacing. One wonders whether this deadly race between the manufacturers of medicines and nature itself will ever end, and if so how! One cannot but feel menaced, knowing that whichever way the dice may fall, it is always nature that emerges as the final victor. If we are to go back to the good old days of comparative freedom from sickness, perhaps it will be necessary to abandon the effort to combat disease with more and more potent drugs.

Whereas my paternal grandparents were extremely orthodox, and strict followers of the Vedic mode of life, my maternal grandfather, especially, paid little more than lip service to the whole matter of religion. It was not that he was an atheist or anything like that. He was a firm believer, as almost all Indians are, due to the conditioning that we receive from the cradle

My Grandparents

onwards. But he didn't believe in rituals. He allowed the women to take care of such things. For one thing he was too busy with his work. He travelled a great deal, and was not much at home in any case. But he was nevertheless a devout person. There was a great deal of superstition to which most of them fell prey. Village life was ruled by superstitious beliefs, and the need to propitiate such spirits or gods as the so-called seers or priests dictated. But I must say from personal experience that there was something too, in those rustic beliefs.

I remember that at one time, perhaps around the year 1939, my grandfather was in serious difficulties. He had a large herd of cattle for the agricultural operations, and also for milk. The herd numbered some 120 to 150 head of cattle. There were two enormous cattle sheds, and a host of urchins to look after them. One day, all of a sudden cattle started dying, one by one. One day it started with the death of two. The next day three died. The fourth day some seven were dead — and then there was a brand of terror that I have never experienced later in my life. It was as if a pall of gloom had descended. There was a feeling of terror even during the day, and of course by night terror reigned supreme. There were several pairs of shoes put around the house, and pairs of *chappals* outside each room, to keep the evil spirits away. There were brooms laid in the corners of rooms. We hardly slept. It was a time of unreason and of a pervasive fear psychosis.

My second uncle's wife, Anasuya, was the only brave one, and everyone sneered at her saying that her education was responsible for her thick skinned attitude to local beliefs! I believe she was a graduate, a rather rare thing in those days when girls were hardly ever sent to college. She kept us all relatively sane. But all her attempts to do so were very nearly ruined when one morning my grandmother found strange marks on her right forearm. I was called to read it, and to my horror, I found there the word **DIE**. The terror in the household can hardly be imagined. There was pandemonium. An astrologer was brought in hastily from Mayavaram, the nearest town, six miles away. Then an exorcist was brought in. He put some honey on a betel leaf, added some mascara to it, gazed keenly at it, and said, "There are evil spirits attacking this house. However I see Lord Hanuman circling the house to protect you all. There is nothing to worry about, but you must allow me to charge an iron nail with my mantras, and take it near the village pond, and drive it into the trunk of a tree there. I will also dig up the front door-step, for I suspect that some evil spells have been laid upon this house long ago. If I find anything, then that must be ceremonially treated and immersed in the pond with necessary rituals." My youngest uncle Ayya confirmed the findings, after himself peering into the betel leaf. Anasuya was able to see it too, but no one else was able to see anything whatsoever — but I suspect that no one really wanted to either!

The exorcist did later dig up the door-step, and a copper plaque was found some six feet below the earth, with inscriptions in Tamil consigning the occupants of the house to a most dreadful hell. Now how is one to explain that? Because the plaque must have been deposited by some evil-wisher when the house was being built — and the house had been in continuous occupation for the previous sixty years or more. And when the mantrically-treated nail was taken to the pond and driven into the trunk of a tree chosen by him, I am told that for several nights there were the most awful and horrible wails and moans emanating from it. I don't know what to make of all this, but the facts of the matter are such as demand at least some acceptance of the fact that paranormal phenomena do exist, and that they do affect human life. Why then do they not affect everyone? Well, the only possible answer that can be given is that only those who have the requisite karma are

My Grandparents

affected by such paranormal occurrences, whereas those who have no such karma are spared the suffering that such frightening phenomena bring in their wake. Further, those who are afraid of such phenomena seem to be more easily affected by them.

In the betel leaf, one of my uncles, Ayya the youngest, claimed to see Hanuman brandishing his mace, and that capped it all. But the manifestations and the death of cattle did not stop. My grandfather faced ruin, for he had retired from service, and agricultural income was the bread and butter of the family. The terror was reduced greatly when Anasuya, my second aunt, discovered that my grandmother must have somehow brought her forearm into contact with the top of a kerosene lamp when it was alight, and the lettering on top, the brand name of the German manufacturer, DIETZ, had somehow got burnt onto her skin, only the first three letters DIE having become so embossed. There was general relief that my grandmother was not under sentence of death, after all, but the feeling of relief was short-lived.

Though my aunt's courage did restore some order, and removed fear partly, it did not stop anything else, and the poor cattle continued to fall dead even as they were standing, their stomachs bloating enormously. Nothing worked — not prayers, not offerings to the gods and goddesses of the temples, not mantras, nothing. There was all round despair. My brothers and I were there for our annual summer vacation, and were strongly exposed to the atmosphere of horror and dismay. My grandfather was always on the move, driven from pillar to post, trying to find a remedy to the debacle that was being enacted before our very eyes, but destiny was against him. From then began his material downfall, from which he never recovered. It was a massive landslide, and there was no way out of it, no escape route at all.

Down Memory Lane

My grandfather had no money sense, and was always involving himself in hare-brained schemes, and this landed him in disaster. He would buy a large property in a neighbouring village because it was going cheap, borrowing money to pay for it. The interest burden that he created for himself by such investments dragged him deeper and deeper into the quicksands of debt, and the result was that he lost all his vast properties piece by piece. I remember that often when he saw a debtor coming to ask for payment of interest — for there was never any thought of repaying borrowed capital, nor indeed the ability to do so — he would escape through the rear and disappear, sometimes for days, plunging the rest of us into a frightened state of despair. If he could not thus escape, he would sell off a few tamarind trees, or something like that, and buy a temporary peace. But how long can things go on in this fashion? The end had to come, and come it did in the form of absolute penury after he was denuded totally of everything that he had ever owned on earth.

I was often reminded of the Dickensian character, Micawber, like whom he was always waiting for something to turn up. Nothing ever turned up. In his last days, perhaps just a month or so before retirement from government service in 1938 or 1939, allegations of a very serious nature were brought against him, and he was suspended from service. All the retirement benefits that were due to him were denied to him — even the life-long pension that he was entitled to, which would have ensured a happy retirement. He foolishly took the matter to the law courts, and fought the government all the way to the highest courts, and in the process beggared himself thoroughly. He lost the legal battle, and that shattered him. It broke that regal person and made of him a crushed and disillusioned man. It was a great fall, and one had to pity that grand old man who had literally ruled his small part of this enormous world with great courage, ability and generosity. He certainly deserved a better deal.

It is the curse of humanity that it cannot tolerate its successful sons and daughters, against whom the jealousy of the not-so-successful is always aimed, often with disastrous results. The petition that led to his suspension was discovered to have been filed by persons whom he had superseded in service, enraging them, and stirring up their jealousy to such an extent that they were able to do incalculable harm to a good person. One can only assume that they could never have foreseen the disaster that followed. If they had, they perhaps would not have done such a thing — or would they have? Who can tell! Human nature, even in those days, was sufficiently depraved, and no one can ever say how a particular person, or group of persons, will behave under any given circumstance. This makes human life such a wonderful thing, and also, on occasion, such a horrible nightmare.

My poor grandmother suffered as no woman should ever have to suffer. Her life was one of long and endless suffering, patiently borne. But the end was indeed a bitter one. Having been virtually a queen for all the years of her life up to 1936, it was a tragedy for her to have to see her family sinking deeper and deeper into debt. Her own jewels were of course the first to go. I remember times when my grandmother had silver basins filled with the gold sovereigns of those days, each sovereign weighing eight grams! When visitors came, for even the most insignificant reason, she would present the child of the family, or the bride, one such coin. She was innocent and generous to a degree such as I have not come across subsequently. And for her to suffer materially, and also to have to suffer the social stigma that always follows a person's or a family's fall, was something we could not bear to see. I don't think we ever felt really sorry for Thatha, because he had created the disaster. But that such an innocent, loving and generous person as my grandmother should have to suffer was something that none of us could accept. We suffered with her, and wept for her.

I was not with her when her end came in the last month of 1955 — the year in which I had been married. But when the news that she was no more arrived, I went to Mayavaram from Madras. I was too late even to see her for the last time, as the cremation had already taken place. I was shocked to hear that there had been no money for medicines, and hardly enough even for food. It was distressing to hear that she died playing with a few coins, tossing them up in the air and catching them as they fell, playing with the coins like a child. May God have a special benediction for her, and grant that beloved departed soul the peace that she rarely enjoyed during her earthly life.

With her passing an era ended for us. The family was held together by her. She was the nucleus around whom everything else revolved till her very end. And after she left, well, everything disintegrated. It was very difficult especially for my grandfather. Poor man, he was like a ship without a rudder. He was miserable in his small rented home. I believe the rent was paid by my aunt, Suli. Perhaps to save that rent, my Thatha went to Bombay to stay with her. But his roots in a village life were too deep, and this massive tree which had grown on that soil did not respond to such transplantation at all. The result was that he frequently left them to return to Mayavaram, where all that was left was his last son, my youngest uncle Ayya. This person who started out with the promise of true genius floundered and went wild, and all the promise of his youth just evaporated. He became a burden on the family, and also began to ill treat my grandparents. Here again my grandmother suffered the most. He exploited her meagre and dwindling resources shamelessly. After she left, he was distraught too, because his only sympathizer was gone. My grandfather went back to this environment of sorrow, despair and lost glory, and there he died in the paupers' ward of the local hospital some years later.

The history of the maternal side of my family was not a happy one. A happy family is not one that is happy in the beginning, but must be happy in the end. It is better to suffer in one's youth, and to make for oneself the happiness that must be the blessing for the sunset of one's life. I think that this is the great blessing that every sane person must plan, work, and pray for. But alas, the contrary is generally true, and humans spend all their energy in drinking to the very dregs such happiness as they can find in their youth, and suffer the consequences of such folly in their old age.

It was my father's protective attention that prevented us from being drawn into that abyss of despair and blighted destinies. He was always vigilant to ensure that we were kept away from too deep an involvement. He occasionally helped my Thatha financially, but did not allow it to harm his own career. When I began to earn after I became employed, I have often sent help to my grandfather when I received desperate appeals. But always when my father discovered this, he would be quite critical of my attitude, and often angry too. He would say, "It is too late to help him. He is too deep in the mess that he has himself created. Any help that you can give will have as much effect as a snail trying to draw out a sinking ship." My wife never interfered in this matter. She knew that whatever I did for my grandfather was nothing more than what my mother would have insisted upon my doing for him had she been alive.

When I look back upon the destinies of the two families of which I am a product, what a contrast emerges between the two! My father's family, starting out in absolute penury, by dint of courageous and indefatigable application rising to almost impossible heights of material and social achievement. And the maternal side of my family, starting out quite well-to-do, affluent, well established, going very fast down the drain, and ending in total penury. What a contrast! But such is the history of a family, a people, a nation! And so it shall ever be, for one must realise that destiny is what one makes of it. We are, and must be, masters of our destinies, and for such of those who have the courage and the fortitude to take their destinies into their own hands, destiny has ample and unstinted rewards to offer. I am happy to have been the product of two such families, each glorious in its own way, both having very important lessons for those who can learn from the lives of others. To all of them, the members of the two great tributaries that makes up the river of my own generation, and particularly of my life, I am eternally grateful.

T. Rajagopala Iyengar (Thatha)

Kuppammal

From left: Kamali, Vathsala, Parthsarathi, Vaidehi, R. Kasturi, R. Vijayaraghavan (Vijay), Rangamani, Srinivasan, R. Narayanan (Ayya), Calcutta - 1944

III

My Elder Generation

My Elder Generation

The maternal side of the family tree has been considerably more prolific than the paternal. The Tupil family has been fecund and therefore we have a well-filled family line on that side though, as I look back, I see the inexorable depletion that Time, the Reaper, has been making. As one lives to an old age, one attends less and less of birthday parties, and has to attend more and more funerals. This is the unfortunate and inevitable price that one has to pay for living a long life. I am always amused and saddened by persons who are always praying for a long life — the prayer being repeated ad nauseum every time they think of praying for something. I am tempted to ask such persons, "What will you feel if the god to whom you are praying grants you your prayer, and blesses you with, say, a life a thousand years long?" Their initial reaction to this question is to give a boisterous answer, "That would be great!" Many persons don't bother to think after that, and exhibit an asinine ignorance of the consequences. In such cases I prod them, and ask, "How would you like to see your children dying off one by one? When they are all gone, your grandchildren will pop off one by one and, in this fashion, you will live only to see generation after generation of your progeny going on into the after-life, with you as a morbid witness. How would you like that?" That naturally sets them thinking, and they become horrified at the bizarre consequences. Then they become a little wiser but, sad to say, the wisdom only manifests itself in the form of renewed prayers for what can, at best, be called a short-long life! Under such situations it is best to remind ourselves of the story of King Midas, the one who had the golden touch. Not much thinking will be necessary if one tries to understand the moral behind that delightful little tale. There is another story, by H. Rider Haggard, called *She*, and its sequel, *Ayesha*, or *The Return of She*. It is the story of a woman who lives century after century, waiting for her long-lost lover to be reborn. It is a poignant tale of a great, passionate, possessive and jealous love. It tells of the lovers coming together again after centuries of patient waiting on her side, while he is led on and on in an adventure that is breath-taking. But the culmination reveals the tragedy of it all.

I personally deplore the fact that modern life has deprived the younger generation of access to the fairy tales of the yester years. They were entrancing beyond belief. But their greatest value lay not in their charm, but in their ability to give children, during their formative years, a permanent foundation of value systems which they absorbed without being aware of the fact that they were learning the most profound values of life. And since such values were implanted deep into the child's inner core of the developing human being, those values remained, to be called upon in later life in the form of hidden reserves of strength and fortitude, when the now grown up adult faced temptations or trying situations in actual life.

What was the secret behind this process? How did it work? I believe that children learn best when they are unaware of the fact that they are being taught. That is why play, perhaps, is so intimately intertwined with the teaching process. The old adage which says, "Work while you work, and play while you play," seems to me to be not a very wise adage. It may be all right for the grown up boy in school. But we must remember that children learn practically all that they are ever going to learn within the first six or seven years of their lives. While this is a fact of modern research, it is an ancient piece of wisdom as far as the old grandmothers of India are concerned.

They too learnt all that they ever learnt on the laps of the yet older generations. I wonder whether this is not one of the reasons for the older generations not having set much store by scholastic education!

There is a small bit of wisdom which I learnt from practical experience as a salesman — and that was that a salesman never sells. Indeed he must not sell! Then what is selling all about? In my experience, the best salesman is the one who makes the buyer buy. This is extremely important if a salesman is to become a good salesman, and make it up the ladder to the position at the top. I used to tell my sales staff, "Don't try to sell, but try to help your prospective customer to buy." Similarly, a good teacher must create the most exciting environment in which a child or a youth must want to learn. Such teachers do exist, thank heavens, and they are the ones who turn out brilliant students. Students who have not merely learnt the facts of the subject by heart, but who have really understood the subject in depth, in its totality.

The word education comes from the Latin root "*educe*: to lead; to draw out; to develop from a latent condition." Teachers must therefore be able to draw out of their students the latent knowledge that is already in them. This is also the ancient Vedic wisdom of India, which says that the mind is like a mirror with dust on it. Education is only the process of removing that dust, and then the mirror is able to reflect all that is put before it. First principles are extremely important, but nowadays, at least in India, the emphasis is on learning ever increasing loads of facts, most of which are never used in later life. Is it then surprising that the youth rebel against the system? I believe that where the educational system provides merely the facilities to mindlessly cram facts, but does not provide true education — which must be the education in the fundamental principles — then that education, and therefore the people so educated, fail miserably.

I remember an episode which occurred when I was a student at the Benares Hindu University. During my holidays, I went from Benares to Dehra Dun to visit my uncle Ramabhadran. He was then the Director of Forest Education, and lived in New Forest in a fine old bungalow with parquet floors, very well polished and so slippery that when the dogs were excited, they would try to get up, barking furiously, but all that their effort achieved was to keep them slipping on the floor until they gained a sufficient grip on the floor to take off. During my stay with Chitya, one day I went to the Forest Research Institute of which he was the Director, to look around the place. My uncle had sent up a graduate physicist to the roof of the Institute to string up an aerial for the radio. I had finished my tour and we had lunch, but still the boy did not turn up. So my uncle and I went up on to the terrace to see what he was doing. Chitya was stunned to see the boy patiently and laboriously shaving off the insulation of the aerial wire inch by inch. When he was asked why he was doing this he replied, to Chitya's shocked and angry amusement, that if the insulation were not shaved off, the aerial would not receive the radio waves! This emphasizes the need to understand the fundamental principles of a subject, without which education in any subject can have not merely amusing but sometimes disastrous consequences.

In India we have a rich and abundant store of mythological stories, which the mothers re-lived with their children, singing them to the baby in the cradle. And as they grew up, the grandmothers would take all the children out in the evenings and tell them story after story till dinner time, drawing upon their own reserves of mythological and other tales from the great epics of this country. The children, all round-eyed, listened entranced, inhabiting for a moment the worlds of the heroes and heroines of the past.

I remember that when children had to be fed, stories had to be told, and the entranced child would quietly eat mouthful after enchanted mouthful of food, which the mother or grandmother, or one of the numerous aunts that were always available in the joint families of those days, quietly put into the mouth of the child. The child literally learnt as it ate! Nowadays it is the fashion to be told that one should 'earn as you learn' — but in the days of which I speak, it was 'learn as you are fed', and it worked wonders in that it seemed to produce well-adjusted children, free from all the psychological traumas that modern children exhibit. They grew up into contented adults who were capable of handling the duties and responsibilities of the adult existence that very naturally, and inevitably, devolves upon all who enter adult life.

We have had to pay an unimaginably high price for such civilization as has been made available to us as a result of nearly three centuries of foreign rule. Not being an economist, I would not risk making any comments about the alleged 'rape' of this country by its former rulers. The only comment that I can see as making any sense is that rulers have almost always raped the countries over which they ruled. It has never seemed to make any difference whether the rulers were local or foreign. Nor have the ruled ever perceived any difference whether the so-called rulers belonged to royalty and ruled as kings, or whether they belonged to other denominations. The sad fact is that anyone who gets a chance to rule seems to be tempted into becoming a despot and a tyrant — and whether it is an individual or a group of persons, too, doesn't seem to make any difference.

Down Memory Lane

The maternal side of my family has been well-populated as I have already remarked. I had three maternal uncles, Kasturi being the eldest. He was born in the year 1905, and was but a few months junior to my father in age. He was followed by my mother, Janaki, and she was followed by Vijayaraghavan born, I think, in the year 1918. Uncle Vijayaraghavan was known as *chinnapayyan* — little boy — until he later on chose to call himself Vijay. In between was Sulochana, my aunt, known to all as Suli. And last came Narayanan, known universally as Ayya born in 1921. As I write this, only Vijay is still alive. He must be aged seventy-four years or so. He has always desired to project himself as a very young person, and I therefore hope that he will excuse me for revealing his age here! The other two are gone. Kasturi left a son and two daughters behind, along with his widow, Kamali. The son, Rangamani, passed away just a couple of months ago, in August 1990, before even attaining the age of superannuation. His two sisters, Vathsala and Vaidehi are both married, and Vathsala, the elder, is settled in the United States, while Vaidehi and her family live in Lucknow. Vijay has a daughter, Geetha, and a son Gautam. All are now in Canada, settled there as immigrants. Ayya, by his first marriage to Suli's daughter Sushila, had a couple of children. As for his second marriage, I am not aware of the details, the whole episode having been given, as they say in India, 'a decent burial'!

My maternal grandfather's younger brother, Anantachari, fathered fourteen children between the years 1914 and 1944. The eldest, a daughter affectionately called Ammani, lives in Baroda — now called Vadodara — in the state of Gujarat. She has several children. We have had very cordial relations with all the members of that family. The youngest, Colonel T.A. Ranganathan, is now in Madras. In between, of course, the flux of time has created a few sad gaps. Their family has provided three sons to the armed forces of India. Raghu, the most loved of all, died many years ago in an air accident. As for the families of my grandfather's step-brothers, I regret to say that we have lost contact with that arm of the family long ago. In fact I think that the last time I saw any of them personally was perhaps in 1955, the year of my marriage. But this much I do remember, that there were several uncles, and at least one aunt. I suspect that since my great-grandfather, Ramanuja Iyengar, married a second time, there were strained relationships between Thatha and the other half of his family. It must have been a rather late second marriage, for my grandfather was even then more than fifty years old!

My eldest maternal uncle Kasturi was a very fastidious person, and liked things to be placed neatly, everything in its place. He would spend a great deal of time cleaning and polishing his wrist watch and similar other possessions, of which he took meticulous care. He graduated from the Madras University and initially got a job in the same government department as my Thatha. Later on he transferred himself to the Central Excise Department, and there he rose to the position of Superintendent, in which capacity he retired from service in the year 1960. His progress was quite slow, and he attributed it to the fact that Thatha had ended his career with a blight on his character. That was of course quite possible, but nevertheless I have often felt that he blamed his father unjustly for his own lack of progress. For after all, his own merit should have had something to do with his progress or the lack of it. In any case he became bitter and disillusioned, and was not a very happy man. This made him cynical, and he could be cruel to others, and especially to his poor wife, Kamali, who suffered greatly as a consequence.

In a similarly illogical fashion, Kasturi blamed Kamali for his love marriage with her — and I never did understand the logic of his mental process in this matter. He also developed an attitude of bitterness against his father who had to sell off, bit by bit, all his extensive properties in fighting a bitter legal battle against the Government over a period of thirty years or more, which he eventually lost — which disastrous conclusion was clear to all except to him right from the beginning. Kasturi felt that his father's foolishness had deprived him of his rich patrimony. In this, too, he did great injustice to my grandfather for, after all, all the wealth that my Thatha squandered was his own self-earned wealth. As such it was his to do with as he pleased. I don't for a moment deny the fact that my grandfather had been tragically unwise in many things that he did — but it was difficult to accept that his sons had any right to blame him for it.

The other two uncles of mine, Vijay and Ayya, also shared this bitterness. Vijay, however, slowly managed to look at the situation more philosophically, and didn't blame his father so much. In the case of Ayya, unfortunately, his bitterness turned to hatred of his father, and since he couldn't do anything to him, he turned all his bitterness and frustration upon my poor grandmother. All the sons had led a pampered existence, and I suppose this made things more difficult for them. Vijay and Ayya were not serious students in college, and led a life of relaxed ease, dressing extravagantly, while picking up bad habits like smoking and drinking along the way. I remember that they would come home from college with a small pill of what used to be called *Jintan* in their mouths to disguise the smell of cigarettes. Occasionally they would be found out, and if my grandfather was there, they would get a good thrashing.

I have heard that when they were teenagers in Tuticorin, they had been caught smoking behind the bathroom, all three of them caught red-handed for once. And my grandfather's younger brother Anantachari and Kasturi himself, though he was one of the culprits, grabbed hold of heavy logs of firewood and gave the other two a sound thrashing! They survived all this. Those were hardy days, obviously! But they never gave up their stylish dresses, nor their smoking. I remember they used to wear suits to college, as if they were English lads, with the latest fashion exhibited in their 'roll collar coats' — and all this in the thirties! Vijay managed to graduate with a degree in Arts from the Presidency College at Madras by the skin of his teeth, so to say, but Ayya was a drop-out.

Vijay managed to carve out a career for himself, and managed his life very well indeed. I am not quite sure of the various jobs that he held. He was a bit of a butterfly in most matters, without much staying power or concentration. He liked to flit from one thing to another, and yet managed to keep himself in service throughout his life, earning a reasonably good salary. He was never disgruntled or bitter, taking things fairly philosophically, and trying to use such influence as he had to change circumstances for the better. He finally got into the office of the Textile Commissioner in Bombay, and led a secure life, and retired honourably. He also worked for private parties after retirement before he emigrated to Canada, after his son had gone there himself. He was married twice. His first wife, Anasuya, came from a rich and well-known family. She was a wonderful woman for whom all of us, her nephews, had great love and affection. She was a plain woman, and perhaps did not find much favour in her husband's eyes. She was also childless, a good reason in Hindu society for a husband to ill treat his wife. Poor girl, she did not live long, and thus spared herself much possible suffering. Vijay's second wife Padma is happily still alive, and they have a son Gautam and a daughter Geetha.

Poor Ayya was unfortunately destined to lead a frustrated life in the village, and was the cause of immense sorrow to his parents. I know that he was employed briefly, but his overpowering arrogance and his fiery temper were against him from the beginning. No employer could be expected to tolerate impertinence and insubordination from a junior-level employee. Ayya never succeeded in finding a job after his first explosive trials. It was unfortunate that his parents lacked the will and the ability to regulate him from the beginning. My grandfather was rarely at home, being always on the move, conducting raids on smugglers and so forth. My dear grandmother had absolutely no effect on him. In fact, once when she refused to give him the money that he asked for, Ayya actually broke her little finger in violent rage!

Ayya was actually a genius gone terribly wrong. There was very little that he could not do in the mechanical world. I remember that once when their car went dead, he diagnosed the problem as carburetor failure, and not having the possibility of securing a new one for a couple of weeks, he carved one out of wood, replaced the useless one with the wooden one, and made the car run perfectly till a replacement arrived from Madras. He also worked on a *veena*, a south Indian stringed instrument, which had gone badly out of tune, and replaced the entire fret system in a matter of a few days, making it a perfect instrument.

But genius though he was, he was wild and uncontrollable, and all his genius went waste. His was a wasted life in every sense of the term. He idled away his time in ill-treating his parents, quarreling with all and sundry, and in combing his hair, of which he was exceedingly vain, sitting before a mirror carefully positioned on the floor, dipping his comb into a glass of water again and again, combing away for perhaps half an hour, until he had his hair set to his satisfaction. So what is the use of possessing extraordinary talents? Persons much less endowed with the gifts of nature went on to make very successful and worthwhile lives, while he rotted in his own mire of desolation, pushing others also into it.

It is a funny thing that Ayya was always apparently busy, but never did anything except to extravagantly spend the diminishing resources of the family. In his middle age he fell very ill. He was returning late at night to Agaravallam, my grandfather's village, along a village road. Just as he passed a culvert, he saw a flash of light and fell unconscious. Even though it was quite late, some passerby noticed him, recognized him, and brought him home in his bullock cart, the only mode of transport in the villages of India. He lost his voice, and used to scream in pain and fear. He wrote that he felt as if his cot was lifted by giant hands, up to the ceiling, and it was as if some agency was trying to crush him against the roof of the cottage. But that never happened. Again priests were brought in, followed by exorcists, and the rigmarole went on for nearly a year and a half, when he suddenly regained his voice, and his shattered courage — for he was one of the most courageous men that I have known. But this episode ruined his health, and he went into a decline thereafter.

Ayya too had two wives. The first was Sushila, the eldest daughter of my mother's sister, Suli. They were married in 1948, if I remember right. It was just after this marriage that all the horror that I have written about struck my grandfather's household. By this marriage Ayya and Sushila had two sons and a daughter. The second was a romantic attachment. I don't really remember whether he married Rukmini or not, but that union also produced three children. I don't think either marriage produced anything but fleeting happiness for them. And of course there was a lot of misery for both the wives, and for the neglected children of the second union.

Ayya wasted away his life in this fashion, doing no good to anyone, least of all to himself, squandering the ever-dwindling and meager resources of the family. After my grandmother died towards the end of 1955, he had virtually no sympathizers. His end was an unfortunately sad one. He managed to catch pneumonia, which turned into tuberculosis. He was a heavy smoker, and was not able to give it up even after the doctors had repeatedly warned him about the consequences. He eventually was pronounced incurable, and was sent to the Tuberculosis Sanatorium in Sengipatti, near Tanjore, where he subsisted from day to day on meagre remittances from sympathetic relatives who still remembered that he existed.

I went to see him on two occasions, and was shocked to see the skeleton that he had become. It was a fearful sight, and the obnoxious stink in the ward was nauseating and I could only put up with it with very considerable difficulty. Poor Ayya. He still had dreams of coming out alive, and of making an enormous fortune which he thought was his birthright. He died a month later, much to my sorrow, for we had been good friends, he being perhaps just six years older than I was. In his last months in the sanatorium he swung from one extreme of hope and longing to the other extreme of despair and fear of death. What a wasted life! What promise there had been, and how much his parents had loved him, since he was the last born, and the last child is always the darling of the family.

My poor, dear grandmother suffered enormously because of him. In all my life I have not sorrowed for anyone so much as I have sorrowed for her — an innocent and extremely loving woman subjected to such misery as is difficult to imagine. May God forgive my grandfather and Ayya, my uncle, for all the misery that they made her suffer.

My Elder Generation

Both Kasturi and Ayya had fiery tempers, of which they were quite inordinately proud too. They rather proudly attributed it to their Tupil heritage! This fiery temper was shared by them with their father, as well as with their uncle Anantachari, whose sons were also inheritors of this unfortunate trait, bringing sorrow and suffering to the all-suffering women of their respective households. Vijay from my grandfather's family, and his cousin Raju, son of Anantachari, were the two exceptions. The later children of Anantachari, such as Raghu and Ranga, also escaped this evil inheritance. In both the families there was always a great deal of tension. My younger grandfather, Anantachari, had a most terrible temper. When he was enraged he could do anything. Once he was very angry with his eldest son, Parthasarathi, known in the family as Pacha. After soundly thrashing Pacha, he put him out of the house and made him stand in the dark in pouring rain all night. The son was equally adamant, and withstood this treatment. Perhaps because of this ability to withstand suffering with an arrogant patience, he joined the army and rose to the position of a Colonel.

It can be seen that life was by no means a bed of roses in the families of my maternal grandparents. How my mother escaped all this, and had such a gentle and loving heart, is one of those mysteries of nature which is difficult to understand. But in fairness to them I must add that all of them could be extremely kind on occasion, and gentle too. One only wishes that such occasions had been the rule rather than the occasional exception that they were. They never realised how much they ill-treated their loved ones, albeit unwittingly, and I hope unwillingly. More, they never understood that they were harming themselves more than they could ever harm others.

I never cease to wonder at the human capacity to generate misery and frustration, when they are equally powerfully endowed with the capacity to create love, harmony and peace. I have always regretted the fact that my dear grandmother had to suffer so much in her life — suffering which could have been very largely avoided. It is one of the greatest failings of human nature that we refuse to be happy and at peace with the world when it is so easily possible, and then chase these very values after we have created a world of unrest and hatred.

I believe that the older generations were very wise in the ways of finding happiness within the framework of their existence, and did not chase ephemeral shadows as the modern generations are prone to do. The essential difference, to my mind, is that they were finding the maximum happiness that they could within their lives, in the environment that they were in, whereas the modern generation wants to create happiness. I believe that this is a fundamental error in approach, as it is rarely possible to create happiness for ourselves, though it is possible to make others happy! One must be able to probe this mystery to understand that Nature leaves one's happiness in the hands of others, nudging one gently to the understanding of the profound truth that if one is able to make others happy, then we will be made happy by others!

On my father's side the main figures are his two younger brothers, Ramabhadran, affectionately addressed by his peers as Raman, and by us as Chitya, and Bakthavathsalan, whom we all addressed as Bakthu. Krishnan, my father's step brother, was unavailable, though we grew to love him. Chitya was away in Assam when we were young, and therefore we had very little personal association with him. We admired him tremendously because he lived in the dense jungles of Assam, having got into the Indian Forest Service in 1930 or 1931 after passing a most difficult competitive examination. I was told that there was only one single vacancy, and the entrants to the examination had to deposit a personal bond of rupees ten thousand in cash, which would be forfeited if the entrant failed.

They of course had no money, but my uncle had a bosom friend who deposited this enormous sum of money. My uncle passed the examination, topping the list, fortunately for his friend, and even more fortunately for himself, and got into the service — one of the elite services of those days. His friend must have had tremendous faith in my uncle, or a real love, or perhaps both, for there was only one single vacancy that had to be filled by the competitive examination — and on that he deposited the enormous sum demanded by the government. My uncle must have had a similarly great faith in himself to have risked his friend's money. The outcome was fortunate, since my Chitya did qualify for that single vacancy, and got the appointment. The friend got his money back, and he also earned the lifelong gratitude of my father for this timely assistance.

My Chitya is supposed to have had a horoscope, or rather planetary positions, resembling those of Lord Rama of the *Ramayana*. He had to spend a large slice of his life in the jungles of Assam. I remember that once, in 1938, he sent us a tiger skin mounted with head, claws and all. He had himself shot the tiger in the jungle. It was put up on one of the walls of our home, from where it glared down balefully at all of us. He was a hero figure for us, though one whom it was difficult to get close to, or become intimate with. Further, he was living with British officers all the time, and had inevitably to adopt an anglicized mode of life. He went to the extent of even dressing for dinner, and eating with knives and forks! It is true that in those days, officers of the elitist services were expected to conform to the English way of life, but he could have adapted easily to the regular Indian habits at least when he came out of that environment; but for some reason known to himself he adopted that mode permanently, with the result that we were intimidated, and found it difficult to break down those artificial barriers that he had erected around himself.

It was only very much later, after we brothers were all married and had children of our own, that some degree of intimacy became possible. By then he had retired from service and had mellowed very considerably. We had always known that he was extraordinarily kind and generous. He kept our family going during the years when my father faced extreme financial stringency, and also supported Bakthu through his education. In fact his financial assistance lasted till we started earning — as far as my memory goes — and for this we have to be ever grateful to him. But gratitude is not the same thing as love, and it is a pity that we were able to show our love for him only very late in life. He hid a very soft and loving heart under an extraordinarily gruff exterior. His gruffness was augmented by perhaps the most bushy pair of eyebrows that I have seen! I think that he had a deep-seated fear of being exploited if he showed his tender personality, and therefore defensively adopted a false personality which denied him the companionship of almost all his relatives. We were by no means the only ones who maintained a respectable distance from him! To my knowledge, my father was the only person really close to him, for even Bakthu was very uncomfortable in his presence.

My Chitya had a very deep and tender love for my father. He also admired my father enormously for the successes that he achieved in spite of all the handicaps and tragedies that he had to suffer. Perhaps it would be correct to say that Chitya had this depth of feeling only for his mother and for his elder brother. My father was something of a father to Chitya. In fact my father was addressed by him as *chinnappa*, which is a Tamil word meaning 'little father'. The Hindu *Shastras* in fact state

From left: Vaidehi, Kamali, Rangamani, R. Kasturi, Vathsala
1944

R. Vijayaraghavan (Vijay)

Anasuya
(deceased circa 1935)

From left: R. Rangachari and R. Sulochani (Suli)

From left: R. Narayanan (Ayya) and R. Sushila

C.A. Ramabhadran (Chitya) with Parthasarthi
July, 1935

From left: Kothandaraman, Vasantha,
C.A. Ramabhadran (Chitya), Srinivasan - July, 1935

From left: C.A. Ramabhadran (Chitya) and Gouri

C.A. Bakthavathsalan (Bakthu)

Shakuntala (Chitti)

From left: C.A. Bakthavathsalan (Bakthu), Shakuntala (Chitti), Ranganathan, Srinivasan, Parthasarathi, Chakrapani

My Elder Generation

that the eldest brother is to be regarded as being equal to one's father! When we came to develop an intimate closeness with Chitya, I often used to feel a deep sympathy amounting almost to pity for him because he had voluntarily isolated himself from the affection and love of his family, while his heart was weeping for warmth and affection all the while.

He was very brave, and many are the stories told of his exploits in the dense jungles of Assam that were his home for approximately fifteen years. I of course never heard them all, but I do remember a few, perhaps the bravest, of his jungle encounters. One day he went for a walk alone in the jungle adjoining his bungalow. He had only an umbrella with him, as it had been raining heavily till then. He must have walked a few miles into the jungle without realising how far away from home he was. Suddenly he came face to face with a full grown tigress, with two cubs near it. Being familiar with the big cats he tried to back away from them without exciting the tigress. He had walked back a few paces when he heard a deep rumble behind him. It was the father of the cubs, with its tail swinging menacingly! My uncle was caught between the tiger and the tigress, and with two young cubs to boot! It was a moment of the gravest danger, and he of course knew it. Just as the tigress advanced with its belly close to the ground ready to spring upon him, with great presence of mind he snapped open his umbrella with an explosive suddenness. This sudden action of an umbrella opening in its face unnerved the tigress, and it bounded away into the jungle, followed by its cubs. Finally the tiger itself bounded off into the jungle. He displayed great presence of mind, for the slightest indecision or sign of fear would no doubt have ended his life there and then.

Of course this was but one of many such episodes in his danger-filled existence. We three brothers had once gone to spend our summer holidays with him. We went by train from

Calcutta to a small station called Haltugaon, travelling thither overnight. Chitya met us with his car — a huge saloon with an open top, which used to be called a tourer model. It was an enormous model, and was called a Marmon. It was said to be one of two or three Marmons in the whole of India. I have never heard of this make of car subsequently! From there he drove us two hours or so to reach his village, where he had a bungalow built upon tall stilts, so that the edifice was about ten or twelve feet above the ground. It was tiger country, and those forests were well populated by this ferocious giant cat. Our luggage followed on elephant back, and reached our home about eight hours later. Each of the elephants carried the trunk of a banana plant in its trunk, this being one of the components of their evening meal. The banana plant was stripped of its petal-soft covering, layer by layer, folded length-wise into a sort of packet, and stuffed with paddy soaked for several hours in water. This stuffed packet was placed in the elephant's trunk, and the elephant swallowed it whole. Each elephant could consume a whole bucketful of soaked paddy thus wrapped into packets for each meal.

We had our bedroom next to Chitya's. It was normal to be awakened once or twice every night by the trumpeting of the wild male elephants calling out from the jungle to our tame female elephants — for the elephants used for forest work were usually females. Chitya was often compelled to fire a round or two into the air to drive away the wild males, as otherwise they could cause havoc, having being known to pull down such bungalows in their frenzy. Generally when we woke up in the morning, Chitya would show us the pug marks of tigers on the loose soil around the flower beds in the garden. It was true jungle wilderness, and we had first-hand experience of it. We enjoyed our stay there, of course, but it was not our idea of a pleasant holiday when Chitya took us with him into the deepest jungle in his car, and there left the three of us alone with an unloaded rifle for company, while he went off on foot with a walking stick to inspect the forests under his stewardship! He disdained the use of firearms, and would generally not carry one with him, though there was always an unloaded one in the car for use in any extreme emergency!

Poor man, his marriage was not a very satisfactory one. After years and years of waiting, since he did not want to take a bride into the forbidding environment of the Assam jungles, he was finally married to Gouri Thambatti, a member of the Kollengode family of Kerala, whom he had met through a friend. I think he married her more out of a sense of chivalry than out of any positive feeling for her. He was the type who could not cause disappointment to another. They were married in Kollengode, with just my father and his cousin brother, Shri S. Amudachari, attending the wedding. The wedding was an elaborate and opulent one, the Kollengode family being a *zamindari* family, the head of the family, Gouri's eldest brother Shri Padmanabha Thamban, having the title of the Raja of Kollengode!

Perhaps this marriage caused some more distance to develop between Chitya and the rest of the family. It was sometimes intimidating to have a so-called princess of the Kollengode family for one's aunt! To be fair to her, she tried, quite successfully I must admit, to come closer to us. She was largely successful with most of the family members. I must thank her for bringing us closer to Chitya by her efforts. She had an easy intimacy of manner which one does not expect from a member of such a wealthy family. Towards the end, Chitya developed a really deep love for my son Krishna, and they became good friends. This companionship developed more and more when Chitya was in hospital during what finally proved to be his last illness in 1977. Krishna used to visit him almost every evening to take him out for a walk along the corridors of the ward.

Chitya was hospitalized for a month, during which period he had to have blood transfusions frequently, about once every three days, as he had a peculiar form of anaemia in which the white blood corpuscles of the blood were not being regenerated. The only treatment was blood marrow transplantation, as it was then known, but one had to go to the U.S.A. for it. He was getting better day by day, though the blood transfusions could not be stopped. One evening after Krishna had come and gone, Chitya's condition suddenly deteriorated. I stayed with him the whole night, silently praying for his life. As the night ended and dawn arrived, he breathed his last. One moment he was there, and the next moment he was gone. Krishna came an hour later, looking happy, with a smile on his face. I met him on the staircase and gave him the sorrowful information — and both of us wept for the dear departed one who had suffered so much loneliness and misery in what should have been an extraordinarily happy and prosperous life.

Since Chitya was childless, my aunt Gouri asked me to perform the ritual acts of final respect for the departed, and also the cremation. So I was compelled to perform this most sorrowful of dutiful acts for my dear Chitya. It was something which I would have avoided at any cost, but circumstances made it impossible to escape this dreary duty. Once again I had to light the funeral pyre of a beloved one, consigning the body to the flames. I had already been compelled by circumstances to perform this heart-breaking duty once before. My family was unhappy about this, because there was a tradition — perhaps it is more appropriate to call it a superstition — that one whose father was living should not perform the funeral obsequies of a male relative. Thus it was that I had this miserable experience of bidding good-bye to two of my beloved uncles.

In the final analysis one is compelled to say that my poor Chitya suffered needlessly all his life. He had distanced himself too much from the reality of the daily life, and created a gap between himself and the rest of the family, so that barring but a few exceptions all were uneasy with him. It was the same in his work-a-day environment. He was a perfectionist — and there is certainly no harm in that — but his vitriolic criticism of poor performance, and even of reasonably good performance, earned the displeasure of all his associates. He had virtually no genuine friends. Such as came to him were mere flatterers who needed something from him, and this deepened his suspicion of human beings in general. Also he seems to have regretted the fact that his marriage to a Malayalee (Keralite, in today's terminology) had in no small measure estranged him from Brahmin society — for the Brahmins are a closed community, with standards of their own. This seems to have made him think that in some way he had ceased to be the pure Brahmin that he was. I have seen him shed tears in temples when the Vedic chanting was going on, repeating the mantras silently. My father knew all about Chitya's state of mind, and they would have long conversations over the telephone, each conversation often lasting fully half an hour! I think what distressed Chitya the most was the feeling that his mother would not have approved of his marriage to one who was not a Shri Vaishnava Brahmin.

What a lesson his life has for others? Here was a man born in an absolutely poverty-stricken family, but with the highest cultural and religious heritage possible. He overcame tremendous odds to get a first class education, topping his class all the way right to the end, and by dint of sheer brilliance entered one of the coveted civil services. He went on to become a success in every sense, making a great deal of money, becoming really wealthy, and a well-known world figure in the field of forestry. He became Director of Forest Education in India, and went on to get into the service of the United Nations, and served with the F.A.O. in Rome for several years. He was later a member of the U.N.D.P., serving in a few foreign countries abroad.

I once visited him in Amman, happily for his sixty-first birthday — a very auspicious day in the life of a Hindu Brahmin — and it was a great pleasure for me to be there for I was the only member of the family to be able to make it. He then told me that at the behest of the ruler of Jordan, he had created a small forest in the desert, the work taking some ten years to complete, and entailing the enormous expenditure of several million dollars! He was very proud of this achievement. Such was his dogged nature, for he had to go down some twenty thousand feet to find the necessary water! And yet, with all this magnificent achievement, he was a miserable man, always brooding upon what might have been. So what is the real value of wealth and achievement? Nil, I should say, if his life is any indicator. He suffered for his mother. She was his magnificent obsession — and his everlasting regret was that he could not help her to lead a reasonably comfortable life. He was also guilt-ridden about his marriage. These two emotions ruined all the chances that he had of living his life in happiness and contentment.

For our younger uncle Bakthu we all had a great deal of affection and fondness right from the beginning. I suppose the fact that he was the youngest of the brothers, and was able to meet us on our own footing, made all the difference. Also, he lived a very simple life, and there was neither fuss nor ceremony in his house. An easy familiarity prevailed, we all often behaving as brothers, rather than as uncle and nephews. Another circumstance was that we all lived together most of the time, whereas with Chitya meetings were few and far between. Bakthu maintained an elder-brotherly familiarity with us, but at the same time we all had to be quite careful, and wary of changes in his moods, since he was prone to suddenly losing his temper, and then we had to watch our behaviour! He had a nasty temper, and on occasion did not spare the rod by any means. But such occasions were rare. He was generally sympathetic and loving, and helped us all with our childish pranks when we were very young children, and helped us to devise more mischievous ones as we grew older. His already great love and affection for us was greatly enhanced because we were motherless!

He suffered from a terrible inferiority complex, and this made him hide his golden and soft interior under a veil of silent gruffness. He was, I believe, awed by the genius of his two elder brothers. They were extraordinarily intelligent, and even though he was not lacking in that department, he nevertheless developed this terribly crippling inferiority complex very early in life. The difference in age no doubt added to this. With my father he was quite easy, though he was quick to angry response if he thought there was even a trace of criticism in my father's attitude or comments. My father took care to avoid rubbing Bakthu the wrong way, but there were always certain thoughtless moments when Bakthu would react with anger or annoyance, and then all conversation would cease. But generally there was love and harmony, and we loved to be with him.

It is a pity that Bakthu did not shine in his scholastic endeavours. I don't think he ever made any serious attempts to do so, feeling that nothing he ever did could lead him to the glorious heights of scholastic achievement of his brothers. In this he did grave injustice to himself, for I have often perceived that he had a latent wisdom which he shielded under a cover of indifference. He could throw up the most astonishing facts from his vast store of the most outlandish information that he possessed. He was a voracious reader — Chitya often remarking, rather uncharitably, that he had nothing better to do! — and this, coupled with a very retentive memory, helped him to become something of a walking encyclopaedia! But he was shy of revealing his knowledge, and I think he was always suffering because he felt uneducated in the presence of his brothers.

I did not follow Bakthu's career very closely, for the simple reason that to us he was a sort of compatriot, playing with us, and so on. I believe that he graduated with a degree in science, and then he joined a special training programme at Bombay where the course covered the repair and maintenance of radios. This was considered to be a very good course, and had been chosen for Bakthu by Chitya. Chitya knew of course that Bakthu would probably not fare well in a paid job because of his intolerance, his sensitivity, and his attitude of reticence. So with the best intention in the world this course was selected for him to enable Bakthu to establish a service outlet of his own, so that he could lead an independent and possibly affluent life.

Bakthu completed the course with good grades, and there everything stopped. He just would not accept the responsibility of taking in radio sets and repairing them. My father and Chitya spoke to him again and again, but all to no avail. He would get annoyed, red in the face, and leave the place, or he would angrily ask, "Who will pay if the set gets broken?" My father would patiently point out that he, Bakthu, had been trained for the job. Bakthu would sarcastically retort, "That does not make me God. Only God can repair sets so that the client finds no blame. I cannot do it. That is all." They kept at him patiently for many months, but Bakthu refused to budge, and eventually that career was written off very regretfully. I believe that by his mulish stubbornness arising out of fear, Bakthu ruined forever all the chances that he had of making a successful career for himself. I know that Chitya told him again and again that if anything went wrong, he himself would take responsibility for any damages claimed by the clients. But it all had as much effect as rain falling on a buffalo's back, as we say in Tamil!

In the end Bakthu sought service with the government, and with Chitya's help at every stage, he did manage to enter the service of the Madras government in the Labour Department, from which service he eventually retired on a small pension. It was by no means a fulfilling career, nor was it suitable for one of his education and his higher-than-average abilities — but that was what he wanted. He chose job security conjoined with the minimum of personal responsibility for job performance, and that was what he got. It is a curse on the south Indian, and more especially the Brahmins, that they have always sought security of service, and landed up with the lowest paid jobs; most of them end up as clerks or stenographers under the shelter of the enormous umbrella of the central and state governments.

The south Indian Brahmins were a timid community, and though they have always had the reputation of being the top brains of the country, and therefore much sought after, they lacked drive and initiative. One should not conclude that there were no eminent south Indian Brahmins. There were, and many of them too. They were the intellectuals *par excellence* of this country, and continue to be so, though intelligence is no longer the virtual monopoly of the Brahmin community as it used to be. There were eminent south Indian Brahmins in the freedom movement. There were great lawyers and judges too. One reason for this backwardness may be that the *Bhagavad Gita* specifies that the Brahmin should not be involved in agriculture and commerce. The chosen fields for the Brahmin were teaching, priesthood and as advisors. Therefore, in the time of the princely states in India, of which there were several hundreds, small, big, and very big, it was quite common to find that the prime ministers of such states were by and large Brahmins, the south Indian figuring quite prominently in this field.

It is heartening that, especially after World War II, the attitude has changed somewhat, and today one can find Brahmins with initiative and boldness, taking risks, and entering the field of business and industry. South India has produced many large industrial houses, and the field is growing. But lack of capital has tended to inhibit the growth of the community as a whole in this direction. Bakthu unfortunately lacked the drive, initiative and the courage needed to take off on his own. He missed a golden opportunity, as just then the field of radio engineering began to expand, and he could even have obtained a good position in the growing number of radio stations that were coming up, one by one, all over the country. But he missed the bus, and had to resign himself to a life of mediocrity. This was of course very frustrating, and I am afraid that it made him something of a cynic. He also tended towards increasing timidity, and would worry about almost everything that one can possibly worry about. His philosophy was that anything that could at all go wrong would go wrong! Naturally he was wary of most things, persons and events, so that he got very little pleasure or enjoyment out of life.

His only pleasure or recreation was in books, which he read voraciously, and with a great catholicity of taste. He was prepared to read anything in print, but his chosen field was novels and, later, science fiction to which we were both addicted. I don't know who got the addiction from whom —

perhaps I was the carrier! I don't think he had an interest in anything else, though he was never averse to joining us in any game or play if we were able to persuade him out of his bed, where he did most of his reading. I was quite close to him, and he would generally not turn down my requests. He was also fond of walking, and he and I used to go on very long walks from which we returned after many hours, tired and hungry. This helped us to know the city thoroughly. I believe that I developed my sense of distance and direction from all those long walks with him. After I entered service I couldn't walk so much, and it is only after many years that I have been able to start walking for pleasure, all over again.

Bakthu was married in 1939, if my memory serves me right. He was just twenty-four or twenty-five years old then. I don't remember whether he had already secured a job or not. I believe he had not. Those were still the days of comparatively early marriages, and the marriages then, as now, were generally arranged marriages. The bride was named Shakuntala. She came of a family which had been very well off, but had fallen on evil days, and were quite destitute at the time this marriage took place. The wedding was celebrated in a small village called Kshetrapalapuram in the Tanjore district. We all went there by train, and found the house to be a very old and decrepit one. The family's poor financial circumstances were obvious, there being no genuine coffee even for the groom's party. What was served was a pseudo coffee made out of fried coriander seeds, and this used to be called, very appropriately, the poor man's coffee!

Shakuntala, who became our Chitti the next morning, was a fair and pretty girl. She instantly adopted us as she was to be our paternal aunt, which conferred upon her the status almost equivalent to that of our mother. She was friendly and affectionate, and went out of her way to earn our affection — which she did without any difficulty.

Her father was a wonderful old man. He had been a business man and had enjoyed a thriving career. I learnt that his business had been with cement, which was then imported from England, there being no local manufacture of this commodity. I was told that just a few years prior to the marriage, one ship load of cement had been unloaded and transported to their place. Not having adequate godown space, the cement bags had been stored out in the open. Even though it was not the rainy season, unseasonal rains had suddenly washed away the entire stock, ruining the family overnight. There was no insurance in those days that I was aware of. Of course I was too young and inexperienced to know of these commercial requirements, but later gossip confirmed this. Shakuntala's father was suddenly faced with an enormous burden of debt. He vowed that until he had paid off all his debts he would not shave, and so when we met him for the first time on the eve of the wedding, he had a long and luxurious beard. He was a most affectionate person, and our close association with him and the rest of his affectionate family was something which was cherished by all of us.

The wedding the next morning was a modest affair. We youngsters were there at the bride's home for a long time — I think it must have been a couple of weeks — because I fell ill, and my newly married Chitti nursed me with the attention that her son would have received. We became very close and intimate, thanks to this illness of mine, and I am therefore grateful to it. She had no knowledge of cooking or of the household duties that she would have to perform in her husband's home. But she learnt most of it thanks to my illness, so that in a sense both of us benefited from that stay. She was just a girl hardly sixteen years old, and marriage did not make any difference to her. She played all the games that boys usually played, and became known as something of a tomboy. She had, in those days, an irrepressible sense of humour, and her laughter would go pealing through the house — much to the consternation of her mother, for it was just not done for a bride, and a newly married one at that, to behave with such abandon. But her father loved her deeply, and would look on with a fond smile at all her antics. I can say that just after her marriage to Bakthu, we were very much like brother and sister. It was only later that she took on the role of an aunt — and by then I too had grown up, I suppose, and a reserve developed in our relationship. I suppose it was appropriate, for she was my aunt.

My uncle, Bakthu, seems to have had a satisfactory married life. He was always gruff and reserved, and with Chitti he was sometimes quite abrupt, especially when he lost his temper. He was not physically active within the house, mostly lying in bed reading. This made my aunt too quite lazy physically, so that in later life she put on weight. Ladies didn't go out for walks, and there was no other form of physical exercise available to them. As girls they were allowed to play in the front and back yards of the house, but after marriage such tomboyishness was frowned upon. She seemed to become less and less active as the years rolled by. But she always retained a little of the freshness of her youth. She suffered much from Bakthu's morbid fears, and from his uncertain temper. But then the lot of women in India has always been a difficult one, and I have very often felt that but for the background of tradition and culture, our women would have rebelled against the circumstances they were expected to consider happy!

Bakthu was just fifty-nine years or so old, and was due to celebrate the completion of his sixtieth year, his sixty-first birthday, to which happy event we were all looking forward, when tragedy struck. It was the year 1974. I had been to

Down Memory Lane

Lucknow and Shahjahanpur, and had just got back home. I was having lunch at home, and I remember the day vividly because as I was eating, a telephone call was received from my office to announce the passing away of Mr. T.T. Krishnamachari, the founder of the firm for which I was working. I had to go to the home of his eldest son, Shri T.T. Narasimhan, the senior partner of the firm of T.T. Krishnamachari & Co., to offer my condolences. I do not remember the exact date, nor is it relevant. Why I remember this at all is because the sad event of my uncle Bakthu's passing away occurred a day or two later.

It was early in the morning, at around 4:30 A.M., that a phone call was received from my Chitti to say that Bakthu was a little unwell. She asked my father to go to their home, which was hardly a mile away from ours. We all decided to go there. When we reached the home a few minutes later, Bakthu was sitting up in his bed, and when he saw my father he said that he was well, and that he had telephoned only because he felt like seeing him! He was perspiring profusely — a cold sweat — and this should have alerted us to the impending tragedy. But we were glad that he said that he was feeling well, and thought no more about it. We all had coffee, and I was just about to return home, as I was to have a much-needed hair cut, when my Chitti called from the bedroom to say that my uncle was taken bad suddenly. I rushed to our family physician, who was fortunately available, and brought him to Bakthu's place. He examined him, and advised immediate hospitalization. There was a private nursing home within a few minutes walk, and we telephoned and fixed up the appointment for an immediate examination. We had to take Bakthu down in a chair, as his apartment was on the first floor. We rushed him in the car to the hospital. He was swiftly taken to the cardiac care unit, and as his ECG was being monitored, he expired.

My Elder Generation

It was a devastating shock which could hardly be believed. We were all benumbed by the suddenness of it all. But life has to go on, and after paying the bills we brought his dear body home to *Gayathri*, telephoned uncle Bhadran, and prepared for the cremation. Bakthu's elder son, Chakrapani, was on the high seas somewhere between Japan and Australia, he being the captain of a ship. The second son, Ranganathan, was in the U.S.A., he having settled there. The responsibility for the cremation of Bakthu descended upon me — a sad and bitter duty which could not be delegated. The saddest part of it all was that, just before I set fire to the funeral pyre my weeping aunt, Chitti, put her arms around me and said, "Oh Pachu, I was depending only upon you to save him."

My aunt was utterly devastated by this sudden bereavement, which left her a widow. Both her sons were away, one permanently in the U.S.A., and the other on the high seas of the world, coming home only occasionally. It was impossible to even imagine her agony. I was especially close to her, and sometimes it was almost impossible for me to even look at her, for fear of breaking down myself. We persuaded her to stay, but after a day or two, she insisted on returning home to their flat, telling me that her dear departed husband might need her there, and perhaps might be looking for her! There was no persuading her to remain with us, and so we took her to her apartment, where a young girl, a relation of hers, came to stay with her.

Some six weeks later I was in Mayavaram, some 180 miles south of Madras. I had attended a wedding there, and just as I finished lunch, a long distance call was received for me. When I spoke, I was told that my Chitti had passed away, and that I should return home immediately. As it was considered inauspicious to talk about death in a house where a wedding had just been celebrated, I pleaded urgent work in my office and left by car for Madras, reaching Chitti's residence at around 6:30 P.M., only to find that her body had already been taken to the crematorium. I went there just as my younger brother, Kothandaraman, lit the funeral pyre. Again both the sons were unavailable, and the final duty to the dead devolved upon him in my absence. It was perhaps forty days since Bakthu had passed away!

The second son, Ranga, arrived some days later from the U.S.A., but he was too late to be of any use. He had not been able to soothe the last moments of his parents on earth. I personally believe that Bakthu had been deeply affected by the loneliness caused by the absence of both his sons, but in his usual reticent manner he never spoke about it. I knew something of it, because I had a suspicion that he blamed my father for Chakra's career in the merchant navy. It had been my father who sent Chakrapani to the *Dufferin*, a training establishment for young boys wanting to adopt an ocean-going career. My father was perceptive and sensitive enough to know that Bakthu blamed him, but he had done it with the best of intentions to improve the family circumstances. But nevertheless, I believe that it was this deep-rooted loneliness that was at least in part responsible for Bakthu's untimely and sudden end. Chitti followed him within seven weeks because life was intolerable for her without her husband's presence, especially with both her sons away.

In India such tragedies have become quite common, because many are the families where sons have gone to the U.S.A. for education, and stayed on there, lured by the glitter and glamour of life in that country. I wonder whether the children of such families ever realise that the loving hearts that they are leaving behind are being broken bit by bit, day by day, often culminating in the death of those they love. The material lure of the Western world, and above all of America, has destroyed quite a few families. I think it is a special blessing conferred upon my wife Sulochana and myself that our only son Krishna returned to India after a three-and-a-half year spell in the U.S.A., during which he took two Master's degrees, one in Industrial Engineering, and the other in Business Administration. Especially following upon the poignancy of the loneliness that beset my uncle Bakthu and my aunt Chitti, we were able to appreciate this special blessing, for which I am ever grateful to my Master, and to my son.

There were other relatives in the older generation who were very close to us. My mother's younger sister named Sulochana, but universally addressed as Suli, was one such person. She was my mother's only sister. Whereas my mother had been dark complexioned, Suli was very fair and quite handsome. She too had poor eyesight, but nowhere as bad as my mother's. She was statuesque where my mother had been slim and tall. Suli too was tall for a south Indian woman. In later life she had to wear the spectacles which she tried to avoid when she was younger.

She was married to Shri R. Rangachari, a very meek and reserved person, out of whom even his closest friends had difficulty in getting a few words. He was also a short-tempered person, trying to cover it up under a superficial cloak of meekness, but it would explode on occasion, and then his real self would be manifested for a brief while. My uncle Rangachari served in the Railways, but in the South of India, and therefore we had not much opportunity of being together. He was an auditor, and served in that department of the Railways.

I believe he was a disappointed person, no doubt having expected life to give him a better deal than what he had received. Being too withdrawn and reserved, he never really let go sufficiently to get some minimum fun out of life. As far as I can remember, his only recreation was the indoor game called *Carrom*, but that too stopped some thirty years back! Even when playing with children he was quarrelsome, and this naturally did not conduce to continued play. He used to occasionally play Bridge, but the games never lasted long because he was always losing his temper with his partner for playing the wrong card! On the whole he was a disgruntled person, carrying a chip on his shoulder, and was poor company at best.

Suli was not by any means a docile person — quite the contrary. She had a trigger-happy temper, and would flare up suddenly, but her temper generally cooled very quickly. She was a very affectionate and outgoing person, and therefore her quick temper never really bothered anyone. Even my Thatha would, on occasion, get the rough end of her tongue! But her affection and concern for others made up for this small deficiency, if it can be at all labelled as deficiency. She was forever buying gifts for others, and I think this generous trait also was part of the reason for her husband's moody nature.

The other person in that family, I mean my maternal grandfather's family, who was always cheerful and outgoing was my second uncle, Vijay. He liked to be cheerful, always saying that life was in any case too short to be wasted in losing one's temper and making everyone else miserable. A healthy philosophy indeed! I think they both inherited their sunny nature from my Thatha who, until his financial debacles plunged him into the deepest depths of misery and despair, had always been cheerful, generally whistling a tune so softly that often we did not know where the music was coming from. He could whistle away for long hours, when he had the time and was in the mood to do so, without pursing his lips. This made it seem as if the music was in the air!

My Elder Generation

Suli mothered us, but without fussing over us as some tended to do. She loved the family as a whole unit, and also loved all its members individually. To her the family was important, and I think she grieved silently when the fortunes of her father's family declined drastically. She did her best to make my Thatha's last days comparatively peaceful and bearable, but she could not do much to alleviate his misery. I never really understood what tortures he suffered, for he must have acutely felt his utter failure after having been one of the most senior officers in his time. I am sure that had she the money, she would have tried to pay off his enormous debts, but no single person could ever have done it — such was the magnitude of his indebtedness.

I realised quite early in my life, perhaps even in my early teens, that her marriage was not really a happy one. But she never made this apparent, though it too would occasionally surface, to be pushed out of the way speedily. She had a character quite opposed to her husband's. He never attempted to change. For her to change would have been of course disastrous. I don't think that he ever really co-operated with her in anything, and though they never stayed apart, they were hardly ever in tune emotionally. This was sad. I feel that she deserved a better deal out of life — though I must say that I had considerable affection for my uncle too. They say marriages are made in heaven. Looking at the marriages all over the world, one cannot but wonder whether this can be true. The only glimmer of reason comes from Hindu philosophy which says that the soul, in its wisdom, chooses its future life-partner (as the spouse is called in India) purely out of evolutionary considerations — and not for happiness or pleasure!

It is amazing how solid the institution of marriage is in India, even today in October 1992 as I write this. At the drop of a hat marriages break apart at the seams in the Occidental world. Divorce rates are so high that one wonders whether such unions can really be called marriages at all. I don't imply any criticism, but am just voicing my concern that words and terms have changed their meanings in the last several decades, often quite drastically.

In India marriage has always been considered to be an indissoluble bond between two persons, one male and the other female. Marriage between persons of the same sex would be considered an utter absurdity, and an abnormality of the most depraved variety. Therefore persons who got married stayed married. There was never any thought of changing the partner. Such a thing was generally considered suitable only to the animal kingdom. I think that the understanding of this fact of the indissoluble nature of marriage, and its acceptance, made the institution of marriage a tolerable one. One set out on the path of married life knowing that one had to make the best of the marriage, and this gave the partners the necessary courage to mould life to their will wherever this was possible. Where it was impossible, it gave them the fortitude to bear what could not be changed. I think this understanding of life produced a healthy attitude to marriage, and made marriage not only tolerable but acceptable as something that had to be used positively if one were to evolve.

I think it is with this evolutionary purpose in mind that the *Shastras* have made marriage obligatory. Perhaps that is also the reason for the early marriages, which custom has prevailed since the dawn of time in India. When something had to be undergone, the earlier the better, seems to have been the attitude. And the evolutionary purpose of this divine institution having been accepted throughout the long ages of this culture, it was inevitable that the element of choice never entered into the scheme of things. Therefore marriages were arranged by the parents of the children. They looked for a suitable bride or groom, as the case may be, paying utmost attention to the other family's history, both spiritual and social. It was not at all as stupid as people in the West would suggest! It made sense to avoid making a choice, because the parameters by which one chose were so absurd — good looks, slimness, fairness of complexion and so on — that it was unthinkable to entrust one's evolution to such flippant considerations. How long did beauty or good looks last, in any case? A few years at best. Then is it wise to sacrifice one's evolution to it? A very firm 'No' was the inevitable, if unwilling, answer. It was not that a young person did not desire to have a beautiful wife — but if destiny decreed otherwise, well destiny had the final say.

On my father's side there was a cousin of his, Mr. S. Amudachari, who was familiar to us. He was a senior advocate of the Madras Bar, and a very staid and sober person. He lived with his family in Triplicane, a suburb of Madras. His wife was a mousy sort of person, very small physically, but very affectionate. I remember that when she entered her final illness, she looked so small on her bed that she could have been mistaken for a bundle of clothes lying upon it. My Periappa — elder father in Tamil — was just the opposite, being a very tall man, quite solidly built, with an imposing presence. Physically they were as mismatched as a couple could have been, but in their marriage they built up a solid family.

There was nothing extravagant about their love and affection. They would receive us with a quiet affection as if we had always been there! We visited them only on our journey to and from Mayavaram on our holidays. We used to be in Jubbulpore in those days. After travelling a few hours from Jubbulpore to Itarsi, we would take the Grand Trunk Express from Itarsi to go on to Madras. From Itarsi the journey lasted around twenty-four hours. When we arrived at Madras, we would take a *jutka* as the horse-drawn vehicles were known, and proceed to my

Periappa's house in Triplicane. We generally spent the day there, leaving for Mayavaram by the night train. My Periappa usually had some money for us — paid to us at my Chitya Ramabhadran's request. When I grew up, I understood that Amudachari Periappa had owed my Chitya a considerable sum of money, and we appear to have received small instalments of the repayment due to him! Very useful to us, no doubt.

I also remember our Amudachari Periappa with much affection because it was he who looked after that other beloved Periappa, Krishnan, my father's step-brother, who had been afflicted with the dreaded leprosy, and who was therefore more or less ostracized from society. He was a very handsome person even when we saw him ravaged with leprosy. He must have been very handsome indeed when he was in his youth. My father had told me that Krishnan Periappa had been a very brilliant student, and had been sent to England for higher studies — and this perhaps in the year 1925 or 1926. He went to England, and it was there that he became afflicted with this awful disease. Before going to England he had married a very beautiful and rich girl, but naturally his marriage ceased to exist when he came back from England. He never exhibited the least bitterness or anger at the way his life had turned out. I thought he was an uncommonly philosophic person, capable of taking every adversity in his stride. He was an inmate of the Lady Willingdon Sanatorium for lepers for well over twenty years. It appeared to me that every day spent there made him more of a philosopher. He seemed to gain something intangible from the miserable existence, cut off from all those he loved, and looked upon with horror by the general public, for leprosy has always been feared more than any other disease.

Krishnan Periappa would come once a month to Triplicane, and sit patiently on the verandah until someone noticed him. Amudachari Periappa would speak with him for some time, and then unobtrusively hand over to him some money. It made no difference to me when I learnt later on that the money which Amudachari Periappa had periodically made available to Krishnan Periappa had also come from my uncle Bhadran. Kindness is kindness, and it matters not a whit if the material giver is someone other than the actual giver.

I believe that what little of human warmth and affection Krishnan Periappa received was from Amudachari Periappa's family. The children too were fond of him, though the nature of the disease necessarily kept them at a safe physical distance from him. I know that my father as well as Bhadran Chitya had the deepest love for this unfortunate step-brother of theirs, but since they were serving far away, they met him only infrequently. It was my uncle Bhadran who kept Krishnan Periappa supplied with his few material wants. I remember the parsimony of Krishnan Periappa when we learnt after he had passed away and been cremated, that he had actually stacked wood patiently gathered from the nearby forests in Chingelput to be used for his cremation, as he did not wish to be a burden on his brothers even after death!

Of such undaunted stuff were the mortals of those days made — men and women of indomitable will and tremendous courage, coupled with a patient faith in their destiny, all of which made it possible for them to live a satisfactorily happy and comfortable life, providing for this life as well as for the life hereafter. The *Gita* asks, "Where can one find peace in this world of non-peace?" Well, there seem to have been such souls in the days of the past — not very distant past at that — and it makes me hope that such men and women will be again born into this world to make it a fitter and a happier place for all of us to live in. May it be so!

C.A. Rajagopalachari (Appa)

IV

Appa

Appa

My father, Shri C.A. Rajagopalachari, was born on the 7th April 1905 at Pudukottai, in the then Madras Presidency. His father was Shri R. Chakrapani Iyengar. My father's name should normally have been just C. Rajagopalachari, for it is the custom in south India to have the father's name as the initial before one's own name. But he had to add on a second letter of the alphabet since there was another C. Rajagopalachari. This person was the famous politician and philosopher who rose to the position of Governor General of India — the last one to occupy that exalted office, because India soon became a sovereign independent republic. My father added 'Aiyangar' to his name to distinguish himself from his famous namesake!

I recall that many years ago, when I was travelling to Salem, I reached the train and walked up to my 1st class compartment in which I had a reservation. I saw a small group of some fifteen persons standing outside my compartment. As soon as I neared the coach, one of them approached me and asked, "What is your good name sir?" I gave him my name. Then he looked at the others, and they all smiled with a trace of embarrassment. I wondered why. Then the person said, "Excuse me sir, we thought you were **the** Rajagopalachari. We knew it could not be he, but we didn't want to make any mistake and miss seeing him." This occurred because Salem was the birth place of that other Rajagopalachari, and he used to go there frequently. So there was reason enough for my father adding on an alphabet to his name.

As one comes nearer and nearer one's own time while recapitulating one's life, past details flood the memory, and there is a general clamour for inclusion. This obviously cannot be permitted. It is as if the woods are obscured by the trees! I used to dabble with canvas and paint once upon a time, long ago in the dim past of my youth. It was a secret hobby, shyly practised in isolation, for I knew that I had no ability whatsoever. But I was encouraged to try my hand at it after I had read somewhere that Winston Churchill had begun painting after he crossed sixty years of age, and had become quite an artist. So once when I went to England I bought up a lot of materials and equipment, as most beginners who are never destined to be anything but beginners, do. I remember from the little experience of those days that for me it was always easier to paint the nearer objects, whereas it was extremely difficult, if not impossible, to paint the distant scenes. Now, in recapitulating the past, I find the reverse to be true!

My father was a giant among men, larger than life, as is said of such persons. To do justice to him several very large canvases would be necessary. I could spend many hours just writing whatever I know about him and his life — but that is of course unnecessary. He was a man of many facets of character, and possessed a whole spectrum of extraordinary abilities, all of which he used with great charm all his life — one at one time and another at another time. His courage was extraordinary, and I think that is what gave him the ability to use his very real abilities! We often fail not because we lack specific abilities but because we lack the necessary courage to give of what we have in the way of qualities and capacities. He did not suffer from such crippling inhibitions, and in that lay such greatness and strength of character as he built up painstakingly all his life.

I have no distinct memories of him pertaining to the early years of my life. The earliest memory is related to the passing away of my mother. That is the first time I remember to have

Appa

seen him. Of course there must have been togetherness before that, but the memory of those days and years have faded irretrievably. Memories can be terrible nuisances, and can even create deep-seated traumas in those who are not blessed with a necessary and desirable strength of mind. I have no doubt that Nature, in her own genial kindness, erased from my memories all that was not necessary for me to carry through life. It is a pity that in our later years we tend to hoard memories, and thus heap upon ourselves a tremendous load of suffering. Observing little children growing up around me, I have nothing but wonder, and a sense of tremendous gratitude, for the amazing rapidity with which they shed memories — of persons, places and things! It may be argued that they thus lose a great deal that was pleasant while it lasted, but one can't have only one side of the coin! Both or neither, seems to be the law, and if one desires one side of the coin, the other will surely make its presence felt.

My father was born of noble parents, steeped in the religion and culture of their epoch. They were persons of standing in the days when wealth was not the sole criterion for judging a person's standing in society. It was often not even one of the criteria. Far from it! Wealth was often considered a bar to a person occupying the higher echelons of a cultured and refined society. In fact those were times when wealth had something dirty about it. It had a fishy emanation, as it were. Rich persons therefore were careful to keep their wealth a private thing. There was no ostentation as is common with the wealthy ones of our times, no brag and bluster. They were wealthy — so what?

I am reminded of the idea that money in vast quantities is filthy lucre! It was very much so in the time of my grandparents. Also, to have too much was to be tempted by the Devil! Wealth was always suspect, and the wealthy ones had to face some sort of odium or disrepute, and were not easily accepted into the rarefied heights of a society which had as its important purpose the preservation of social, cultural and moral values in the day-to-day existence of the people. The poor were never blamed for being poor, as they are these days when a man's success is measured only in terms of the wealth he has amassed. So though my father and his brothers faced extreme privation, they did so without any ignominy being tacked on to their situation. In other words, it was possible to be poor and yet lead an honourable life, earning the respect of all. In India there has always been this tradition that the truly great are rarely wealthy, their wealth being 'not of this world.'

My father was in his early teens when he had to face the stark tragedy of losing his father. It was a crippling loss, whichever way one looks at it. He was barely twelve or thirteen years old, and had two younger brothers aged ten and four years respectively. The pension that the family received could have hardly fed one adult, and here it had to feed a family of four! Their education was a very long way from completion, and in the case of the youngest, Bakthu, it was far away even from the beginning. There were no wealthy relatives to help them through those difficult heart-breaking years of misery and frustration, coupled with severe privation. There was the brother of my grandmother who lived in the village of Kuttalam, who had some landed property there. My father has told me that this uncle used to help them whenever he could. But such help was not a permanent feature, nor even consistent enough to be called regular.

After their father's death, they continued to stay on in Triplicane, moving to a very small place to save on the rent. My father told me that it was just one room with a tiny verandah. My grandmother, Rukmini, did such cooking as was necessary in that room, and she slept in it too. Her life must have been unimaginably difficult, for the women of Brahmin households had to follow the orthodox Brahmin rules of cleanliness, purity and so on. The boys slept out in the open. Private toilets and bathrooms were unheard of. They had to share the primitive sanitary facilities with a dozen other families, all living under the same conditions of privation and penury. Lesser mortals would have reeled under such conditions of life, and many were driven to the extreme step of even attempting suicide. But my father and uncle Bhadran were made of steel. They had to perform what today would appear to us to be extraordinary tasks just to keep body and soul together. They were deeply concerned that their beloved mother should never feel any sorrow or deprivation, and they did everything possible to keep her cheerful, and as happy as was possible under those soul-stifling circumstances.

It was a blessing that Chitya was friendly with all, being something of an extrovert. He therefore managed to borrow school textbooks from the numerous friends he had, and to study so well that literally he never paid any school fees, always qualifying for some sort of a scholarship which made free education possible for him. My father has often humourously remarked that Chitya had numerous rich school friends, and he was so popular with them — since he helped them with their studies — that he was often invited for lunch or tiffin with them. My father was equally brilliant, and managed to similarly avoid paying fees throughout his academic life. They were two of a kind in this matter. They studied under the street lamps at night as there was no money for kerosene lamps! The only expense they had to provide for was therefore the pittance of a rent for their mean lodgings, and for food. The rent could not be reduced, and so they reduced their expenses on the only other item, namely food.

One wonders at the state of their finances when one remembers that the monthly rent for rooms such as they occupied could hardly have exceeded a few rupees! My father has told me that my poor grandmother often went without a meal for days. The Brahmins of those days were accustomed to fasting frequently, and this training must have helped them very considerably. When many years later I read the famous novel *Siddhartha* by Hermann Hesse, I was reminded of my father and of my uncle Bhadran. They both shared with *Siddhartha* the incomparably useful ability of being able to fast and to wait!

My youngest uncle Bakthu was protected from the harsher impacts of their circumstances of living, and this of course meant less of everything for the mother and the elder brothers. But his suffering was perhaps no less than that of the others, though he was too young to appreciate the need for all the parsimony that had to be exercised in spending the few rupees that were available to the family. I believe that the monthly pension was eight rupees! It is impossible for me to even try to appreciate the true state of their existence. Today one can perhaps have a simple south Indian breakfast for this sum of money — nothing more than that!

It is true that suffering moulds human beings as nothing else perhaps can. It is the crucible in which the dross of human weakness and frustration can be burnt off, and the metal refined, strengthened and ennobled. It is not to be wondered at that saints and sages have always advocated the voluntary acceptance of suffering if one wants to achieve the highest goals open to human endeavour. In such crucibles were my father and my uncle Bhadran moulded. It was their strength of character, and their capacity to endure everything, that later on enabled them to scale the heights of career achievement. They had the resilience necessary to help them, as otherwise they

Appa

might have broken down under the load that they were carrying.

My uncle Bhadran, especially, had tremendous faith in himself and in his destiny. He seems to have sensed early in life that he was there for a purpose, and this gave him enormous strength. In the case of my father I believe it was the consciousness of the onerous responsibility that had been thrust upon his young and inexperienced shoulders that gave him the necessary strength of purpose, shunning fatigue of the body, mind and perhaps even the soul, to plod on and on towards an undefined goal. I don't think that he could have known what he was expected to do. Nor do I think that he could have had even the vaguest idea of whither they were bound, or in what direction lay such redemption as they must have wept and prayed for in the dark moments of despair.

Such moments of silent and tearful despair, often in the deep silence of the night, are common to all mankind, and I don't think that my father or uncle Bhadran could have been exempt from it. But their strength lay in not succumbing to such moments, but plodding on and on, waiting for the dawn after the dark night of the soul. It is fortunate that young Bakthu could not have experienced such despair, for he was too young to feel such things. His fate was more charitable in that his lot was more of physical deprivation — hunger perhaps, and the deprivation of toys and such things in which children delight.

My father made tremendous sacrifices to help his younger brothers exist in reasonable comfort. As the eldest male in the family it was his duty to do so, but it was his love and generosity that made him convert this duty into something of a pleasure. This was the reason for the love and respect, amounting almost to devotion, that uncle Bhadran lavished upon my father all his life. Bhadran was the more successful of the two, but this did not take him away from my father. His gratitude for all that my father had done for him during those days was ever present, and he tried to manifest this in everything that he did. To Bhadran, my father was something of a god! I do not exaggerate when I say this. Their relationship was something profound and deep, beyond time as it were.

There have been stray occasions when I have differed with my father. On such occasions Chitya would take me for a drive far away and, in the solitude of some forest or desert, would plead with me not to say 'no' to my father for anything. "You can never know how much your father has suffered, and how much he has sacrificed. I know because I was there. He may be wrong in asking you to do some things which you can't accept. He is neither a super-human being nor a god. I know he has been wrong in many things, and will be wrong in the future too. But please do this for my sake, remembering all the suffering that he has undergone." Thus would he appeal to me, and I could never disagree with him, knowing that everything he said was true. My uncle of course knew his brother inside out, but knowing his weaknesses did not dilute his love for my father even a bit.

I believe that where there is true love, one must love the person and not what he does, or what he becomes. Nor must love change if the person changes. When I was in the Benares Hindu University, I once approached the Vice Chancellor, Dr. S. Radhakrishnan, for an autograph. He was a world-renowned philosopher-statesman, and went on to become the President of India. He wrote in my autograph book, "Love is not love which alters when it alteration finds." My father and my Chitya loved each other in this remarkable way, and we in turn loved them for it, as it set before us an example to follow. But alas, emulation comes not so easily, especially where the heart is

Appa

concerned. I have more or less come to conclude that the capacity to love truly is a divine gift.

Such was the love that these two brothers had for each other, that often when they were together one felt that for them nothing existed except the other. They ignored all the others, and only when they had finished whatever they were talking about — and they could talk and talk for hours — would they think of the others present. This often made my aunt Gouri very annoyed, and she would remonstrate with my father saying, "Chinnappa, why don't you two realise that there are others in the room? You are behaving like school children going into a huddle. Please break it up and join the others." I am convinced that it was this love that kept them going all those years of utter misery. It is also what kept that love alive when life became more easy and pleasant and comfortable. If it had not been there the family might have split up, each going his own way to try and make his way in the world. Their love for each other, and their limitless love for their mother, was what made life endurable, and made their subsequent victory over circumstances possible. In the final analysis it is love that emerges as the victor!

My father had his education in the Hindu High School at Triplicane in Madras. It was a famous school in his days, and perhaps one of the few then existing. In those days Madras was a small town indeed, and the different suburbs of the present-day Madras were all different villages, separated by immense groves of coconut plantations through which only the intrepid few would walk, even by day. Those groves were populated by small families of toddy tappers, and there was generally a floating population of drunkards in and around the toddy shops. Such drunkards, drawn from the uneducated poorer classes, were naturally prone to lose whatever self-control they may have possessed when sober, and therefore drunken brawls were the order of the day. Naturally such places were shunned by the educated classes. The main suburbs were Triplicane and Mylapore. The only 'modern' means of transport was the tram. It was very cheap too. As an alternative one could take the horse-drawn vehicle known as the *jutka* which was many times more expensive. I don't know whether bicycles existed when my father began school. My father and his brothers mostly went everywhere on foot, because even if bicycles had existed they would not have been able to afford one!

My father was a brilliant pupil, and had a grasp of subjects that has been called instinctive. He excelled in everything that was included in the school curriculum, and was always at the top of his class. This enabled him to make his way through school without paying any school fees as he was the recipient of scholarships entitling him to free education. My grandfather's passing away when my father was hardly twelve years old, thrust upon my father an adult view of life to which he had to rise, and to perform as if he was many years older than his twelve years. He excelled in mathematics. In his days they had question papers containing more than the number of questions to be answered. For instance, a question paper could contain fifteen questions, out of which only ten had to be answered to get full marks. The beauty of the system was that those who answered all the fifteen questions correctly would be awarded 150 marks out of 100! My father always answered the full paper, and thus was able to stay ahead of the whole class, for not all were brilliant in mathematics. Indeed the subject was usually forbidding, the very mention of it sending jitters through most students. This system enabled the brilliant pupils to be well ahead of the general bunch — and from this my father profited enormously.

I have always been afraid of mathematics myself. I believe that the way the subject was taught was totally faulty, and put students off the subject. I have not known many that were actually at home with the subject. Most were automatically afraid of it. This is a pity, because it is such a necessary and elegant subject. I actually began to want to study it later, but by then of course it was too late. It is amazing how, in those days, students could ignore the way subjects were taught, and get on with the job of mastering them by themselves. My father has told me that the teachers taught from notes that they had prepared, and were largely dependent on such notes for their classes. Those notes were almost never changed, but went on from year to dreary year. It is no wonder that not only did the students not derive any pleasure from education, but most of them suffered from the tedium of repetition, with the teacher amply sharing that tedium! It was all a dreary business, with virtually no joy in the process of education.

I think it was a very good thing that the students of those days were generally compelled to pass their exams, as otherwise they would not have got any jobs. This situation gave them the necessary impetus to get on with their own education without having to depend on their teachers. A very good thing for persons like my father, if looked at in this way. In a sense one can say that the system favoured the truly capable students. It was an unconscious, and no doubt unintended, weightage in favour of the intelligent. I think it was better like that, for today we have the opposite phenomenon of everything being inordinately weighted in favour of the weak-minded, and that is certainly not a good thing for the nation, as it only serves to fill the offices with ill-educated mediocrities!

Anyway, my father and Chitya made their way through school by leaps and bounds, since the system also provided for double promotions — that is a student could be promoted from say class four to class six, skipping class five. They both got such double promotions a couple of times each! This helped them to pass out of school considerably earlier than the others. They saved a few years like this, and therefore could enter college that much earlier.

One rather unexpected phenomenon was that since students seeking entrance into the colleges had to be of a certain minimum age, such brilliant students who passed out of school much earlier than the educational system planned for had generally to falsify their ages to get admitted into college. My father obviously did not do so. He gave his correct age. I do not know how he managed it, but that is the fact. But I know many who had to retire before they had actually reached the age of superannuation because they could not change their ages back to the correct one! Further, the pressure of life was such that most students had to study well, and therefore many ended up in college at the ridiculous age of thirteen years, and some geniuses even younger than that! Something perhaps unusual in the western world, where regulations are stricter, and enforced with greater discipline. I have heard that the great Lord Kelvin was admitted into the University of Glasgow when he was just ten years old — and that too in the year 1834 or 1835! My father was no Lord Kelvin, but matters obviously were about the same as far as speedy progress of the brilliant ones through schools and colleges was concerned. This fact was so deep in my mind that when I first went abroad, and found so-called boys entering college at the age of twenty-four or twenty-five, it was quite a shock to me. In the India of my father's youth, persons in their mid-twenties were long out of college, if they had not dropped out of the educational system altogether, and were often married, and fathers too!

After finishing school education at the Hindu High School, my father joined the Presidency College, being admitted into the mathematics honours course. His earlier brilliance accompanied him to this prestigious institution, and he fared

Appa

very well there too, topping all classes. But here tragedy struck — in the insensate manner of all tragedies. He was a student of astronomy, which was then part and parcel of the mathematics curriculum. Once while observing a solar eclipse through a telescope, he looked at the sun with the lenses undarkened. The lenses of those days had to be darkened with soot, and this precaution was tragically forgotten. The result was that his right eye suffered severe damage, and he had to be hospitalized. A criminally stupid doctor gave him an injection into the eye without taking the elementary precaution of sterilizing the needle, and my father contracted septicemia.

My Chitya told me that my father's right eyeball bulged out so much that it looked as if it would fall out of the eye socket. It was in terrible shape. They then consulted a British doctor in the General Hospital, one Dr. Wright. This doctor exclaimed upon seeing my father's eye, "Which fool did this to you? He ought to be shot." I agree with him wholeheartedly! But the damage had been done, and it was too late even for the great Dr. Wright to do anything for the eye — but he was able to save my father's imperilled life. In spite of this tragic accident my father went on to graduate with honours in mathematics, his professor giving him special facilities at the time of the examination.

I have often thought that he would have preferred to die rather than have to endure the rest of life with but one eye! It is fortunate that he had no choice in the matter — otherwise this account may never have been written! Dr. Wright gave him loving care, treating my father as his own son, and suffering his anguish with him. He was a humane doctor, and after saving my father's life, he went on to have expensive artificial eyes obtained for him from England. I understood that my father did not have to pay anything at all for all these loving services that Dr. Wright rendered to him. I have seen my father with the artificial eye, and I can say that few could have ever known that he had only one eye, so perfectly were they made. Dr. Wright had several made for him, and they lasted well into the fifties! They were originally made of glass, they required great care to maintain them. He exhausted the stock of artificial eyes that Dr. Wright had supplied him with, and then came the problem that Dr. Wright had passed away, and the modern era had ushered in artificial eyes made of plastic. They were not the same, and my father never again had eyes which either fit him or looked right.

There was something of a by-product of an irritant resulting from the eye surgery. The eye socket had been scooped clean, even the skin at the back of the eyeball being removed. My father needed a skin graft to close up the mutilated eye socket, and the only acceptable skin had to be taken from his own thigh. Even though the skin had been treated in all possible ways surgically and medically to make it appropriate to replace the lost skin, some of the hair roots had escaped being removed. They used to grow, and the hair growing behind the glass eye was a recurring irritant, and someone had to carefully cut out the hair from the root. Otherwise the surgery was a definite success. The glass eye was so beautifully matched with his good eye for colour, shape and size that no one could have easily noticed the difference. I often wondered why my father decided to hide behind his dark glasses, for they were certainly unnecessary.

My dear father had to suffer greatly because of the loss of his right eye when he was perhaps just eighteen years old. He told me that it took him several months to get used to living with one eye. They had to use ink pots and quill pens in class, and it was an enormous education for him to learn to be able to dip the pen into the ink pot, since he had no parallax vision. Everything needing binocular vision had to be patiently remastered. The thought that he had been able to do the very same things almost without thinking about what he was doing — well it was often too much to bear. One wonders how he avoided the psychological trauma of such a crippling loss. I can only surmise that the terrible responsibilities that he had to fulfill kept him sane.

Chitya admired him more than anything else for the bravery with which he suffered this loss. What could not be cured had to be endured — and endure it my father did, with utmost self-control, and eventually with enviable nonchalance! But initially he must have suffered from some degree of self-consciousness, perhaps diffidence too, because he wore a pair of dark glasses all his life. He had perfect eyesight in the remaining eye, and needed no glasses. In fact the lenses were of plain glass, only dark, so that his eyes could not be seen. Late in his life, perhaps around the year 1975 when his eyesight weakened, he finally discarded the dark glasses once and for all.

A grave consequence of this loss of one eye was that he could not seek government service. That was terrible, for the Brahmin youth relied on the government to provide them with safe service till they reached retirement age. Such government jobs were poorly paid, but they had job security, and that was what mattered. India has never been a safe place in this context. It has always been a difficult thing getting a job. It has always been extremely difficult to get a second job if one stupidly managed to lose the first. For some time after graduation from the Presidency College — for graduate he did, with the stubbornness born of absolute need to survive — he taught in the Hindu High School. He was almost persuaded to continue teaching there, and had he done so he would no doubt have eventually retired as the Head Master of that institution in which he had been a student himself.

He however chose to seek service, and this he did, resorting, I am sorry to say, to subterfuge. He applied for government service, and easily passed all the written and viva voce tests with flying colours, topping the list of candidates as usual. But then came the frightening hurdle — the medical examination which was mandatory. One could not be awarded a government job unless one passed the medical tests conducted by the government itself. Here came the subterfuge. He told me that for the eye test he mastered the charts by memorizing them, and at the actual eye test he recited from memory what he was supposed to see and read out — and this was never found out, so that he did get the job! It was but the job of a clerk, on the royal salary of thirty-two rupees a month, but it provided a safe and secure berth for the rest of his life. He always considered himself to have been extremely lucky that during the earlier years of his service no one discovered the fact that he had only one eye, for had someone got on to the deception, he could have been summarily dismissed from service.

He joined the Great Indian Peninsula Railway as an accounts clerk, and was posted at Bombay, the headquarters of the G.I.P. Railway. Till he left for Bombay to take up this job, he was an orthodox Brahmin youth, with a sacred tuft adorning the top of his head, and the caste mark on his forehead. But once he entered service at Bombay, he thought it necessary to go in for one of those modern hair cuts in fashion in the British days. But he never discarded the caste mark, which continued to adorn his forehead all his life.

He used to tell us the amusing story of what followed that momentous change in his appearance. He came home to Kali, their native village in the Thanjavur district, on a short holiday. Not finding his mother at home, and hearing that she had gone to the village tank for water, he followed her there. She was there, and after filling two brass vessels with water, holding

Appa

one on the hip, and carrying the other on her head, she returned home. He was amused that she had not recognized him, and followed a few yards behind her. When she reached her door, she turned around to see who had been following her. She looked closely at him, recognized him, and said, "Is that you Rajagopala? What have you done to your head? Go straight to the barber and have your sacred tuft restored. Then go to the tank and have your bath and come home." And that was what he had to do!

Very orthodox days they were, and nobody thought of rebelling either against hoary tradition, or against parental authority. That my father had his hair cut in the modern fashion was in itself an act of bravery. It certainly was not rebellion, because his intention was merely to conform in the minimum possible way to the modes of a society into which he had somehow strayed. He never gave up his orthodox ways of Shri Vaishnavism, performing all the daily rituals diligently. He taught us many of the prayers early in our lives, and we were able to successfully memorize them. But in his outer attitudes and in his dress he certainly changed to the necessary extent, and that certainly bespeaks of an ability to adjust to circumstances. There was no fanaticism at all in his attitude to religion. Also, Hinduism is not a fanatical religion, preaching tolerance and charity towards all as the highest virtues.

My father must have been married prior to the accident which cost him his right eye. The only available evidence that I have with me, my mother's greeting card, shows that he was married in 1923, or perhaps earlier, in 1922. I assume this to be a fact because I cannot see how my grandfather could have given his most beloved daughter away in marriage to a one-eyed person. They were a very prosperous family, and he could have certainly found a far better son-in-law for himself. One wonders how he ever thought of my father as a suitable groom for her! The story is told that my Thatha's younger brother, Anantachari, came to know of my father through friends, and went to the Presidency College one day to see him as he came out after his classes were over for the day, without himself being seen. He had heard that my father was a brilliant person. When my father came out of the college gate, Anantachari saw that my father was a fairly tall person, very fair, and handsome. And this combination of good looks with brilliance must have been what made them offer their daughter to my father in marriage. It is certain that matrimony was quite far from my father's mind, given their circumstances.

I am sure that my father could not himself have taken any initiative in the matter of his marriage. It was simply not done! Among the Hindus the tradition is that the father of the girl has to go around looking for a suitable groom for her. There is the question of first of all matching the horoscopes when a boy thought to be suitable is found. Friends and relatives assist — one way or the other — in the matter of locating a suitable boy. The family astrologer then enters the picture, looking suitably grave as befitting the occasion. There can be a degree of skullduggery at this stage, because the astrologer may be willing to stretch a point, or to even turn a blind eye to adverse planetary influences! In certain cases it has been discovered that a wholly new horoscope has been cast, if the people were influential enough and could pay for this skullduggery. Then if he gives the green signal, as we say in India, the boy's people generally desire to have the horoscopes matched by their own astrologer. If and when this rigmarole ends successfully, the boy goes to the girl's home to 'see' her.

I know of one case involving a close friend of mine who went to see a girl for marriage, and liking the girl, he gave his approval. The marriage was duly fixed to be celebrated a few months later. On the day of the marriage, after the preliminary

Appa

rituals had been performed, when the girl was led in he found to his consternation that it was a different girl from the one he had seen. He could of course have aborted the marriage there and then, but he was too much of a gentleman, and went on with it — though he suffered from this deception for many years. Sad to say the poor girl, who perhaps did not know anything about the switch, suffered a great deal too.

It is a humiliating thing, this matter of a boy seeing a girl, for while a boy can disapprove of girl after girl — and many have a great deal of fun in this way — the girl generally has not the same liberty of saying 'no' to a boy who has come to see her. Nowadays things are slowly changing, and one comes to hear of the stray case where a girl has rejected a boy as unsuitable for her! It used to cause some consternation in male circles, naturally, but now it has come to stay, and I consider it a very good thing that a girl has an equal right in the matter of choosing her spouse. In India marriage has very often assumed the appearance of a market transaction, and that has been a blight on this society.

In my father's case too the same procedure was followed. However, things were relatively easy for my grandfather because I understand my father did not make the usual fuss associated with this stage of the negotiations. For after the boy and girl have met, and the boy has approved of the girl — and this after a mere cursory look, followed generally by a song by the girl — begins what is politely referred to as 'negotiating the terms' of the marriage. In reality it is the time when the boy's relatives make their often exorbitant demands for dowry. Many a girl's family has been broken by this evil system, ruinous and demeaning, as it smacks of nothing more than a commercialized union. The dowry system is a shame upon the fair name of the country and its people. Often things become so nasty that even after the marriage the boy can send the girl back to her parental home with further demands. In recent times there has been a nightmarish turn to this in that brides have actually been burnt, or otherwise made away with, when they could not, or would not, approach their parents for more of the material wealth that the boy lusted after.

I surmise that my parents were married early in the year 1923, but perhaps no earlier than that, and that my father lost his eye only after his wedding. My mother was a brave girl — for girl she was — because she must have suffered silently from this devastating blow to her dear husband. She loved him dearly, by all accounts, and must have anguished over his future. His was a blighted future, for had he had both his eyes, he would surely have gone up for the civil service examinations, and found a place in the coveted Indian Civil Service. Then his destiny, at least on the material plane, would have been vastly different, and he would have been of the elite of India. It shows his strength of character that I was never able to discern any bitterness in him for such lost opportunities denied to him for no fault of his own. By the time I entered the scene sufficiently mature for me to understand him, he had lost all signs of any such bitterness — if there had ever been any!

It saddens me when I brood over the fact that I could have so easily asked him for answers to many such questions, which perhaps would also have had the effect of consoling him. It is a melancholy fact that sons often have difficulty in getting really close to their fathers. It is so much easier to communicate with the father through the medium of the mother! I suppose this is the same the world over. But that does not make it any easier to understand why there should be this difficulty in a son getting really close to his father. I know that almost all sons have the regret that during the lifetime of the father they never became intimate or even friendly with him. I suspect that this is also the case between mothers and their daughters. This

Appa

suspicion has become hardened into a sort of belief after I began to meet abhyasis having problems with their parents — and it is a tragedy of the human situation that in almost all cases the problems are, at least in their origins, of this nature. It is one of those matters which is more appropriately left to the psychologists to deal with and to explain, remembering that, "Fools rush in where angels fear to tread!"

One always assumes that one has all the time in the world, but all of a sudden the inevitable happens, and we are left high and dry. My father rarely, if ever, spoke about my mother. Her loss was a deep wound to him, from which he suffered all his long life. He never volunteered any information about her or about their marriage. I could have garnered all the details from my grandmother, but with her too I missed the opportunity. She died in December 1955, six months after my marriage. In any case the elder women of those days rarely had a head for dates and times. Those were the days when the lady of the house noted the fact that a baby had been born with a bit of green leaf! They rarely noted the date. As for the time, clocks were quite rare, and their accuracy could not be relied upon as there were no other clocks for comparison, or for setting the time by! I remember that even the daily milk account was thus written on the kitchen wall, vertical lines indicating whatever measure of milk the housewife had in mind. Such records were irretrievably lost when smoke from the wood fires blackened the kitchen walls, or during the rare occasion when the walls were done up — a rather infrequent affair!

I suppose therefore that my dear grandmother would have been unable to furnish such data — and anyway, she would have forgotten everything related to such a painful memory after my mother had passed away. My grandfather would have been a more reliable source, but he never liked to discuss anything concerning my mother, except to say that she was his world, and with her passing his world became totally dark. Poor man, he suffered enormously because he could never express his grief. Women can be quite cruel in these matters because they assume that they suffer more than their men when they are bereaved, but I think this is not true. Women are more expressive, whereas the culture of the world prevents, and perhaps even forbids, men from open expressions of grief. The men always suffer silently, and my Thatha suffered all his life in this way. Anyway, dates and times are not all that important, and when they are not available one has to do without them.

My father was a very handsome person, having a very fair complexion and a well-formed head. His one eye was lustrous and extremely expressive. He was of medium height, being five feet seven inches tall, and always had a commanding presence. Though a cruel destiny compelled him to join the subordinate services of the government, his spirit remained at all times unsubdued, and nothing could cow his indomitable spirit. He was never ostentatious about his personal appearance, but was always dressed appropriate to the occasion. He had very clean personal habits bordering upon the fastidious. As a Vaishnavite Brahmin, he performed the stipulated rituals every day with flair, though I have often doubted whether he really believed in their efficacy, either for this life or for the life hereafter! He was very attractive to women, and had a very engaging charm which he used very naturally. He was always gentle with the fair sex, and they reacted to him in a reciprocally special manner too. He had a courteous old-worldly manner with them, taking presents of flowers whenever he had to meet a lady. He was ever courteous, charming and friendly.

Given such an attractive and manly personality, and the attraction that he had for women, I have often wondered how he escaped a second marriage. I know that he was under constant pressure to marry again so that his children would have a mother to look after them — even though it would only be a step-mother! In India this sort of second marriage was a very common thing, given the child birth mortality of those days. Mothers died off like the proverbial flies, and infant mortality was also rampant, so much so that the combination of both these factors made it almost imperative that a young man newly bereaved generally remarried. I think what prevented this in my father's case was his inherent mistrust of a step-mother. He knew that it was almost proverbial for a step-mother to ill-treat the children of her predecessor, and he did not want his children to be exposed to such ill treatment. He was himself the eldest son of the second wife of his father, one must remember. This shows to what an extent he was prepared to sacrifice his own life for that of his children.

Even though my mother passed away in the year 1933, he was always the honoured son-in-law of my grandfather's family right through to the end of their lives. He was always given special regard and respect, and they went out of their way to honour him on all occasions. Remembering that my grandfather lived till his eighties, I wonder how my father could maintain pride of place in their hearts, and retain their respect and love for practically half a century after my mother departed this mortal existence. To them he was always **the** son-in-law of the house. It did not matter that he was only technically a son-in-law, and had really no claims on their affection or regard after my mother passed away. To them it was as if my mother's presence was there, undimmed by her physical absence, and therefore to them there was no difference at all. It was most unusual, this relationship between them and my father. Normally when the wife passes away, relations with her family gradually fade away. In this case the opposite was the case, and if anything their relationship seemed to grow stronger and stronger with the passing of the years. I have always honoured my grandparents for their attitude of love and respect towards my father. It was very unostentatious and natural, but it was there in an almost tangible sense — and for this I shall always be grateful to them. Theirs was an old-world charm, and everything they did was done in the unobtrusive manner of the elder generation. May God grant them the peace in the hereafter that they deserve!

Among his colleagues too my father enjoyed the same respect and esteem. They all looked up to him as some sort of a superior person, and sought his help and guidance whenever they were distressed by the officialdom of the British Raj, or by the stupidity of their superiors. In India there has always been this hypocrisy that the superior officer is, ipso facto, always wiser than his subordinates, and always right. One supposes that the British Raj had to perpetuate this myth of the superior person to be able to effectively govern such a vast country. But there has always been a great deal of mental suffering because of this, especially in Government service where to give advice, or to point out errors of judgement, could be construed as insubordination, and punishment meted out.

My father was never cowed down by such attitudes, and was always the champion of lost causes! He was ready to shoulder the problems of those weaker than himself, and played a major role in the professional associations of which he was a member. Strangely enough, I found that he had a very healthy relationship with his British officers, who all had a uniformly good opinion of him. It was due to them that he was able to rise in the service fairly rapidly, much to the jealous anger of those whom he superseded. He did not enjoy the same confidence with his Indian superiors. Perhaps in him they sensed a possible rival. This was a senseless fear of course, but there it was, and nothing could be done about it. He had a fairly difficult time after the British left India because of the jealousy of some of his officers who went out of their way to try to harm his career interests. But all this bothered him not a whit, because he had a courage and a trust that defied such petty chicanery.

For these admirable attitudes of self-confidence, indomitable courage and helpfulness his assistants loved him, his peers admired him, and his superiors respected him. I have seen how they all would come to visit him even many years after he had retired from the service in 1960. They were happy to call on him, and to exchange news of their old service for which he was always eager, for he had an excellent memory and was hungry for details, though they had no bearing upon his current life. Even many of his former superior officers used to thus visit him, and he behaved with them all with the same unfailing courtesy, enriched and garnished with a great deal of affection.

While he was very friendly and courteous, he was also a very strict disciplinarian, and insisted upon the highest standards of performance. It speaks for the affection that he enjoyed that all his co-workers responded to his demands and successfully performed — to their own benefit more than anyone else's. They were thus able to develop qualities of leadership which enabled them to advance rapidly up the rather fatiguing rungs of the official ladders of promotion. In those days promotions were not easy to come by. One often had to wait for so-called time scales to bring them to the proper position from which one could be promoted. And time scales were a weary business, with so-called efficiency bars interposed every few years, which had to be passed successfully. In this process one had to contend with an obnoxious report, called the confidential report, which the immediate superior officer wrote, and which was not made available to the person concerned, unless he wished to appeal against authority in a quasi-legal manner. These confidential reports were instruments of gross misuse, and were used by jealous officers to wreak their vengeance upon a brilliant but unsuspecting subordinate.

I do not know anything about his career before the Jubbulpore days. In Jubbulpore he was well thought of, and enjoyed the confidence of his bosses and the friendship of his subordinates. This was a rare sentiment in those days of British discipline when hierarchical structures were quite rigid, and the lines dividing the classes quite firmly drawn. Only the very cheeky or the very intrepid could transgress across such barriers. It speaks volumes for my father's popularity that our house was often the gathering place for subordinates as well as superiors. He was well thought of by the divisional engineer, an Englishman, and I believe that his satisfaction with my father's work, and his confidence in him, was responsible for the relatively rapid promotion my father received to the post of divisional accountant.

Our house was the meeting point for the members of the Brahmin community of Jubbulpore, especially on festival days such as the annual day when all Brahmins renewed the old sacred thread for a new one after ritualistic prayers and offerings to the departed forefathers. There were qualified priests to recite the ancient *mantras*, of course, but the degree of respect that my father received, though he was then only around thirty-two years of age, was something to see. I was quite astonished that one so young should receive so much respect from persons not very different from himself in age. He had the basic learning in the religious texts, of course, and this must have been a factor. But I think that a much more important factor was his bearing and his aura of authority that made most persons respect him. We had guests frequently, many of them from Madras and places further south. It was good for us, as it served to somewhat mitigate our loneliness. It also kept us in touch with our mother tongue, Tamil. This

Appa

may seem somewhat surprising, but many were the families in which the younger generation had lost touch with their mother tongues, and conversed with their parents in Hindi. My youngest brother, Seena, did not know to write in our mother tongue. Nor did I, for that matter. We all had to learn to read and write Tamil as we grew up in Jubbulpore — and I am somewhat ashamed to say that even today I am unable to read fast, and my Tamil handwriting is awful.

My father was an important part of the movement to create a South Indian Association. One had existed earlier, but had lapsed into almost total inactivity. He helped to revive it. Not only that, he was also active in helping to raise the funds to build the association's Jubbulpore centre building. We were there on the day it was formally inaugurated. It was not really very imposing, but then it was there where none had existed earlier, and that was a matter of joy for the South Indian community. I remember that the floor had not been laid, nor had the walls been plastered, and the place was full of bamboo poles supporting the newly laid concrete roof, and scaffolding sticking out everywhere, on which we bumped our heads repeatedly. Notwithstanding all this we all had a great deal of fun, and of course there was the inevitable feast to enjoy, without which nothing in India is ever really complete.

Hospitality has been, and continues to be, the bedrock of the Indian cultural tradition. No visitor was ever sent away without something to eat, and a cup of tea or coffee to drink. It would have been unthinkable to send a visitor away without some refreshment. *Atithi Devo bhava,* says the ancient Vedic text — which means that the guest should be treated as if he were a deva. This is how the text is normally understood. Generation after generation of Indians down the centuries of Indian civilization have honoured this instruction with all their hearts. The wandering *sannyasis* and monks have been able to survive on their long and arduous religious pilgrimages only because of this hospitality, for they were always sure of a meal and a place to rest in at all times everywhere. Even beggars received their mite, for it was the tradition that a wandering *sannyasin,* a *parivrajaka,* must beg his daily meal.

A householder had to be careful that a high soul was not ignored or insulted by refusing him a meal, or by the show of a sour face — for who could say in what disguise a nobly born one might come to one's door with a beggar's bowl? To my mind it seems that an invited guest does not really qualify as an *atithi.* In my understanding, this word means untimely. I therefore derive the meaning of *atithi* as one who comes at an untimely hour, unexpected, uninvited, and unannounced. Do we treat such a person as an honoured guest, or do we frown and refuse him food? I think that is the real test of one's hospitality.

I remember the story of Lord Krishna, who had been invited by the great *rishis* to dinner in their *parnashala* — their Vedic lodge or ashram. Lord Krishna had agreed to go for dinner at midnight. The *rishis* had prepared a feast with great devotion and purity of body and mind, and were waiting for the Lord. Precisely at midnight a giant wild boar wandered in from the jungle surrounding the ashram. The pig is considered unclean. The *rishis* were shocked to see the unclean animal inside their *parnashala* and drove it out, beating it with sticks. Wonder of wonders, each and everyone present felt the beating on his own back. The wild boar ran away before the *rishis* realised that it was none other than their Divine invitee, Lord Krishna, who had come in the form of a boar, presumably to test them.

The Buddhist tradition too makes the seeking of alms mandatory upon the monks. The Buddha himself did it, and all his monks had to follow his high and noble example. They were enjoined to seek alms, partake of what they needed, and to give away the rest to another needy soul. In perhaps no other land could such a tradition of religious and spiritual search for one's Being have survived all these long centuries! India has therefore been known for its hospitality from time immemorial, and there are many moving tales from the Puranas to exemplify this tradition of austerity and charity. The two, in fact, seem to go hand in hand! They are twin sisters, as it were.

The day when India ceases to be hospitable will probably be the day on which the ancient traditions of austerity and piety will also cease to exist. May such a day never dawn in this ancient land, so resplendent with the hoariest and grandest traditions, with its visions of the Absolute unsurpassed for their clarity and immediacy to the seeker. India has always been holy, and this holiness is sustained, at least in part, by this tradition of hospitality.

I remember that my father had a friend who lived in the Venkatesh Nivas in Bombay. He had lost a dearly loved younger brother with whom he had been very close. This person somehow familiarized himself with certain yogic techniques, and after attaining a certain degree of ability, he was able to exhale out of his own self the essence of his life, and with it to create a human body. After doing that he invoked the soul of his departed brother into the body he had created, and played with him for several hours every day, laughing all the while. This matter came to the attention of our neighbours because the man was losing weight drastically while at the same time eating really enormous quantities of food. When he started locking himself into his room, and they heard all the sounds of playful laughter, someone looked in through a sky light, and found there two persons instead of one! Then the cat was out of the bag. Some friends took him to the *shankaracharya*, who advised him against such practices saying that if the soul of his brother had become embodied again, the act of invoking his presence would leave his present body dead, and if someone stumbled upon it and cremated it, then the soul of his dearly loved brother would have to wander as a disembodied soul until it found another opportunity to incarnate.

My father's friend was a changed man. My father told me that a few days later this person walked into the Thana creek in his office-going dress, took off and threw into the creek all his clothes, bathed there and put on the ochre robes of a monk, and walked out of that life. He turned up many months later in Jhansi, to which station my father had been transferred. He heard that there was a south Indian living there, and when he was brought to him, he found that it was his old friend, my father. He stayed with my father a few days, eating only the tender leaves of the neem tree, with an occasional glass of milk. He stayed there only three days, and then "left for the Himalayas." Many months later my father received a post card from him saying that he had reached his goal — the Ramakrishna Math in Almora. That was the last my father heard from him, or of him!

This tradition of going to the Himalayas for spiritual regeneration, and for the more serious purpose of finding the Self, has been possible only because such wanderers in search of their soul could rely upon a night's resting place, and a meal anywhere at anytime. I may be so bold as to say that spirituality has been the soul of India only because of its hospitable people, which in turn has been kept alive as a tradition because of the ancient teachings which has made it part and parcel of the Indian psyche. Many years later, after I came into contact with one who became my spiritual Master, I heard from his lips the praise for this very hospitality of the Indian people. He told

Appa

me, "Nowhere in the world can such hospitality be found as exists in India. It is something unique to India." And when our young aspirants were going abroad for higher education, or for jobs, his parting advice to them always was, "Go an Indian, and come back an Indian!"

My father was extraordinarily impressed by this episode, and often remembered his friend. However, my father never developed the urge to seek the higher values of life until he reached a fairly advanced age. Perhaps the early struggles for existence had made him too cautious to be religious. I know that this was the case with my Chitya, Bhadran. My father was an ardent materialist, and the need to earn a living and to bring up his motherless children were the sole considerations that motivated him. He was regular in his religious practices — all ritualistic of course — but I always had the impression that he never really believed in what he was doing. Perhaps he did it out of a sense of duty. Perhaps he did it to inculcate in us something of the Hindu way of life. Or perhaps he did it because during his mother's time he just had to do it. Whatever the reason, he did all those things regularly and with a sense of duty, not cutting corners as the priests are wont to do.

I have never heard him railing against his fate or calling God names as many have been prone to do when adverse circumstances assailed them. He believed in carving out his destiny for himself, and in the process perhaps he felt that there was only self-reliance that one could count upon, and that destiny, or the belief in destiny, was for the weak-minded alone. It was not atheism or anything like that. He was quite theistic in his outlook, but no doubt he felt that after all the trials and miseries he had been put through, God was not to be entirely relied upon, and that it was certainly better by far to rely upon oneself. As I say, these are the thoughts that I had about Appa in relation to the performance of rituals. Whatever he did he did with gusto, and rituals did not suffer for lack of attention to detail, whatever may have been his private opinions about their validity or their efficacy.

It is a funny thing that in India there is this widely held opinion that performance of rituals is good, even though no one may have actually derived any benefit, or felt any transformation in himself because of their performance. Also, the scriptures enjoin their performance as duty, and duty is never performed with ulterior motives, expecting returns! There is also the implied threat that non-performance of duty is a sin, punishable in the hereafter. Most persons go through their ritualistic lives because of these ideas, but I am sure that my father never did what he did out of fear of punishment, or out of temptation for rewards. As I have said, he was one of the most fearless persons that I have known. It has been a matter of wonder to me how I have been such a timid creature, afraid of so many things in life, cowed down by adversities, and shy and lonely, even after having such a courageous person for my father. Wonders will never cease, and if every son were to be like his father, the world would be a very stale and boring place indeed. Being an avid reader of that genre of modern literature known as science fiction, I am familiar with the idea of cloning, but though the idea is no doubt fascinating, there is also something very frightening about it. Imagine the world peopled by innumerable Hitlers, for instance, or by numberless Mussolinis! Can there be anything more awful than a world populated by such frightful creatures? Nature always knows best. And in her endeavour to produce perfection upon this earth, she produces type after type, endlessly and tirelessly. And that is all to the good, for otherwise there would be only a drab world bereft of any variety or colour.

My father's progress was slow. Promotions were few and far between, and it took a great number of years for one to move up the time scales, bit by excruciating bit. But all the same his progress was sure. In those times there was no frantic hurry for quick promotions, and the people were generally contented. Something which is sadly lacking nowadays. Since prices of goods and commodities were stable over long periods of time, some prices not varying by even as much as one percent over a year, there was no scramble for ever-increasing incomes as we see today. People were content, and even on the small incomes of those times people were generally able to put something by for a rainy day. People also lived simply and frugally, the habit of eating out not having yet come into the picture. In fact eating in a hotel was thought of as something undesirable, something fit only for travelling salesmen and such other undesirable and disreputable persons! There was also the matter of hygiene, for hotel food was thought to be not prepared under clean conditions — and truth to tell such was indeed the case. Conditions were generally deplorable, and food was served on unclean plates, and the surroundings often dirty and noxious. Therefore few, if any, ever ate out.

Then of course there was the religious question, and Brahmins especially were strictly enjoined to eat only food cooked by Brahmin cooks. It was almost impossible to find a Brahmin eating out in a hotel in those days — such places being only for the lesser folk. Times have changed drastically. I remember an episode soon after I arrived in Madras after being transferred from Bombay. I was legging it on my sales rounds, and one afternoon being quite hungry walked into a restaurant with the name Buhari's. I asked for the menu, and saw that it was full of non-vegetarian stuff only. I asked the waiter whether there was something vegetarian, adding for his benefit that I was a Brahmin. He laughed and said, "You are a strange person. Mostly it is Brahmins who come here to eat all these delicacies." I was naive enough to be shocked — and went hungry that day for all the vegetarian restaurants had closed.

I remember a story which my father used to tell us which concerned his father. My grandfather was such an orthodox person that he could bathe only in a river or with well water. After his bath the daily *puja* had to be performed which ordinarily took several hours. And only after *prasad* had been offered could the family eat — and it was generally midday by then. The habit of eating breakfast had not yet invaded such orthodox households. The children, very young ones to be sure, were of course allowed to eat some thing, and given milk. If such orthodox Brahmins went to the toilet, then they had to wash their feet and their face, again in the river, or using well water only. Taps were unknown in our villages, and even in the smaller towns, piped water supplies were a rarity, available only in the biggest cities such as Bombay.

It so happened that once my grandfather had to go to Bombay where my father was then staying. This must have been well before 1918, for my grandfather passed away in that year. My father could not have been more than twelve or thirteen years of age, and one wonders what he was doing in Bombay at that time. I have no idea why he was there, or with whom he was staying. My grandfather came from the village in Tanjore to Madras, an overnight train journey easily undertaken without disturbing his rigorous daily regimen. Then he set out from Madras, and that was of course a much longer train journey taking twenty-six hours. He had to carry with him his holy and sacred *saligrams*, many of them in a woven reed basket, as he had to perform the daily *puja*.

The *saligrams* are objects of worship to the Vaishnava Brahmins. They are fossils from the rivers of Nepal, and thought to be holy by the Shri Vaishnavites, perhaps because

Appa

they represent a formless god! Anyway, there he was in the train with the basket of sacred religious paraphernalia on his lap, for the basket could not under any circumstance be laid down upon impure ground. He could not go to the toilet as he could not wash in the impure water provided by the railways — so he sat it out, all the thirty or more hours of his journey from my Periappa's home in Triplicane till he reached the place where my father was staying in Bombay. He could not speak, as he was forbidden to speak until he had his bath! So many awful injunctions, poor man, to conform to. But conform he did, with cheerfulness and faith.

When he arrived in Bombay my father took him to the temple where there was a well, and there he performed his daily ablutions as we say, and then cooked a meal of sorts. After that he performed his daily *puja*. And then only was he free to eat his frugal meal. Such was the character of the orthodox Brahmin of those days. My father never tired of repeating this story to us to emphasize the dedication to ideals that the elder generation cherished, and according to which ideals they strove to lead their lives, humble though they were, and of extremely moderate means.

There was another occasion, also concerning my grandfather, which generated another story. That episode concerns his going to attend a marriage in a somewhat distant village. This must have been quite a few years before the Bombay episode related above. He was sleeping out under the sky, but as it began to rain he went in to the corridor and slept there. At night some lady got up to go to the toilet, and not knowing that he was sleeping in the corridor she stumbled over his sleeping form. He had an awe-inspiring beard, fully grown with a lush growth. He could not speak till he had bathed — and so when she shouted out asking him who he was he remained silent. There was no electricity, of course. Mistaking him for a thief she raised a hue and cry, hearing which a few males rushed to her rescue. But even to their questions my grandfather would not reply.

It was a large gathering of persons, all present for a marriage, and therefore many of those present did not recognize him. When he remained silent, refusing to answer their queries, and since he looked fierce, and like a thief as they put it later to my father, they gave him a few blows, which he patiently accepted. Hearing the commotion my father suspected something, and rushed in to find that his father was being assaulted. He explained to the others the predicament my grandfather was in, and then only did they realise that they had in fact been raining blows on an honoured guest!

There is a different sort of story to illustrate the fearlessness and grit that the members of that generation displayed. This concerns my great-grandfather, Shri Rama Aiyangar. He too was an extremely orthodox person, living a simple life in their village near Pudukottai. The borders of villages are generally protected by enormous stone or clay images of the village guardians called *ayyanar* in Tamil. They are often extremely fierce looking, and may range in size from something resembling the human to the gigantic. They may be alone, seated on a horse, or there may be a whole troop of them, all extremely fierce and well armed. Their village had a whole troop of such *ayyanars* all mounted upon horses. The village folk generally had an annual celebration when these *ayyanars* were honoured, and sacrifices offered to them — a whole day affair in which the entire village participated with zeal and fervour. The Brahmins did not participate as the *ayyanars* were after all only guardians of the village, and according to the religious faith they did not qualify as gods. They were therefore not entitled to worship.

Appa

My great-grandfather was an early riser, up well before dawn, going to the village tank to perform his daily ablutions so that he could return ready for the daily *puja*. There was no piped water, and had there been any he would not have used it, of course. Generally all the males went to the local tanks — ponds or lakes — for their ablutions. The women bathed at the well generally located at the rear of the house. When the tanks went dry, as happened every summer, then the men folk too had to use the well. All the washing, whether of clothes or the cooking vessels, had to be done there too.

One morning my great-grandfather got up and went out to go to the lake. He thought it was dawn, for there was much illumination, and also there were a few crows already cawing. He had gone hardly a hundred yards from his home when he saw a troop of horsemen coming towards him. They all looked very fierce, and bore arms which looked very lethal. But he was not perturbed, being fearless, and was thinking only of his walk to the tank. When the troop came near him, the chief of the horsemen accosted him and asked, "Oh Brahmin! What are you doing outside at this hour? This is our time. Your time has not yet come. Go back home and come out at dawn." My great-grandfather answered that the day had in fact dawned, and did not the chief of the troop hear the crows in the palm trees? The troop leader laughed and told my great grandfather, "Oh Brahmin! Look up at the sky!" My great-grandfather looked up and saw the full moon riding serenely across the heavens.

He was quite chagrined when he realised that the light of the full moon had beguiled him into thinking that the day had dawned. That the crows too had been misled by the moonlight was of course no compensation! He apologized to the troop leader and returned home. The troop of horsemen drove on. It was only later that he realised that they had looked extremely familiar. He then realised that it was the troop of *ayyanars* outside the village, at the village border. They were indeed the village guardians doing their rounds to see that all was well with the village and its residents. These stories sound so unbelievable and inexplicable, but it shows that to those who had the fearless vision to see reality, such things did manifest themselves.

Coming from such stock it is not surprising that my father had such a tenacious nature. He was bold, courageous, fearless and charming. He never thought of failure when he took up any work. To him success was a matter of self-effort, and if one failed, it was because the requisite degree of effort had not been expended upon the job. God was of course there — who could possibly deny His presence? But my father did not seem to depend upon Him too much, not overtly in any case. The Indian, and especially the Hindu, has always been too dependent upon the deity, which is not a bad thing by any means, but it has been a dependence without any personal effort. I believe that the theory of karma, which has been so deeply implanted into the Indian psyche, has been grossly misinterpreted, and the result has been disastrous.

The people of India have somehow been made to understand that karma has already decided what a person will achieve in this life. So they wait for whatever it is that they are supposed to achieve without making much of an effort to achieve it. The westerners are quite right in calling the average Indian a fatalist — because that is what he is. The karma theory nowhere says, to my knowledge, severely limited though it is, that a person will get anything without working for it. It must appear the most absurd of propositions that a person will be entitled to anything at all without labouring for it. At least to most people outside India it has appeared the supreme absurdity. I cannot see how any one can argue with such a position. The *Gita,* too, seems to agree with this, because Lord Krishna emphasizes that even He, the Supreme Lord, cannot remain idle for even a moment, because if He did so the universe itself would collapse. This message is clear, and there for all to read. The only thing that Lord Krishna says is that one should not be attached to the fruit of one's actions.

Personally I have derived the greatest benefit from the teaching of the *Bhagavad Gita,* and especially this statement about karma yoga. Lord Krishna says that the only difference between Himself and the rest of creation is that He has nothing to do as a duty devolving upon Himself. Secondly he emphasizes that the fruits of His actions do not affect Him. Going through this again and again, I have felt that in this teaching is contained a great liberation, as it were. All our doubts and fears are because we are attached to the fruit of our actions — the results that we expect from our labours. Fear that the expected reward may not materialize is bad enough. The greater fear is of failure. Therefore I believe that what Lord Krishna's exhortations really amount to is that if we think of the fruit of our labours, we shall be condemned to impotence from the very start. It is not as if Lord Krishna is telling us to work for free. He only tells us not to think of the end result, but exhorts us to get on with the job. I believe that there is definitely the implication, perhaps the promise too, that right labour **must** be followed by the right result. This is not explicitly stated but I feel that it is, it must be, implicit. Right thought leads to right action, and right action then must lead to right result. This is the law. Further, how can anyone deny the fruit of right action if the fruit of wrong action cannot be withheld?

I wonder why there should be any failure if the job has been properly done. It is this aspect that has been misunderstood by enormous sections of the population of India from time immemorial, and it is this misunderstanding that has brought India to the sorry state that it is in today. The apathy that one sees in the people of this country is something too awful even to imagine. The people are just waiting for something to happen to them, which will lift them out of their sordid and miserable existence and bestow upon them a life of pleasure and happiness — *Ram Rajya,* or the rule of Lord Rama of the *Ramayana* which the people of India have been fondly waiting and hoping for. If one has the courage to tell them that such a thing will never happen unless they take the trouble of making it happen, they will just stare in angry disbelief and call one a liar and an unbeliever! The faith is there, of course, but what on earth is the use of a faith which is slumbering in the individual? More, what on earth is the use of a faith which is misplaced? The desire to be great, or to be at least something in life, is there too, but again, what on earth is the use of such a desire if one has not the ability to make the effort to realise the desire as an actuality in one's life? I wonder when the people of India will wake up to the fact that things happen only when we make an effort to make them happen. The divine will has to co-operate in it, no doubt, but what will the divine will co-operate with in the absence of a human will applied to the achievement of its purpose?

It is a sad fact that the religious leaders and teachers have not cared to point this out to their flocks, but have rather tended to keep them in the darkness of ignorance. It is a pity that few persons read the texts and try to understand their meaning by themselves. Within the ancient texts of India is available all the wisdom that one needs to conduct one's life in a satisfactory and fulfilling manner. There have been great scholars of this literature — *pundits,* as they are called — but it seems rather curious, and very tragic too, that all the knowledge in the world did not help them to lead a life of fulfilment and joy.

Life was certainly meant to be a joyous and growth-oriented existence. That it is not so is certainly not to be blamed on the creator, but upon ourselves. What have we done with all that ancient wisdom and tradition that we have inherited, and which many have also studied? I believe that in the end, as Carl Jung the world famous psychologist has pointed out, it is a question of the moral fibre of the individual whether he applies all that he has learnt to his life or not. So it is not education that decides what the life-content of a person's existence shall be. It is also not intelligence. Nor is it worldly wisdom. It is the moral fibre of the individual that really and truly matters. If this is lacking, anything else being present or absent has no significance. If it is present, it multiplies enormously all the other faculties and strengths that a person may possess. In this lies the value of being trained to lead a moral life, or a life filled with moral purpose.

I believe that my father had intuitively developed such a moral strength within himself, and that was what gave him the ability to build his shattered life in such a manner as to make it bloom like a desert flower — a life of fulfillment and joy in substantial measure. His successes came slowly but surely. He was never after success really, but did everything that he had to with a passionate application that was an education in itself. For him it was never too late for education. In India there has been this rather egotistic thought that education is only for the young. Adult education was an unknown thing till recent years. It seems that the elderly individual felt it demeaning to study when he had passed out of school and college, not realising at all the truth of the statement that true education begins only after one leaves college.

I think that here again there was a misunderstanding of the ancient teaching which divided the stages of man into four — *brahmacharya, grihastha, vanaprastha* and *sannyasa*. Education was supposed to end with the *brahmacharya* stage, the stage of the celibate youth. Then one entered the *grihastha* stage, the stage of the married householder. That was the time for material pleasures, sticking of course to the pleasures approved by the Vedic texts, and for bringing up a family. When this stage had been adequately dealt with, in the sense that one had married off one's daughters and ensured that one's sons had been established in life by finding them something to do, and getting them married too, then it was time for the *vanaprastha* ashram to be entered. One left home with one's wife and took to the forests to begin one's spiritual life, so that the life hereafter could be adequately taken care of. Rather late in the day, one would think, but that was the way it was put. When that ended, the male could seek *sannyasa*, renouncing the family and the responsibilities that go with existence, and become a mendicant, a monk.

It was very much later in life that I found justification for my early beliefs in the teachings of my Master, who was also my father's spiritual Master. Under the scheme of the four-fold classification of human existence, it was as if everything was being put off. At least that was the way the scheme was interpreted. Also it seemed to put each stage into its own water-tight compartment, rigidly sealing it off from the next one. So education was not supposed to intrude into the life of the householder. A sad misinterpretation indeed, in my opinion. What a contrast in the western world where no one is ever too old to go to school! Is it any wonder that the peoples of those lands have prospered so fast and so wonderfully, while poor India remains a land of darkness and ignorance?

My father always stressed the need for right understanding, because without it nothing was possible. He used to teach us the *slokas* — chants to the divine — in Sanskrit, as part of our religious instruction. They were drawn from the *upanishads,* and we loved to repeat them whenever he asked us to recite them with him. There was neither a ritualistic

Appa

atmosphere nor an atmosphere of *puja*. We just recited them whenever he wanted us to do so, and it was generally when he was occupied with some other manual work. I do not remember whether he performed any daily *puja* in those days in Jubbulpore. I believe not, because he was frequently on tour to neighbouring stations on the G.I.P. network. Also, once a month he had to go to Bombay for comparing the divisional accounts with those maintained at the Headquarters of the railway. This often took three days. On such occasions when he went away, the house would appear darker, and assume a melancholy atmosphere.

I must say that till we boys grew up my father's life was definitely a life of intense suffering on the physical plane, and no doubt on the mental plane too. We were frequently ill, and had to be carried to the doctor's clinic, especially when we were in Bombay, for he could not afford visiting fees for the doctor. There were several occasions when Kothand and I were both ill, and then he would carry us, one on each shoulder, and walk a mile to the doctor like that. Life in Jubbulpore was definitely more relaxed. His income was such that we could have better food and clothing, and the atmosphere of the house with its enormous garden, the largest that we have ever had, was truly healthy and invigorating. It was the largest house that we have ever inhabited. And we have never had a bigger garden since then. One cannot begin to even imagine the horror of some phases of his existence. He told me that when he was just eight or nine years old, an epidemic of smallpox attacked his village, and eleven out of the fifteen members of his family were down with this dreaded killer disease. While my father and two of his aunts nursed them, they died off, one by one, until only five members of the family remained alive. He does not know how he survived that nightmare.

In those days villages were attacked at night by gangs of *dacoits* mounted on horses, carrying lighted torches with which they would set fire to the thatched roofs of the village houses. Terror reigned at night, but my father was never afraid, and helped to drive them away. Such attacks were frequent, and police help negligible or not available at all. Villages generally had one police constable, and that was all the protection that the government provided the villages with. And though they were supposed to be brave, their bravery was restricted to the occasions when there was no danger around! There was also the suspicion that the police were hand-in-glove with the *dacoits*, which opinion is still widely held, showing that things don't change all that easily.

Then there were other robbers who moved stealthily into a village at night who, using crow bars, opened up a hole in one of the mud walls of the house, and entered feet first into the house. Generally they went unnoticed. They made away with much of the property of the householders in this fashion. Even when they were noticed, the inmates of the house kept quiet, as they did not want to risk their lives in trying to defend their property. I asked my father why they entered feet first. The reason that he gave me was that they originally used to enter head first, but some alert persons waited for the digging to be over, holding a lethal *aruval* (a curved knife, very large and sharp, used to harvest paddy) in their hand, and as the head of the robber appeared through the hole, they just cut off the head as the robber was still half in and half out, and quite helpless. The head rolled inside, and when produced helped to track down the rest of the gang. Therefore to avoid danger to the whole gang they changed their tactics and started entering feet first — for then all that they lost was a pair of feet. And this had the additional merit, a very important one, no doubt, that the feet could rarely be used to identify the rest of the gang!

.A. Ramabhadran (Chitya) standing; C.A. Rajagopalachari (Appa) seated; C.A. Bakthavathsalan (Bakthu) on floor

From left: C.A. Ramabhadran (Chitya), C.A. Bakthavathsalan (Bakthu), C.A. Rajagopalachari (Appa) - 1939

C.A. Rajagopalachari (Appa)
standing in doorway of mobile office (saloon)

From left: C.A. Rajagopalachari (Appa), Chakrapani, Srinivasan, C.A. Bakthavathsalan (Bakthu), Shakuntala (Chitti), Parthsarathi, Gouri, Kothandaraman, C.A. Ramabhadran (Chitya),

Appa

"And the meek shall inherit the earth," says a famous text. I wonder what the poor and timid Brahmin families thought of that one! For the Brahmins were the ones who were generally attacked, being known for their timidity and non-violent nature. The habit that the Brahmins had of inhabiting a whole street or a section of a village made the job of such predatory gangs all the more easy. The places where the Brahmins thus huddled together — a whole street generally — was known as an *agraharam*. With the Brahmins giving up agriculture, and deserting the villages to seek jobs in the towns and cities, such Brahmin *agraharams* have largely disappeared.

This business of the high-souled ones being timid and non-violent has been a puzzle to me all my life, and more especially after I came into touch with the spiritual life as a practising aspirant. I am familiar with many of the stories drawn from the ancient lore of India — and have been especially fascinated by the great epics, the *Ramayana* and the *Mahabharata*. All the great stories deal with the spread of evil and violence on earth to such an extent that even the *rishis* were prevented from performing their *yagnas* in their forest ashrams. Finally matters become so bad that the *rishis* have to go to the Ocean of Milk — the *Ksheera Sagara* — upon which the Ultimate Godhead, Lord Narayana, is reclining upon the great serpent Vasuki. After arriving there, the *rishis* stand in profound respect before the Lord, and pray to Him to relieve the world of its miseries. Their prayer being favourably heard by the Lord Himself, He tells them to return to their world and to await His coming. An emanation of His own Self — an *amsa* — leaves the Lord, and He is born on earth as an *avatar*. Then there is the rest of the epic detailing how He, in His incarnation, destroys the evil doer, protects the virtuous, and re-establishes *Dharma* again on earth before returning to His divine abode. This threefold purpose is the purpose of an *avatar*.

Now what has been puzzling me is that the *rishis* are said to possess immense powers, acquired by virtue of their patient and dedicated *tapasya (askesis)* lasting, in some cases, as long as twenty thousand years! If they possess such awful and divinely endowed powers, then why don't they use them themselves, instead of petitioning the Lord Almighty every time they are in trouble? The stories tell of the *rishis* having to continue with their *tapasya* under the protection of the Lord's *avatara*, such *yagnas* being conducted for the sake of the welfare of the world and its inhabitants. The whole matter has been puzzling to me, because I couldn't discover a reason for their non-violent attitude, especially when they possessed such powers themselves. If they didn't, or couldn't, use them, then why did they acquire such powers at such tremendous effort? Some answers emerged to this and to many other questions only after I came to the Divine feet of my Great and Benevolent Master, Shri Ram Chandraji Maharaj of Shahjahanpur, of which more later.

I think this line of thought must have rubbed off on me, so to speak, from my father. But whereas he became more and more self-reliant and effective, it has not been the same with me. In one sense, and in one only, it may be proper to say that Appa actually defied the gods in his attempt to create his life afresh from the ruins which his destiny had made of it. I may venture the suggestion that his was one of the few cases that have come to my notice of a person having been able to remake his destiny, remould it, to give it a shape that it would never have had had he been a spineless believer in an unchangeable destiny. It would be too facile an argument to say that to be able to do so, too, must have been predestined. The one characteristic, above all else, that I would put as dominant in Appa's character was his indomitable will.

Appa

I do not know much about my father's life in Calcutta except that it was a very busy one. He lived in the Ballygunj area in South Calcutta, while his office was at 6, Esplanade East in one of the busiest areas of Calcutta. We continued in Jubbulpore as our studies could not be interrupted. Further, there was the general feeling that one could not say what would happen during war time, and therefore it was far safer for us to stay on in Jubbulpore, far away from any theatre of active warfare. But I must say that in the absence of Appa we only felt more and more insecure, though we were quite grown up by then, my age being fifteen years. Nayudu mama looked after us all with great affection, and visited us at least twice a week. But a father is a father after all, and we missed ours very much indeed. We of course had no telephone. I wonder whether I had even seen one in those days till the end of 1943. There were instruments which the Railways used, which had a handle to crank, and which enabled communication between a few stations, and within the railway network only. Such things, which have become a necessity these days, were practically unknown in those days. The telegraph was there, of course, but restricted to the conveyance of only urgent matters or 'matters of life and death.'

On one occasion my father was transferred, and we had to stay on in Jubbulpore in the railway quarters with the new incumbents, Mr.T. Raghavachari and his loving family. Now Mrs. Raghavachari had a most wholesome terror of a telegram. I remember that every time one was received she would sign for it, go to the back yard and vomit copiously, come back into the house, pray before the shrine they had set up in the *puja* room, and then only ask someone else to open and read out the telegram. She was terrified of it, always assuming that it contained the worst possible news. When she heard the good news that a telegram often brought, she would once again head for the back yard, this time to vomit out of relief! She would then smile at all of us most affectionately, and pretend that nothing had really happened. Telegrams were not resorted to frequently. A telegram was a messenger of death, to the common people!

We used to wait impatiently for our father's next letter, for it was not possible for him to write to each of his sons separately. Those were the days when family news concerned everyone in the family, and so generally only one letter would be written, to be shared by all. The idea of individual privacy which has, in my opinion, destroyed a fairly large part of family oneness and togetherness, had not yet invaded the minds of the innocent people. Looking at it now, I am amazed at the fact that even a letter written by a husband to his wife was generally read out before all — for was not the marital harmony of the couple a matter of the deepest concern to all in the family? Could the family exist in an atmosphere of harmony, satisfaction and peace if even one member had problems which he or she withheld from the others? Certainly not! Therefore all was of common concern.

This system ensured that everyone, literally everyone, knew all that was there to be known, and all advised where advice was necessary. All shared the joy of togetherness when that was the occasion, and all of course shared the sorrows of life — of which there has never been a dearth in Indian familial existence. As the eldest in the house, it was some sort of a dubious prerogative that I enjoyed of reading the letter out for all to hear. Then the others would read it for themselves. Sometimes my father would address the letter to one of my younger brothers, and then if I insisted on opening it and reading it, there would be hell to pay!

Appa

I remember one particular letter that my father wrote to my youngest brother, Seena. My father had been telling us the story of the *Three Little Pigs,* and Seena had been fascinated by it. Later, when Appa was in Calcutta, he wrote Seena a letter in which he addressed my brother as "My darling little pig", and this made Seena inordinately happy. We were of course anxious to read it, and managed to take it from Seena's hands with the minimum of persuasion. Little did we imagine that it would rebound upon us, because Kothand and I became the middle pig and the big pig very naturally — and that was not at all what had been desired or even anticipated! A loving appellation in a letter is one thing, and for a similar appellation to be used in a derogatory sense quite another thing. I think Seena had his quiet revenge, and the last laugh on that occasion.

Some of the privileges and prerogatives that I enjoyed as the eldest had to be retained at much expense — unless one was prepared to fight to retain them. Even though I was the eldest, I was also the weakest, and suffered from the added disadvantage of wearing spectacles — glasses as they were usually referred to. So I had to be prudent not to provoke my brothers to even sham violence, knowing that what began as play often could degenerate into the real thing.

It was naturally by telegram that my father had to be informed when I suddenly fell sick one evening as soon as I returned from school. In spite of his own severe illness — he having collapsed in the office, and having had to be hospitalized — he rushed over to Jubbulpore to look after me, little realising that it would take nearly four months to get me back to health. After my recovery he went back to Calcutta, while we continued in Jubbulpore. It was my final year in school. I completed the Cambridge School Certificate Examination —

the Senior Cambridge, as it was also called — and then we all moved to Calcutta.

My father's sacrifices were great, and I relate an instance of it. Till I left school I had been a little fellow, four feet ten inches in height, and weighing just about 84 lbs. I had been the weakest in class, and even though I participated in some of the games, I was no hero to anyone, least of all to myself. One day my father suddenly dragged me to a physical culture institute called the Bajranga Vyayamghar, run by one Shri Krishna Kali Banerji. He enrolled himself, and suggested that I too should undergo the course. I agreed. He started me off on it, and after going there with me for a few weeks he stopped, making me carry on. I shall always be grateful to my father for this, for it helped me to grow considerably taller, reaching a height of five feet ten inches and a weight of 144 lbs in just one year. At that stage new clothes had to be made for me, as all the old ones were too small. Few persons recognized me, and it was fun having to introduce myself to all those who had known me for many years.

During the period from January 1944 to the middle of June 1946, we lived in a large house situated on Raja Basanta Roy Road, near the Dhakuria Lakes. My father used to leave for work very early — even for India — and return late at night. One advantage of staying in Calcutta was that we saw more of our uncle Bhadran, who was then in Assam as a District Forest Officer, and later as an Assistant Conservator of Forests. He used to come to Calcutta several times a year, and so we had closer contact with him. My father was very happy for this. Bakthu also lived with us, and so the three brothers could meet more often than it had been possible after their mother passed away. For some time my maternal uncle Kasturi, aunt Kamali and their children also stayed with us. Kamali used to do the cooking, grumbling about it most of the time, though she had a servant boy to assist her in everything. I remember that as my involvement with physical culture increased, and as I grew bigger and bigger, my appetite increased proportionately — and it was by no means unusual for me to eat a dozen dosas for breakfast! She would grumble all the time about my "elephantine appetite" as she put it, but this annoyed my father for it amounted to casting an evil eye on a growing boy. But it went on all the same, and added some spice to our life. Life was a very happy thing in those days, mainly because there were so many in the house.

Joint-family existence was a really great thing, but now it is a thing of the past. It is a very great pity that it has been almost completely phased out in modern times. There was a great deal of love and protection in that way of life which it is impossible to find now. It was possible in a predominantly agrarian economy, and when the ways of life changed with the advent of 'industrialization', much that had been good and wonderful was thrown out. There may have been a great deal of innocent and silly superstition in the old days, but there was tremendous good too, and when social changes of a profound nature came in following the growth of industrialization after the war, the abandonment of much that was not merely good but essential to the Indian way of life was like 'throwing the baby out with the bath water.'

For one thing, respect for the elders almost disappeared. This was a serious blow to Indian culture, and has caused enormous damage to the concept of family oneness based on mutual love and respect. The true proportions of this erosion of the minimally necessary etiquette has not been realised by most even today. It is facile to say that society can be benefited by the erosion of the cultural base of a society or of a civilization. Remembering all that had been wonderful and beautiful, with tremendous powers of integration, in that way of life in the distant past of my own childhood, I can only mourn for all that has been lost, perhaps forever. This has greatly impoverished the way of life in India. The strong will always be strong — it is almost a truism of course. But the weaker have been made progressively weaker, and that has not been at all a desirable thing for a country like India, where the joint family way of life had shielded and protected the weak, and which had given them a chance to live their lives with a degree of self-respect which has gone with the wind, as it were.

The elders had the duty of looking after the whole family. That gave them a sense of purpose, and a quiet dignity, a dignified dignity I am tempted to say, which was a remarkable thing. It brought a sense of belonging to all, and there was the feeling of being not only protected but loved too, for such elders had of course to make tremendous sacrifices in their own personal lives to look after the general welfare of all. It was more or less a general feature of life in those glorious times that the eldest member of the family was generally the economically weakest, for he would generally have sacrificed even the chance of higher education for himself to enable his brothers to have it. This was more the rule than the exception. I have known of but few families where the selfishness of the eldest robbed the younger ones of their opportunities.

An even more demanding sacrifice often became necessary by the eldest son of the family. If the eldest daughter happened to be less than pretty, she often remained unmarried because of the difficulty in finding a bridegroom for her. In India marriages are generally arranged marriages, and the girls had virtually no opportunities of finding husbands for themselves. Romance has generally been a post-marital affair between the spouses in this society! I have written elsewhere of the lack of a romantic period in the life of Indian youth. Marriages were supposed to be made in Heaven. Destiny had already produced a girl's groom, and he would appear at the destined time. Why therefore did a girl have to hunt for a man on her own? Indian marriages were staid and sober affairs, to be handled with great care and prayer. In comparing Occidental mores with Indian ones, it was often said that romance in India was a cold pot of water which, after marriage, began to warm up as if put on a fire, and went on getting hotter and hotter until it boiled. Occidental love affairs were said to be like a pot of boiling water taken off the fire, which inevitably went on cooling until it became like ice!

The job of getting the daughters married was of course that of the parents, and the eldest brother had to share that responsibility if he was old enough to be included in the scheme of things. An ancient Sanskrit phrase says that the eldest brother of the family is like the father to the other children! And if unhappily the father of the house had expired prematurely, this role of the father did actually devolve upon the often immature and weak shoulders of the poor young person who had the misfortune to be the eldest son of the family. Such instances are by no means rare, my father himself being an outstanding example of having been thus pressed into the role of a father to his younger brothers. If for any reason the eldest daughter of the house remained unmarried, the eldest boy would remain unmarried until she had 'been married off' as it is said! Because if he or the younger sisters were married before the eldest sister, then people would think that there was something wrong with the girl, and this would ruin her chances of matrimony forever. That was how the thinking went.

I know of so many families in which this sort of thing has happened, creating enormous unhappiness and frustration, but there was no recourse. This sacrifice was a cruel and demanding one, but the eldest boy of the family generally did accept it as part of his duty. Younger sisters would remain unmarried, but with the passage of years, some sanity would descend upon the family and the younger ones would be slowly married off. This sacrifice gave them tremendous strength, and a respect in society that does not exist today, when personal development and advancement have become the order of the day. Such a steep fall in standards where the rule is, "Let the other fellow go to the dogs so long as I make it," has created a society which is cursed with selfishness, greediness, avariciousness and all the evils of a life devoted to personal advancement only.

I have seen that the people of those times were generally less guilt-ridden when compared to the present generation. They did their duty to the best of their abilities, and sacrificed all that they possibly could to do it. When one has done one's best, there is hardly anything to feel guilty about! That was their reward! In modern times when the family has been given the last place in life, and self-seeking is the order of the day, the joint family system has almost disappeared. Guilt has reared its ugly head. For where is the son today who does not feel guilty for having given his parents a rough deal, or for having left them to their destinies? It is generally argued that the children of these times have very little choice, for in a competitive world one has to make one's way in the world somehow. But if filial duty is thrown overboard for the sake of personal advancement, then such a situation will surely breed guilt, and make the latter part of such a person's life miserable — and if unfortunately the parents are dead, one has to carry a sense of shame and guilt right into the grave, as it were.

My father was quite happy with his shift to the Defence department, for he had an excellent boss, Mr. Lockhart by name, whom he was praising all the time. Since Appa was always more able to get on with the British bosses, it suited him very well. I believe the sole reason for this was that the Englishmen in India were not a jealous lot. They had no reason

Appa

to be, for their future was back home, in good old England, and so they did not try to interfere with the careers of their subordinates. It was very different with the Indian bosses, for they have generally been a jealous and frightened lot, looking at every promising and brilliant assistant as a potential menace to their own career, and therefore nipping all brilliance and initiative in the bud. This has, in large measure, been responsible for the utter mediocrity of Indian administration, particularly in government departments.

Our next door neighbour was Mr. G. Vanmikanathan Pillay, known generally as G.V. Pillay, and to all of us of the younger generation as Pillay mama — uncle Pillay. He introduced Appa to the marvellous healing system of Homoeopathy, of which he had been totally ignorant before then. Calcutta has been pioneering this system, and we witnessed several remarkable cures while we were there. Pillay mama was our doctor during our Calcutta sojourn. He was one of the most affectionate persons I have ever known, and was able to mix freely with persons of all ages without any inhibitions. This is a rather rare quality in a human being. Whenever we had problems we would go to the window of the bedroom facing his house and shout across the intervening few yards, when he would come to his window and then there would be a conversation, a discussion. Then we would go to his place half an hour later to take the appropriate medicine. He taught all of us the fundamentals of Homoeopathy, and all of us became deeply interested in it.

Pillay mama and Appa became fast friends, as we say of intimate friends, and Appa had a great deal of respect and regard for him, which Pillay mama fully reciprocated. We valued this friendship, which ended only a couple of years back in 1989 with the demise of Pillay mama at the age of nearly ninety! He was healthy in all respects and had his wits about him to the very end, suffering only from an impaired vision. He became something of a *paterfamilias* to us, and when we had complaints about Appa, we would go to him for consolation and advice. He was always very understanding, and took the place of Nayudu mama whom we had left behind in Jubbulpore, and were not to meet again for very many years. He was also something of an adviser to Appa himself, and Appa valued this friendship which lasted from 1944 for very nearly half a century. It was Pillay mama who wrote the book about some of his very close and intimate friends, all of whom he greatly admired for one outstanding reason or other. In that book he wrote a whole chapter about Appa, referring to him as a modern-day Bhishma. High praise indeed! I am glad to honour Pillay mama's memory with these lines about him. I shall perhaps have to refer to him later on in this narrative.

For us youngsters, Pillay mama was an everlasting source of strength and wisdom. After our stay at Calcutta, we left for Bombay in 1946, and then we lost touch with him for many years. But the roots of the friendship were too deep to be affected by a mere decade's absence — and in our case absence definitely did make our hearts grow fonder. In fact when we met him again after many years of silence, it was as if there had never been any parting at all. He was some years my father's senior in age, and after he had retired from service he settled down in Trichy, about 200 miles south of Madras, in the suburb of Tennur. There he established The Tirukkural Prachar Sangam. Apart from his mastery of Homoeopathy, he was a Tamil scholar, and especially of the Tirukkural, perhaps the most famous of Tamil philosophic works which sets out the duties of a human being during the various stages of his existence, dealing with them under the three broad classifications of Duty, Material Existence and Love — *Arathuppal, Porutpal* and *Kamathuppal*.

Appa

He became a disciple of the Shankaracharya of the Kamakoti Peetham, and took up the religious life with fervour and ardent dedication. He spent a couple of hours every morning on his *puja,* and grew a very impressive, if somewhat forbidding, beard. His wife was sickly, and Pillay mama's last years were spent almost exclusively on his *puja* and in looking after his wife with great devotion. A model life worth emulating. But whenever I spoke to him about spirituality, he would no doubt extol my spiritual life, and praise some of the books that I had written, but never turned towards it himself. It has been a great disappointment to me that I could not be of any service to one who had given so much of his loving attention to us.

By the time my father's services were returned to the railways, I had passed my Intermediate Examination from the St. Xavier's College, Calcutta, and so I went to Bombay too. The Bombay life was totally different, full of hustle and worries. One had to run around a great deal, commuting by suburban electric trains or by buses. My father was posted in the Lower Parel Workshop of what had now become the Central Railway, and worked as an Assistant Controller of Stores. It was a shift from the Accounts Department. Someone he had believed in all his life, one whom he implicitly trusted and with whom he had been friendly for decades, brought about this shift to favour someone else, and my father's career interests were substantially damaged. After his war service record he should have moved up many rungs of the ladder of the railway administration, instead of which he had to fight for survival. A strange turn of events indeed. He used to become very angry, but he never let it affect him. He went on with his job, but with a pain in his heart at having been so betrayed. What I admired in him was that he still retained the friendship of the person who had virtually ruined him, without allowing the betrayal to effect any change in his own behaviour. Eventually the other person realised the enormous harm he had caused to my father, and I believe that he apologized to him too — but it was of no use, since it could not help in restituting a damaged career.

While at Calcutta Appa had taken a rather dilettantish interest in learning homoeopathy. He didn't really get his teeth into it, but was able to treat the usual mild disorders in the family with sufficient efficacy to obviate the need to go to a doctor for relief. He lost interest in going on with that, and then turned his attention to learning Hindi. He was already forty-three years or so old, but that did not deter him from attempting to master a new language with which he already had some familiarity. He spent hours every day, and attended classes conducted by the Hindi Prachar Sabha. In a few years he managed to pass the degree equivalent to a Master's degree in that language. He became quite a scholar, though his spoken Hindi was never as good as it ought to have been.

He joined the St. John's Ambulance Brigade and became a keen member of that brigade. He was proud of his uniform, and was diligent in attending the frequent parades. Here too he rose to high rank, and continued his interest and active association with it for well nigh six or seven years before he was forced to abandon it because of a severe attack of arthritis which nearly crippled his right arm. Allopathic medicine was useless, and finally his doctor in the railway hospital put him under anesthesia and twisted his arm to break the lesions in the right shoulder — causing enormous pain to my father who, still under the influence of the anesthetic, was screaming with pain. There was temporary relief, but the problem returned. Finally he learned that a doctor, Shri Benoytosh Bhattacharya, living in Naihati near Calcutta, was able to treat such illnesses by different means. Appa wrote to him, and was asked to send a

Appa

copy of his photograph, which he did. Dr. Bhattacharya was a famous Indologist apart from all his other achievements. He treated my father who became completely well in just one month. The arthritis problem never recurred till the end of his life.

One element of his treatment was very simple. He advised Appa to cut a lemon in half at night, and to soak the two halves in water, the water just covering the upturned cut surfaces of the lemon. In the morning he had to squeeze the juice of the two halves into the water in which they had been soaked overnight, add a spoon of honey, stir well and drink it first thing in the morning. We have later recommended this to a large number of suffering friends and colleagues who have all benefitted by it.

When in Jubbulpore we had started a stamp collection of sorts. We had no knowledge of stamps, but collected them for the sake of their different shapes and colours. Our main interest lay in exchanging the duplicates that we had, without knowing anything about their value. This hobby helped us to brush up on our geography — and I still remember the exotic-sounding names of countries such as Johore, Kota Baharu, Estonia, Latvia, Lithuania and so on. Many of those names had disappeared from our geography books to resurface only recently, in late 1991, when enormous changes have brought Estonia, Latvia and Lithuania back on the world stage as independent sovereign nations. One hopes and expects that new stamps by these Baltic nations will re-emerge to enliven philately again.

The reason for my mentioning this hobby is that my father took over this collection of a couple of thousand stamps, and taking a serious interest, he began to tackle it very systematically and professionally. I know that he even began buying stamps from dealers to make up his collection of chosen themes. Eventually he concentrated on stamps issued by India, and began a highly specialized collection of stamps issued by the Republic of India. He became an exhibitor, and won many prizes in exhibitions in India and abroad. This hobby became a passion with him and threatened to ruin his eyesight. We had to request him to take it easy, and not work during the night. He became a respected philatelist and graduated into a judge-examiner at exhibitions.

It was his nature to become passionate about anything that he took up, whether it was learning a language or a technique, or just simply a hobby. To him anything that deserved to be done deserved to be done as well as he could do it. He was a seeker after excellence in any and every sense of the word, and he would not rest till he had achieved what he wanted. I have forgotten to mention that he had the soul of an artist, and an eye for colour and beauty, both of which he developed by undergoing a course of instruction at the J.J. School of Art in Bombay. I do not know when exactly he did this, but it was definitely before his marriage. Later on, during our Bombay days, we used to go to a hill station called Lonavla, in the western ghats, a mere couple of hours journey by train from Bombay on the Poona route. In those days he made a couple of oil paintings which even today adorn the walls of my brother's home.

Passion is one word which could be used to characterize him. I am not referring to the lower type of passionate nature, which manifests itself in mere selfishness and in a base physical existence, but to a passion he exhibited in undertaking anything that attracted his immensely varied interests. I believe that this variegated interest in the many subjects that he mastered kept him youthful and gave him a fillip in enabling him to find some happiness in life through such achievements. They also created a channel for his enormous energies, and that

Appa

was surely a good thing in itself. It rounded him off, so to speak, and he matured into a very capable and wise person, ready to love and to help others in all possible ways. He matured steadily, and got rid of such failings as he had.

He was always extraordinarily courageous. One instance of this comes to my mind. During his tenure as District Controller of Stores in the Central Railway, he had his work place in the enormous Parel workshop which employed around 15,000 persons, mostly labourers and workers. On one occasion there was a strike in the workshop, and the Railway administration was quite agitated over it because of the possibility of violence during an extended labour strike. The senior managers were reluctant to enter the workshop, and remained at the Victoria Terminus headquarters of the railway, discussing the situation. One day Appa decided to study the situation at first hand, and went to Parel and walked up to the immense gates of the workshop which were closed by the striking workers. He called out to the assembled leaders to let him in, and much to his surprise they opened the gates but said he could not enter. He ignored them and boldly walked in. The crowd of 15,000 or more workers meekly parted to let him pass, shouting anti-management slogans all the time. He stayed the whole day in his office, unharmed and unmolested, and returned safely home in the evening.

Life was a sedate experience after Appa's transfer back to Bombay. His work was going on well. He had reconciled himself to the career prospects that were available, and this gave him a degree of contentment that had perhaps been lacking in his earlier life. His other interests kept him busy and happy, and social life became very fulfilling for him.

For the first two years I was away studying in the Benares Hindu University at Benares. When I returned after getting my

Down Memory Lane

Bachelor's degree in Science, he had quarters in Thana, a suburb of Bombay about twenty-five miles to the north. We had to take the electric suburban train to get to work. He was then working from the railway headquarters at Victoria Terminus, and commuting to work was fairly simple as he had direct trains from Thana to V.T. I had secured a job with Indian Plastics Ltd., and had therefore to go to Kandivilee everyday. My journey was a long and tedious affair, since I had to take a train south to Dadar, change to the B.B & C.I. network, and take a train going north to Borivili, alighting at Kandivilee. From the station I had to walk nearly two miles to the factory where I was employed. Notwithstanding all this, life was pleasant and there was a fair degree of contentment.

A year or more later my father was allotted quarters in the suburb known as B.B. Matunga, since it was Matunga next to the B.B & C.I. Railway network. We lived in two Nissen huts put together which though looking awkward was very comfortable inside. There were eight quarters for the officers of the Central Railway — as the G.I.P. had become — and so we had a great deal of company and fun. We had monthly dinner parties out in the open, each family hosting the dinner by rotation. While here, I secured a Government scholarship to go to Yugoslavia for training in plastics technology, and I was away for approximately eighteen months. I had to take leave from Indian Plastics without salary, but it was no great loss for the meagre salary I was drawing in those days — a mere 175 rupees per month. There was the implicit understanding as part of the scholarship that the Government would employ me upon my return — it was a commitment from my side in any case. But much to my chagrin the job that should have been mine went to someone else.

I had to go back to Indian Plastics again. They were not too happy to have me back, as they had to pay me a salary

Appa

commensurate with my training. Normally they should have paid me a minimum of Rs. 650.00 per month, which is what I would have got in the Government of India job, but they sneered at my request and said that I was welcome to go to the Government! Jobs were difficult to come by in the Plastics Industry, which was as yet in its infancy in India, and after some argument with the General Manager, I had to agree to a measly increase of Rs. 25 per month, and rejoined them on a salary of Rs. 200 per month.

When I was away in Yugoslavia, my father was quite lonely, since he had to live alone with a cook. My brother Kothand was studying in Jamalpur after completing schooling in Calcutta. He was also away from home. Seena, my youngest brother was on the training ship Dufferin preparing for a sea-going career. My father seemed to be condemned to a lonely existence for the greater part of his life, but he took it all very philosophically. He retired from Railway service in the year 1960 upon completion of fifty-five years of age. His last pay was a mere Rs. 1,150 per month, whereas it should have been at least thrice that, had his career taken its normal course. His retirement pension was therefore a meagre six hundred rupees or so. It naturally became necessary for him to seek employment again to keep the family kitchen going, as my own salary was a mere pittance too.

He secured a good job in Ranchi with the Heavy Engineering Corporation Ltd., a Government of India undertaking. An old friend from the railways was there in a very senior position. He helped Appa in getting the job. As we had to vacate the railway quarters, we bought a small flat measuring 520 sq.ft., in Sion, another suburb of Bombay just north of Matunga, for a price of Rs. 15,600 — which seems so unreal now, for the same flat now costs somewhere around Rs. 350,000! We separated once again, Appa going to Ranchi and I shifting into this tiny flat with my wife Sulochana, for we were married in June 1955. Appa made the flat as comfortable as he could before he left for Ranchi to take up his new job there.

It appears as if our family was destined to separate, reunite for a brief period and separate again, and so on all our life. Kothand had a long course lasting about five years to pass through in Jamalpur, after which he was posted to the Southern Railway at Madras as a probationary engineer. Thus he entered the Railways for a career in Engineering. Seena completed his training aboard the training ship Dufferin and went away to sea as a second officer on a ship, and his sea going career lasted a good twenty years. Therefore it was I who was more often with my father. Yet such occasions passed too briefly.

To my happiness I had to leave Indian Plastics and seek a job elsewhere. After an idle period lasting ten months, if my memory serves me right, I secured a job as a sales representative with T.T. Krishnamachari & Co., a trading organization based in Madras, on a salary of Rs. 200 per month. I joined the Bombay office of that firm on the 2nd of January 1955, and went on to serve that organization till I finally retired from its service in July 1985. After an initial period my services were transferred to the head office at Madras, and by then Appa had also quit the service of Heavy Engineering, and decided to settle down in Madras. So we were once again together. We rented a small apartment in Sri Ram Nagar, and Appa started construction of a house in a nearby plot of land. This house soon became ready and we moved into it on the 11th of September 1962. Kothand married the next year, and moved into our home *Gayathri,* and we were all happy to be together again.

My father could not remain idle, and though we no longer needed the money since I was drawing a very good salary, and

Appa

Kothand was a class I officer in the Railways, he nevertheless sought employment and joined the Standard Motor Co., as a purchase officer, and went on to serve that company till he finally decided to retire in 1965 when he attained the age of sixty years. This period of his service with the company which manufactured cars was a period of hectic activity in the house, more especially for Sulochana. My father had to leave for work at 6:30 A.M. every morning as he had to go to Vandalur, some twenty miles to the south of Madras. This was also the time when he was most religious, and had to perform his ritual *puja* every morning before leaving for work. This meant that he had to be up by 4:30 A.M. every morning, have his bath, and begin his *puja* well before 5:00 A.M. *Prasad,* which was also his breakfast, had to be ready by 5:30 A.M.

Sulochana had to get up even before my father was up if all this was to be possible, because she had not only to cook the *prasad*-cum-breakfast, but she had also to cook his lunch to be packed and taken with him. The tension in the house cannot be imagined, since Appa was always in a hurry and tended to lose his temper! I was generally very angry in the mornings because Sulochana's getting up out of bed naturally disturbed me, and I was irritated. Poor Sulochana, she had to bear the brunt of all the bad tempers that my father's *puja* created. I have always felt that Appa could have managed with a couple of sandwiches, but he was the true Indian — he had to have a cooked lunch every day!

Now the completion of sixty years of a person's life is considered to be a major turning point in one's life. The first hurdle in life is the completion of one's first year of terrestrial existence. Therefore when a baby completes the age of one, there is a religious ceremony of cleansing and propitiation. The child's horoscope is not cast till it completes the first year! The second hurdle is completion of the sixtieth year, and if one does it — for life expectancy in India was very low — then that necessitated a major celebration called *shashtiabdapoorthy*. There is the third and final hurdle, and that is the *satabhishekam* — which is celebrated when one has "seen" a thousand and eight moons — generally the completion of eighty years of life on earth. Few lived to celebrate this great event, given the appalling living conditions in the India of those years.

My father's *shashtiabdapoorthy* was celebrated — or rather almost celebrated — in 1965. All had been readied and the religious rituals had already begun very early that morning. At about 7:00 A.M. my father was supposed to bathe for the second time that morning in a large pot of sanctified water purified by Vedic chanting. He had just gone for this ritual purificatory bath when his step-sister, my aunt Kanakam, who had come for the celebration and had been perfectly well till that moment, suddenly took ill. She had in fact had her breakfast just a few moments earlier, and had gone to the bathroom for a wash. There she felt giddy, and we helped her to my father's room just a couple of steps away. She called out to my father, and he came running from his bath. She was faint, and clearly very unwell. We sent for the doctor who was living in the next house. My father sat on the floor and took her on his lap, and there she died a few moments later, even as the doctor arrived.

There was of course chaos and consternation in the house. The guests started leaving immediately, and those who were just then arriving turned away from the gate when they heard of the sudden tragedy. Death seems to have this awful and fearsome effect upon people — even the best of them. Literally no one wanted to be there. We were just one year old in the Shri Ram Chandra Mission, but nevertheless many guests were mission abhyasis, and even Dr. K.C. Varadachari had come from Tirupathi. He had come the previous evening and spent several hours in our home. He came soon after my aunt's passing, and he too left after calling my father to the gate and saying a few words of condolence to him. So did Shri R. Vira Raghavan, the preceptor of our Madras centre. So did everyone else. Suddenly a house that had been full of people, filled with joy and laughter and happiness, became a deserted house full of sorrow and fear.

There was the superstitious fear that since Appa's *shashti-abdapoorthy* celebrations had been interrupted thus by sudden death, some dire consequences were in store for him. It is difficult for others to even imagine the atmosphere that prevailed. To cap it all my aunt's son arrived after she had departed this world, and so did his sister. There was some agitation and confused talk among them. "How can she die so suddenly when she was well just this morning? What happened to her? She was well when she left home yesterday evening. What could have happened between then and now that she has died so suddenly?" Such were the annoying questions, accusatory in nature, that were thrown at us. As if death would send in his visiting card and then enter to take a soul away with him! Relatives can be so unnecessarily cruel when all that the situation demanded was sympathy for the living and a proper disposal of the dead.

Anyway, arrangements had to be made for the cremation of the old lady who had been my aunt, and everything was done as prescribed by the all-pervading *Shastras,* for her family had pretensions to strict orthodoxy. A house of joy and festivity had suddenly become a house of death, but the traces had to be picked up, and life had to go on as the living had still to be looked after and helped to continue to live. We were an orthodox Vaishnava family and my father was a very respected member of the community. Therefore many temples in south India had sent temple honours in the shape of garlands of flowers that had adorned the Lord, *prasad* etc. All the garlands went to adorn my aunt's body, and she went on her final journey looking like a bride. Such is life.

From then on my father lost some of his spirit. Death had visited the house, and that was not a visit that could be easily forgotten. He was familiar enough with death, but as one advances in age, death seems to assume a greater poignancy, and the mystery associated with it seems to deepen and deepen until it is a total mystery. From my observation of life, I may say that when we are very young, death is perhaps no more than a curiosity. There is some element of nervousness perhaps, because that which was moving has suddenly, and for no apparent reason, ceased to move. This causes the curiosity. And when the young child sees the elders weeping, then it too senses that there is something wrong, and sets up a sympathetic wailing. It is strange, this phenomenon of fear. One does not understand how exactly it works, for when that which has been moving ceases to move, there is fear. At the same time if something moves that has never moved in one's experience — a statue for instance, then that too causes not merely fear but consternation.

I have always felt that if the idol in the temple ever became mobile, there would be mass evacuation. I have discussed this with friends and abhyasis often enough, but no one has ever cared to answer my question as to what they would do if the idol to which they were offering prayers suddenly, and most unexpectedly, opened its eyes, stepped down from its pedestal, and asked, "My son, what do you desire?" I personally have no doubt about the reaction that such a situation would instantly provoke. It would cause consternation and horror! There would be fear and pandemonium, the devotees would no doubt run for their lives. So much for *bhakti* and devotion, and for that much vaunted commodity — love of God!

Appa

Appa intensified his ritualistic *pujas,* even though he had commenced meditation under the Sahaj Marg system the previous year. He went to consult the palm leaf oracle, as the westerners call it — the *Kowmara Nadi* — which he had consulted in 1954 just before my marriage was settled. He wanted to know something about his future, but it was all very hush hush, and I came to know about his consultation only several years later when he accidentally put the book containing his readings in my hands. Death has this effect upon people. But alas! The effect does not last long enough for it to bring lasting change in individuals.

There are two types of *vairagya,* or renunciation, spoken of in the Hindu tradition. One is called the *smashana vairagya* while the other is known as *prasava vairagya.* The former refers to the renunciatory attitude that follows a visit to the cremation ground when we see a dead body being cremated, and we come away from that sacred place feeling a deep sense of foreboding and also a sense of the utter futility of life, and vowing never again in our minds to all the follies that we have committed in life — for death does teach us this lesson, but only temporarily! In the *Yaksha Prashna* of the *Mahabharata,* when the *yaksha* asks Yudhishtira, "What is the strangest thing in the world?", Yudhistira answers, "Men see death all around them. But no one ever thinks that he himself will also die sooner or later. This is the strangest thing in the world."

The *prasava vairagya* similarly seems to mock the human being. It refers to the renunciatory attitude that comes over humans when they see the suffering of women during delivery. Then the men say, "Never again, poor thing, never again." But such a renunciation, even when sincere, is merely temporary, and hence the tradition mocks at the merely human being who, during times of such extreme sorrow or suffering and stress, makes vows which he himself knows he will never be able to live by. I do not know whether Appa took any decisions regarding his own life, and the need for him to change in certain aspects, but he did change, for the change was almost palpable. I used to feel sorry for him, because he who had faced so many deaths all his life was now facing one that threatened to bring about a major shift in his outlook. This was all to the good, for he had been "an ardent materialist" as the *Kowmara Nadi* reading had accurately revealed, and it was necessary for him to go inward towards his inner roots to bring about major changes in his life.

He still continued to do the daily *puja* of which he had been so fond, and to which in a sense he had been addicted. However he now meditated with somewhat greater zeal, and developed a progressively closer nearness with the Master to the extent that Master became quite fond of him. This was a major and extremely desirable change, for which I am grateful to my Master. My father's life continued to acquire a new tranquillity, and with increasing work on the spiritual front — for he was made a preceptor in the Mission in 1969 or 1970 — he began to travel to centres of the Mission outside Madras and built up a personal popularity, especially in the Rayalaseema and Nellore districts of Andhra Pradesh, which was quite enviable. This gave him a deep sense of satisfaction, arising out of a devoted acceptance of himself by the abhyasis which perhaps had been rather rare in his life till then.

His activities as a preceptor in the Mission gave a new direction to his life. In 1970 he went to Italy to meet Bhadran, his younger brother, and that was his first ever journey out of India. He was thrilled to have the opportunity to travel, as he was a wanderer by nature, and generally was happy to be on the move. My uncle paid for his travel. In Italy he started working for the Mission, and was responsible for starting the centre in Rome. By the time he left Italy, there were about thirty

Italians practising Sahaj Marg meditation. Master was very pleased with his work.

While in Rome a rather strange thing happened. He received a letter from Copenhagen from a lady unknown to him, who invited him to go to Copenhagen to help her with spiritual practice. She wrote that she had come to know of his presence in Europe and desired to take advantage of the opportunity. He wrote back accepting her invitation, and did go to Copenhagen. She refused to reveal how she had come to know of his presence, but this invitation gave him the opportunity of establishing a second centre of the Mission in Europe, in Copenhagen. This was how Shri Ram Chandra Mission began its activities outside India on foreign soil. Therefore it is my father who deserves credit for commencing the Mission's activities outside India. My Master was very pleased with this development and lavished praise upon him. Later on my father was put in charge of all foreign centres of the Mission.

It was around this time that Master took a decision to strengthen the Mission's official bimonthly spiritual publication, *Sahaj Marg,* which was languishing for want of proper attention. The editorial functions were restricted to merely receiving articles and publishing them from the Mission's press. Initially the printing was done outside, but later it became necessary to buy a small press. There were editors for the Hindi and English sections of the magazine, but they didn't know what to do — and so the magazine was very literally a shambles. It was cheaply produced using the cheapest possible materials, and contained articles of very poor standard, and was always late. The printing was awful, and if one counted the errors on each page, one would surely feel that there were not merely printer's devils, but that he was in the printer's hell itself!

Down Memory Lane

My father was appointed as the Editor of the English section, and he took up his new responsibility with great zest and application. But it was a thankless job, at best, because the standard of the articles could not be improved. There were so few articles available for publication that he had no choice in the matter. As a matter of fact it was a difficult thing to keep the magazine going at all, for there was a permanent paucity of articles both in Hindi and in English. Appa's editorship lasted a couple of years, and then as his eyesight was failing, and he couldn't be burdened with this sort of work, I was given charge of the English section.

Perhaps this was Appa's happiest period in his life. There were grandchildren in the house — for Krishna, my son, was born in May 1957, and was followed by Janaki and Sudarshan, both Kothand's children. Our house *Gayathri* was full, and there were always abhyasis at home, and life was a full and satisfying experience for him. He had also his passion — stamp collecting — to attend to and that kept him busy for the major part of the day, and sometimes even late into the night. We had to remonstrate with him to stop peering into the stamps after sunset, but we could not regulate his activities as we had our bedroom upstairs, while he had his downstairs.

All went well, but trouble is always lurking around the corner, as it were. Master summoned Appa to Shahjahanpur to assist him with the first overseas abhyasis visiting Him. This was in 1971, and there Appa seemed to have fallen early in the morning, and was discovered unconscious near the bathroom at 5:00 A.M. by sister Birthe Haugaard of Copenhagen, the very same abhyasi who had invited Appa to visit her in Denmark. Master assured me by telegram that there was no danger to life, but after a few days he summoned me to Shahjahanpur, and I went there to find Appa at death's door. There was no doubt that he was in a critical condition. Shahja-

Appa

hanpur is a very backward place, and the medical facilities available were poor and comparatively crude. Diagnostic facilities were of the lowest variety only. It was clear that Appa had a brain damage, as he was vomiting continuously round the clock at intervals of a few minutes. He was feeling giddy all the time, and was unable to move by himself. It was necessary to request a neurologist to visit from Dehra Dun, and the young physician came immediately, took a spinal fluid sample, and diagnosed that there was no brain haemorrhage — thanks to Master.

Master had been most concerned that Appa had this accident in his home. He was with Appa every day for at least an hour. He kept reassuring me that there was no danger to his life, but of course he himself was concerned too, as was evident to all who were with him. We were in Master's house, naturally, there being no other place to go to. We were reassured after the visit by the neurologist, and thereafter there was a somewhat relaxed atmosphere. But we had to stay on in Shahjahanpur for more than three weeks before it was possible to move Appa. Kothand had arrived to see Appa. It was on this visit too that Kothand had a talk with Master about Sahaj Marg, and started meditation directly with Master himself. So that was one good thing that came out of Appa's fall.

Finally we were able to leave Shahjahanpur, taking the night Lucknow Mail which left Shahjahanpur at just past midnight. We had reservations in the Ist class air conditioned coach, but it was difficult to get in at that hour, and when we got in we found that there were a couple of senior government officers occupying the lower berths. We requested at least one of them to move up to an upper berth, but notwithstanding the fact that he was a senior officer in the Government of India, he refused very churlishly, and we had to make a real effort to put Appa in the upper berth. But that was not the end of the story, for an hour later Appa wanted to go to the bathroom, and we had to move him down, escort him to the bathroom, and then put him back up on his upper berth — a real job full of risk in a moving train in India! Had he fallen it would have been fatal to him.

We reached Delhi in the morning, and with the help of abhyasis who met us we went up to the retiring room in the railway station for rest. That afternoon we went to the airport to take a plane back to Madras. Appa was taken to the plane in a wheelchair and put on board an hour before departure, but just a few minutes before the time of departure, we were informed that there would be a delay of a couple of hours, and so Appa had to be disembarked and brought back into the lounge to wait there in pain and considerable discomfort. Everything must end, thank God, and eventually we were on board the aircraft and reached Madras. Appa was enormously relieved to be back home again. I suspect that he had decided that he wouldn't return home, but thanks to Master he did, and that was a great thing. Just before we left Shahjahanpur, Babuji Maharaj, my Master, spoke to Appa and told him, "Rajaji, you will live for twenty years more because you have to do a lot of work for the Mission." But very cannily he called me aside and told me, "I have told your Appa that he will live twenty years more, but life and death are in God's hands. It is impossible to say anything precisely, but I am sure that he has a long life ahead of him, may be a few years more or less than what I have said."

Appa was never the same after this accident, for he had not only fractured his skull in two places on the two sides of his head, just above the ears, but there must have been some inner damage to the brain — though there had been no haemorrhage — because soon after we returned to Madras he developed what is called Parkinson's disease. He had to be

Appa

continuously under medication for the rest of his life, and the medicines had to come from Germany. Thanks to the generous assistance of a preceptor of the Mission in Munich, this was not difficult, and he was well supplied with the necessary medicines.

Appa's troubles and sorrows were not over yet. In 1974 his youngest brother, Bakthu, passed away after a sudden heart attack. A telephone call from my aunt Shakumtala at about 4:30 A.M. that morning called for Appa to go over to their home a mile or so away, and we all went there at once. We found Bakthu sitting up in bed. He was sweating profusely, but appeared cheerful. He was apologetic about having sent for Appa. All appeared well, but an hour later there was a sudden deterioration in his condition, and we had to move him to a nearby hospital where he was rushed to the cardiac care ward. While under examination he passed away at about 7:30 A.M. This tragedy that struck our family fell upon us like a thunder bolt. Bhadran Chitya came soon after, and the body was taken to *Gayathri* from where Bakthu was taken on his last journey to the crematorium. The saddest duty in one's life — that of having to light the funeral pyre of a beloved person — fell to me. His two sons were both away, Ranga the younger in the U.S.A., and the elder son Chakrapani on the high seas somewhere between Japan and Australia, captaining his ship. This horrible duty could not be avoided, and I had to perform the last rites.

Appa was deeply affected by this death in the family. He kept saying that he should have gone first, and how sad and unnatural it was that the elder should live while the younger departed this existence. But that was not to be the last shock in poor Appa's life. Our aunt, Chitti as we called her, Bakthu's wife Shakuntala, was of course the most affected, as she was alone without even her sons to help her get over this enormous tragedy. We took her with us and she stayed at *Gayathri* for perhaps a week, but then decided to return to her home saying that Bakthu would look for her there, and she could not be away when he needed her. I was away at Thanjavur on work when a phone call came from Madras to inform me that she had passed away. I hurried back by car, but arrived too late as her body had already been taken to the crematorium. I rushed there, to find my brother Kothand going through the dreary funeral rituals prior to cremating the body. This time poor Kothand had to shoulder this sad burden, and thus passed away another member of our depleted family.

Chitti had been staying all alone, with only a maid to assist her. It appears that on that fateful morning she had felt unwell, and had gone to the opposite apartment to ask for help. While she was there she became serious, was taken into her flat, and there she collapsed — the whole shocking episode taking hardly three minutes. It was good that she had gone to the neighbours, for otherwise she would have remained locked in her own flat, and her death may not have been discovered till at least the next morning.

Sad to say this death, too, did not end the series of tragedies in our family. In 1977 tragedy struck again. Our uncle Bhadran was taken ill after an eye operation. He passed away after a month of hospitalisation. My father was shattered by this tragedy. It was difficult to console him. I don't think that he ever recovered from the shock of his two younger brothers dying while he was still alive. He felt that in some way he had betrayed them — and that it was also in some way a betrayal of himself.

Appa was totally devastated by this second loss of a younger brother, his only surviving brother. He was inconsolable, and mourned for this sudden loss deeply, often crying in

Appa

the night as we discovered, for they had been very close, these two. But nature's demands are inexorable, and she knows no affection, or laws of seniority and juniority, but picks up each life as the time for its temporal sojourn comes to an end. I believe that Appa even developed suicidal tendencies during this period, but by the grace of our Master he curbed those tendencies.

I believe that with this bereavement Appa entered a phase of definite decline, though he was active and could look after himself. He even managed to go abroad again, and that was for the last time in his life. His wanderlust had to be shelved, and he had to content himself with excursions within India, but soon that too had to stop as he entered the senile phase, and after that his visits were restricted to Bangalore to stay with Kothand. Krishna had gone abroad to the U.S.A. for study, and so whenever Sulochana and I travelled out of Madras, we would leave Appa in Bangalore. Appa's *satabhisekham* had been celebrated in Bangalore too.

It was in Bangalore that Appa's end finally came, on the 13th April 1987. He had completed eighty-two years of age just a few days earlier. We in Madras had just had lunch when Sudarshan called from Bangalore to say that Appa had taken suddenly ill, and that he would call back after sometime since the neighbouring doctor had been called in to examine him. The call did come, but only to announce Appa's end. It seems that Appa had lunch and retired to his room where Narayan, Kothand's second son, had put him to bed and covered him with a blanket. Some twenty minutes later Narayan wanted to go to the bathroom in Appa's room. He saw Appa in what appeared to him to be a rather peculiar posture. When he called out to him Appa did not respond. He had obviously passed away peacefully in his sleep at 13:27 P.M. It was a peaceful and painless end to a long life well lived. Kothand had gone to

Bombay on work, and so he was not at home when Appa passed away.

Krishna arranged for all of us to go to Bangalore, and we reached that place a few hours later. Appa's body was laid out, and visitors were already present. Appa had a set of abhyasis who were very close to him in Bangalore. I had expected to feel some emotion, but Master's training no doubt kept my balance intact. The next morning, the 14th of April, I had a wonderful experience. I was sitting in a chair next to my father's body, and suddenly felt transmission coming to me from a point just above my father's chest. I closed my eyes and went into meditation. I could clearly see my father transmitting to me. It was a very tender, love-filled transmission, and lasted about fifteen minutes. Then suddenly the source shifted to a position a few inches to the left, and I saw my Master, Babuji Maharaj, seated there transmitting to me. It was as if Babuji Maharaj had come to show me that Appa was with him, and that there was really nothing called death, and to reassure me that all was well with my father.

Soon after this experience it was time to take my father's body on its last journey to the crematorium. It was an electric crematorium, but the ritualistic requirements had to be gone through as my father had desired that I dispose of his body in that manner. Soon it was all over. We then took the ashes and drove some thirty miles to a river where the ashes were immersed according to tradition, this being the final ritual that my father had enjoined upon me. I removed my sacred thread there and threw it away with the ashes, conforming in this too to his wishes. Thus ended a long life of eighty-two years and a few days, a life fully lived, courageously lived, satisfyingly lived, lived with enormous effort, and backed by very considerable achievement in many fields of endeavour. With his passing an era came to an end.

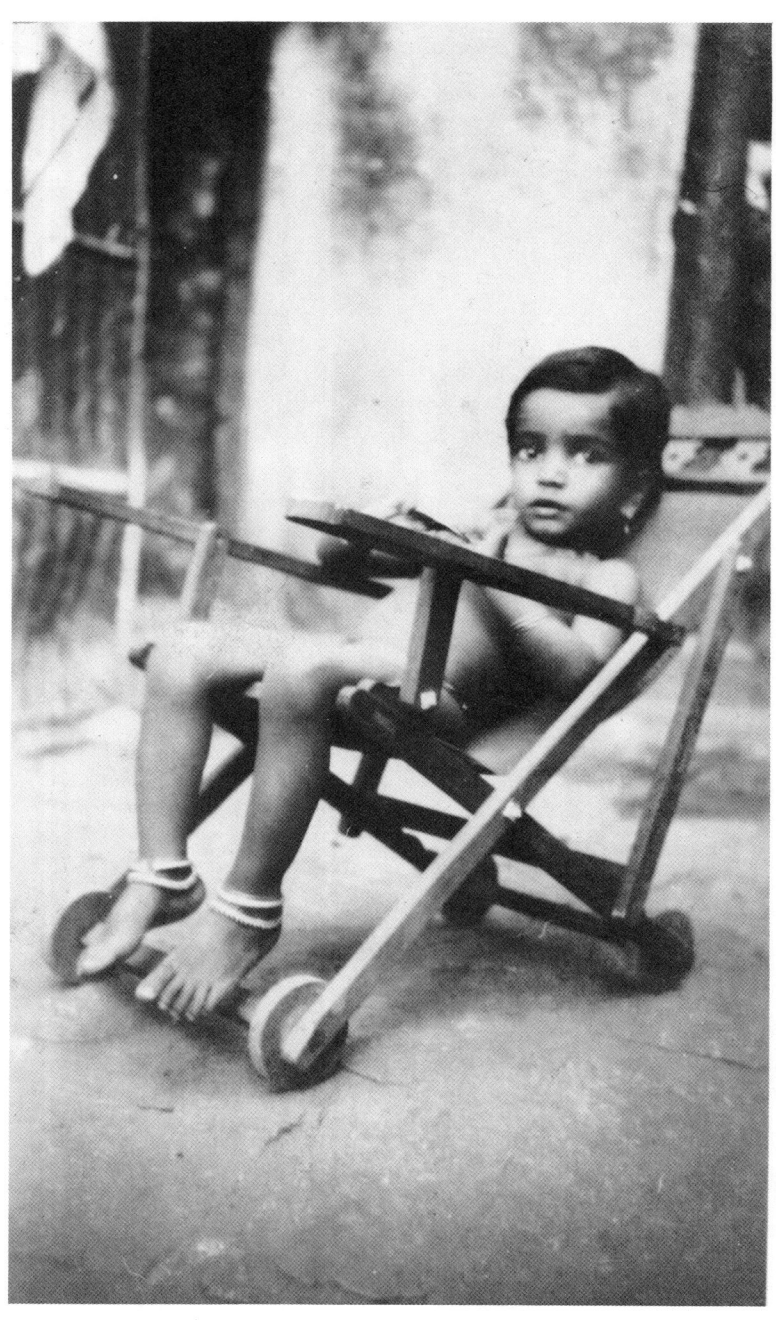

Parthasarathi - 1928

V

The Early Years

The Early Years

The first born of my parents, I was born at 11:35 A.M. on Sunday the 24th of July, 1927 at Vayalur, a sea-side fishing village some thirty miles north of Madras. My grandfather was serving there in the Salt & Customs department of the then Madras government. In India it is the custom for women to go to their parental homes to be delivered of their babies, especially for the first pregnancy. My mother had gone to be with her mother at Vayalur, leaving my father at Madras. Appa was then teaching at the Presidency College. Our home — I do not know whether I can say 'our', as I was yet unborn — was in Triplicane, a small suburb, near the famous temple of Lord Krishna, in his role as Parthasarathi, the driver of Arjuna's chariot.

The custom of a woman going to her mother's home for her delivery is a very sensible custom, in my opinion, and is still generally followed. A woman is very naturally and lovingly looked after by her mother. Emotionally this is a very good thing for the mother-to-be. She feels entirely at home, and, especially in such a time of stress and physical suffering it is a very sane and safe custom indeed. The destruction of the joint family way of life has ruined so many wonderful and time-tested systems in India and, unfortunately, this system too is slowly going the way of all systems of the past. This is very unfortunate for the women of India. Nowadays there is the modern fad for the husband himself to take charge of the delivery of his wife, and even when the delivery is in a hospital or a nursing home, the husband desires to be present! I wonder whether any woman can ever tolerate this for, in the mind of the woman, it is a secret and a sacred matter, this bringing into the world of her baby, and therefore a male presence only makes profane an essentially sacred event. At least in India this is the widely held attitude, and that is why deliveries were always conducted by females qualified in this matter. They were not doctors, nor were they medically qualified, but they went about their business with the help of their vast experience, and on such knowledge as they had based on the ancient lore of wisdom.

My father received the telegram announcing my arrival into this world at around 2:00 P.M., and as was his habit he went to the Marina beach a mere furlong away, for a stroll. There he met his friend and regular walking companion Mr. Vasudeva Rao who was an excellent astrologer. When Mr. Vasudeva Rao was excitedly informed by my father about the birth of his first child, he asked for the time of birth, and quickly drew my horoscope on the beach sand. After studying it for a few minutes he told my father, "Raja! You will never have to worry about this child, for he is destined to be a leader of men!" My father has repeated this story to me, and to many others, again and again throughout his life, repeating it with a great deal of conviction after I reached my current situation in life.

Soon after that my father left for Vayalur to have a look at his first production. This involved a short journey of about thirty miles by train from Madras Central to a station on the Calcutta line called Ponneri, where a horse and *syce* — a groom — waited for him. He rode the horse seven miles to Vayalur, the poor *syce* running behind him all the way, as was usual in the British Raj of those days. Since my grandfather had to inspect several square miles of salt pans every day, the government provided him with a horse, as other modes of transport were non-existent. Nor could any vehicle have navigated the sandy terrain. The jeep had not yet been developed! I never

The Early Years

knew what he thought of me when he first saw me. He never said anything about it, and I was always too shy to ask him about it.

Since I had been born under the star Rohini, the same star under which Lord Krishna himself had been born, my maternal uncles could not look at me direct, but had to see my face reflected in a pan of oil. This was a ruse to escape harm at my hands. Lord Krishna had been responsible for the death of his own maternal uncle, Kamsa, the tyrannical king of Mathura. That created the superstition that any child born under the same birth star was *ipso facto* a danger to its maternal uncles!

Whatever my father may have thought about me, I know my mother was inordinately fond of me from day one. My grandparents too were excessively fond of me, as were my maternal uncles. It is the grace of my Master that this was the case, for after my mother passed away in 1933, the maternal side of my family was responsible for a great deal of assistance in our upbringing. I know that my grandfather, too, had given my father financial assistance as my father's income was but a mere pittance. My father has acknowledged this fact to me on several occasions, but yet he was averse to our associating too closely with that family. He felt that they were too easy-going, and lacked discipline in their every day living. Whatever it was, we owe a great deal to my grandparents, and this debt of love is such that it can never be repaid in this life, except by prayer for their welfare.

Having been born under the birth star Rohini, and our house being within a stone's throw of Lord Krishna's temple, it was inevitable that I be named "Parthasarathi". This was my given name but I was universally called Pachu, an affectionate diminutive. My uncle Bhadran would appear to have been very fond of me, as I was the first child in the family. It was only later, after he entered the Indian Forest Service and went away to the jungles of Assam, that he became somewhat reserved and distant. My younger uncle, Bakthu, was part of our family, and we grew up together. In fact we developed an easy intimacy that came out of that early togetherness.

Bhadran does not appear to have had any great opinion of me, however. I was always too shy and reserved, and he, being something of an extrovert, could not take kindly to my reserve. I remember that once I wrote a letter to him from Jubbulpore, and he wrote to my father saying, "Your boy has a very poor handwriting, and you must do something about it. It is said that great men are poor calligraphers. Even if Pachu does not become actually great, I nevertheless venture to hope that he will amount to at least something in life." Not a very optimistic thought, I felt. But he did answer my letter, and that was something, coming from the great man that he had by then become. It was gratifying, in later life, when I had 'amounted to something,' to be treated with a measure of admiration and respect by him. It is always the case that when an individual of whom not much is expected comes to achieve something, much is made of that person. In this respect I have been lucky!

My brother Kothandaraman, generally addressed as Kothandu, was born on the 8th day of November, 1929. The next brother, Srinivasan, called Seena, was born on the 30th day of October 1931. The last child Vasantha was born in 1933, so that the four children came in regular succession, one every two years. Family planning being unknown in those days, had my mother survived her fourth delivery, more children could have been very reasonably expected to follow Vasantha!

There was a method of birth control available even in those days, indeed from ancient times. And that was the way of abstinence as set down in the religious texts. It of course entailed exercise of one's will power, as conjugal relationship was permitted only on limited occasions. For instance such a relationship was forbidden on the full moon and new moon days, as well as on the succeeding two days. It was also forbidden on the eighth and thirteenth days following the full moon and the new moon days. Other forbidden days included those days when rituals for the departed ones were performed. In short, if the religious prescriptions were followed absolutely, then a couple would have no more than a very restricted number of days per year.

In fairness to the couples of those days it must be said that many did follow them with great sincerity. My paternal great-grandfather was one such individual. My father has told me that my great-grandfather had a physical relationship with my great-grandmother only once a year — and the holy event, for holy it became when such an attitude was brought to bear to such a mundane activity — was planned well in advance when the lunar calendar for the succeeding year was published. Such an activity, when it was dealt with in a holy manner, necessitated the choice of the right and appropriate day for it, and it was chosen with the greatest care, bearing in mind the birth star of both the partners, among other details. On the selected day my great-grandfather would get himself shaved all over the body, have an oil bath, and thus prepare himself for the sacred event — for sex was indeed, and should be, a sacred thing, being an act of creation, and therefore the sole human activity in which a human being could partake of the nature of the creator, albeit temporarily!

By and large the recollections of the early years are understandably dim, but the memories are there all the same. Inevitably, perhaps, such memories tend to be the cherished ones, and have an air rather of fantasy, of illusion, and therefore are more loaded with nostalgia than the later ones, which tend to be more down-to-earth. Therefore childhood memories are so warm and sweet, as if they bear an enchanted quality that the memories of one's later years lack. The early years are very far behind one, especially when they are sought to be brought into focus after a lapse of some sixty years or so, but this too adds to the magical and rather unreal quality of those memories — as if one is looking at a scene through the wrong end of a pair of binoculars. I expect my own memories of the early part of my life, from age one to around twelve, will suffer from such inevitable though sweet distortions. Nevertheless, they form the basis for one's future life, and especially for one's psychic existence. They are therefore extremely important, for through them the later life of the individual is guided, as it were.

My life has been perhaps somewhat different, for the recollections of the earliest part of my life have been hidden behind a mist, perhaps by a conscious act of memory erasure. I conjecture that those years were painful ones, sad ones, and perhaps the most unhappy ones, for otherwise there would emerge at least the faint memories usual to that period of one's life. All this is, of course, conjectural, and should not be taken as some sort of psychological truth. Far from it. But judging from the scars that those early years have left upon my subsequent life, I know that such was the case, and therefore there is some sort of deductive authority for such a surmise.

The trauma of the early loss of my mother played havoc upon our family life. My father had to be both father and mother at the same time, and since he was but a humble clerk in the railways, bread-winning to keep the family going was itself a whole-time occupation. He had to go to work far away by electric train, leaving the home at around 8:00 A.M., and was generally not able to return home to our one-room apartment in Matunga before 7:00 P.M. The wives of neighbours played mother to us, and I must state that they were really and

The Early Years

truly our mothers in those woebegone days of utter loneliness and misery. My father's misery was there for all of us to see, though he strove manfully to hide it under a stern and gruff exterior.

His suffering is hard to imagine, for life itself was a burden in those days, and for the lower middle classes to which we belonged, life was a permanent struggle 'to make both ends meet' as it is said in India. And over and above all this to be saddled with a family of four motherless children was a burden no male could normally be expected to put up with. That our sister Vasantha was with our grandparents in the village in Tanjore district hardly amounted to any reduction of the burden. If I remember right my youngest brother Seena, too, was with Thatha at the village. For the first few years only my younger brother Kothand and I were with my father at Bombay. But since we were a sickly pair, Appa's burden was a tremendous one.

To those surrogate mothers we owe our upbringing, and gratitude for all the love that we received during those years of life in Bombay. Life was very difficult as we had only one room to live in. It had a water tap in one corner, which served for all our needs. It provided us with drinking water, and it was also our bathroom, where we used to bathe one by one, with all the others standing outside to give the minimum of privacy to the one inside. Even women had to bathe like that, filling the water into a bucket and then pouring it over themselves with a small vessel. And to top it all, the cooking too had to be done in that very same room. And of course it was our bedroom too at night! In those days an attached bathroom was unheard of. All the tenants living on a floor of the building used one of three or four W.C.s (water closets) located at the end of a corridor which was generally quite dark even by day. At night there was some feeble illumination provided by a single bulb hanging by a cord, the light being severely diminished by the accumulation of dust and smoke covering it.

There was electricity in those days in Bombay, of course, but since economy has always been a stringently practised virtue in India, lamps were few and far between, and the bulbs were generally of low wattage, so that only the dimmest of illumination was provided — the toilet after all being not a very respectable place! It was not just the fact that we were compelled to live in cheap lodgings. Even the houses of rich persons did not have attached bathrooms, as it was considered dirty and unhygienic to have the toilet within the living area. And of course for the orthodox Hindus it was unthinkable to have the toilet within the house. What would the gods think of such a thing, for heaven's sake! Such were living conditions in Venkatesh Nivas, the building which we inhabited in Matunga for several years.

Those mothers looked after us with love and devotion when our father went off to work. I am sure that we must have tried their patience to the very limit every second of the day, but they never bothered about our childish pranks and tantrums, but treated us even better than they treated their own children. Among such mothers, the outstanding one who has played a large part in our lives, and whom we have loved with a full heart, is Mrs. M. Krishnamoorthy. She and her husband have been very close to our family, and very dear to us. Whenever we had problems with our father in later years, it was to Krishnamoorthy mama that we went for solace and guidance. It is a matter of much sorrow to me that mama died a few years ago at the age of seventy-seven or thereabouts. He was my father's close colleague in the Railways, and a constant source of strength to us. May God grant him peace in the hereafter. In childhood grief lasts but for a short while — thank heavens! And it was no different with us. And what with the innumerable children available all day long for us to play with, life was not as unpleasant as it was for the elders.

The building we lived in was composed of several single-room apartments such as the one we occupied. Some of the more lucky ones occupied two rooms. In that four-storied building there must have been at least twenty families living cheek and jowl. Each family, on an average, consisted of four members, so that our building housed almost a hundred individuals! It was all very noisy and hectic, with screams heard all the time, sometimes screams of agony when someone was suffering acutely, but more generally screams of joy from the playful children who far outnumbered the adults. Indian families have always had an abundance of children. It was good that it was so, for children are a blessing, endowed with the simple innocence and love that can soothe the most cruelly hurt hearts of the elders. I believe that with the modern ideas of restricting the size of the family this joy of having children around us all the time, deriving much joy and comfort from their innocent play and affection, has been lost.

On the contrary adults nowadays seem to worry more and more about their children, controlling their every day lives with the intention of planning for a safe and successful future. Children suffer from an over-abundance of restrictive discipline which is not merely abhorrent to them but also to old-fashioned persons like myself. Such unnecessarily strict discipline tends to mould the children into products of a straight-jacketed intellect combined with a very narrow attitude to life. This has produced many of today's cramped and constrained individuals who have nothing more than their enormously bloated egos and extravagant ambitions to show for all the so-called discipline that they have received.

Down Memory Lane

Modern education, tailor-made to suit such materialistic ambitions, has produced considerable misery in those so educated. It is a pity that such individuals, many of whom are very successful, spend a lot of their energy and time in trying to hide their inner insecurity and fears under a false cheerfulness and bonhomie. Success and achievement have become the gods of modern life, and such spiritual values as were inculcated into the growing and developing minds of those former years has been replaced by a cheap substitute called 'prayer class' in school, restricted to the mere chanting of some prayers before the formal beginning of class. With the proliferation of more and more schools devoted solely to the purpose of 'educating' children for materialistic success, this disease has grown enormously.

There is no denying the fact that many of today's adults are more successful than the adults of the times that I recall here, but it is a moot question whether they are even an iota happier or more contented than the members of that generation to which I belong. Also, they have sacrificed the true inner culture of those times at the altar of success, and therefore today one finds boors at the highest levels of public and private life — boors who may be highly educated in their money-earning disciplines, but boors nevertheless. I remember the statement that I used to hear in England that while a gentleman may not be a king, the king **must** be a gentleman. The charm of manner and the unfailing courtesy of the past have gone, perhaps forever. And this is not merely a cause for unhappiness, but has become a matter of concern to all, for the steady erosion of values that has eaten into the very fabric of a society where inner values and achievements were the hallmark of culture and breeding has made life in India today quite a traumatic one. One has to live not only with one's neighbours but with a host of persons that one has perforce to deal with during the daily drudge. The almost total lack of civility in public life today in India is truly appalling.

Slowly but surely the cultural values of India have fallen, until today they are at possibly the lowest ebb, all because of the tendency to ape western ambitions and achievements, not being content with the strength of the inner life of tremendous serenity that has been our birthright and our ancient heritage. Whatever may be said about the occidental world, they are to be praised for their unfailing courtesy and their civility in dealing with other members of the race. They are keen on rendering the maximum possible service, whereas in India people think that service is demeaning! What a fall in values, and concepts!

It is tragic, and perhaps somewhat comic too, to find that human beings are graded for pedigree by false and artificial values, very much like cattle and our canine friends, except that money and status have become the indicators for such grading! Even the holy institution of matrimony has been invaded by these corruptions, and it is not uncommon today to find marriages being made with nothing more than the idea of a joint career of immense profit. Love? What is that? Do we have to look far for the reasons behind today's love-less societies throughout the world? Mammon has replaced not merely Cupid, but all the other gods of the past!

I do not remember going to school during the period of our stay in Bombay. I realise that we must have been there from the time of my beloved mother's death in 1933 till some time in 1936, but I am unable to recall the period exactly. Things were so very vague in those days. The calendar was rarely, if ever, consulted. In fact dates were so little taken into account that many persons of those days did not even know their dates of birth — and I am not now referring to the illiterate people of the villages! When questioned for such details, they would reply, with a serious look of introspection upon their faces, that such and such a person was born when such and such an event happened, as for instance the birth of a calf, or the death of an aged relative, or some such event.

Time seemed not to have much significance in those leisurely days. It was a great event for one to get one's first wrist watch. I remember that I did not get one till I was twenty-one years old! In the villages such new-fangled objects were viewed with considerable disdain — for was there not the cock to crow at dawn, and could not one see the sun rise? And did not the cow Kamala moo for her first feed precisely half-an-hour before dawn? Persons who needed to see a watch to know the time by, were thought of as cranky, city-bred individuals who had lost touch with nature, and with the ways of reading nature's signs. The lunar calendar was followed for all significant events such as births and deaths, as well as for all religious festivals, and this has continued right into the present.

I remember that my old grandmother in our village used to make marks on the walls with a leaf, or with a piece of chalk, to mark significant family events, along with marks for maintaining the daily milk supply received. This was a sort of primitive calendar which the women of the house used. It is not surprising that such marks got covered over by the dense smoke of the wood fire of those days, for the women used the kitchen wall for their calendar. Therefore there was hardly ever any accuracy regarding dates, and much less about times. I think that the registration of births and deaths too must have been virtually non-existent, at least in the remote villages, though such events were supposed to be reported to the nearest authority — often many miles away. And who had the time for

The Early Years

such funny things when agricultural chores were so pressing all the year round?

I mention this only to show that it was not very surprising for even town dwellers to not remember dates and events — for after all the most important events in their lives took place in the villages of their origins. For me it was much more difficult to remember whether I had any schooling during the Bombay years because of my young age. I can only assume that we were not sent to school then. It was quite usual for children to be at home till the age of seven. The Kindergarten schools were unknown, and in any case it was thought to be extremely cruel to send a mere child to school. "What for?", was the question usually asked — and I cannot remember anyone ever being able to produce a sensible answer. Girl children were rarely sent to school. It was thought that education would 'spoil' them and render them unfit, in some mysterious and inexpressible way, for marriage — and were not girls meant only to be married 'off', as we still say in India? As far as I can remember, it was only in the towns that girls were sent to school. Village girls rarely had this privilege. Nowadays of course the pattern has changed, and education is available to all without distinction of sex.

Those were the halcyon days when male children wandered around naked till well into their sixth or seventh year of age. Girls were treated somewhat differently, of course, but even they wandered around till age three with a fig leaf — generally of gold if the family could afford it — suspended from a thick thread going around the waist to cover their nakedness. Thereafter they graduated into the short skirt, worn knee-length, passed down from the elder sisters in the family. Hand-me-downs were the order of the day, and it was only the lucky eldest that got new clothes. The festival of lights, *Divali*, was an exception when all were presented with new clothes.

Down Memory Lane

Those were happy and carefree days, especially for the children who were pampered and loved beyond belief. They were considered to be the treasures of the family and treated as such, though there was also stern discipline, and often punishment, when certain boundaries were exceeded.

The only significant event of that time was again a tragic one. It was the death of our only sister, Vasantha, at age three. It was attended by circumstances considered very mysterious, and that is what makes it a part of my memory, even though I was not present at our village to witness events myself. My youngest brother, Seena, had fallen very ill and was dying. It was thought that he had no chance of recovery, for the owl, one single owl, had been sitting on top of our roof in the village home and screeching, *"shaa, shaa"*, which in Tamil means, "die, die". My grandmother used to relate endlessly how they all went out to shoo the bird of evil omen away, and how it returned again and again to screech out untiringly its message of death. So my brother was virtually written off, and the whole family was waiting for the tragic and unhappy event when, all of a sudden, Vasantha became ill, for no reason whatsoever, and died a few days later. Simultaneously Seena started recovering miraculously and regained complete health within a week or so.

So died our little sister Vasantha whom I cannot remember having ever seen. There are two photographs of hers available in the family album, showing her at about the age of three. It was a tragedy which I don't think anyone ever mourned, except for my poor grandmother, for was she not virtually an orphan living away from her father after having been responsible for the death of her mother? Poor dear child, to be blamed for something for which she was in no way responsible! Children received so much love and affection in those days, but there was also so much unconscious, and no doubt unmeant, cruelty arising out of superstitious beliefs and practices. Indian society has always exhibited this ambivalence which few non-Indians have ever been able to understand.

The joint family system generated a great deal of care, love and well-being. Children, especially, flourished and grew into wholesome adulthood under the love and care lavished upon them by all the members of the family. Discipline was also there, for there were always minor transgressions of one sort or another, and someone was always waiting to correct the transgressor — but the discipline was immediately tempered with a great deal of love which made the discipline acceptable. Under such circumstances discipline really worked. Nowadays there is either the one or the other, and always in excess, so that children are truly bewildered by the extremes to which parents swing off and on. Under the old system all lived together in harmony, the well-to-do contributing to the general welfare of all. There was very little selfishness. The old received as much care and attention as the very young, and the children were shared by all as a sort of common wealth, and a source of joy and happiness.

A little did go a long way, for things were shared by all. I remember that when we were young there was only one packet of tooth powder in the wash place, and all used it to brush their teeth with. A whole family generally shared one cake of soap. Similarly one towel was shared by the whole family, the head of the family enjoying the prerogative of using it when it was dry! There was the idea of 'ours' which has been supplanted by the selfishly possessive idea of 'mine'. And of course a house in which so many persons lived together meant, automatically, protection for all, care from one source or the other, any number of persons to help with the numerous chores that had to be performed day after day, and a common platform for all to share their ideas, thoughts, sorrows and joys.

More than anything else, such a life made for vastly better mental health of the individuals. The people may have been less educated, and perhaps many did not have even the minimum of schooling, but a society has to be judged by the mental health of the people, and by such a standard the people of those times were definitely superior to the present generation. They were well adjusted internally and externally to face the demands of life. One must remember that the demands were more pressing and immediate than those of today. There is no exaggeration in this. One must have lived in the India of the thirties and forties to know the reality of the nature of the demands under which people lived, and lived quite happily and successfully too.

In general our life at Bombay was agreeable, and time passed swiftly. I am unable to say when we arrived in Bombay — I mean my brother Kothandu and myself, for of course my father had been serving there for several years. Nor can I recollect when we left it. We were both often sick, and my poor father had a hard time looking after us. I suffered from the dreaded typhoid, and had to be hospitalized for a period of three months according to my memory. It was a trying time for all of us. On another occasion I had to have my tonsils removed. The surgery frightened me, but the post-operative care was a pleasant thing because I was fed nothing but ice cream for the next twenty-four hours — a treat in those days when Brahmin children were forbidden all edibles other than those made at home!

But the worst was to come. It came as an attack of tuberculosis — a much dreaded disease, for it was a killer in those days when antibiotics were yet far in the future. It started as a fever, and I was treated by our family doctor, Dr. N.P. Narayana Iyer. He was a very mild mannered person, and quite efficient, having his own compounder and a dispensary where the prescriptions were compounded. That was the system then prevailing, and medicines, generally powders, and liquids in large bottles the sides marked off for doses, were compounded on the spot and delivered to the patient. Pharmacies were relatively unknown.

The fever persisted, coming on as a mild fever, gradually rising towards the evening. It resisted the efforts of Dr. Narayana Iyer, and eventually a specialist had to be consulted. My father brought him in one morning to examine me as I was too weak to walk. He tapped me on the chest, examined me with his stethoscope, turned me over and thumped me on the back at several spots, looked very grave, and said, "He is suffering from tuberculosis. It is advanced, and if he is to live you must take him away immediately from Bombay." My father asked him where to take me, and he replied that I must be taken preferably to a village where the air would be clean and wholesome, as medical treatment was not available, and one had to depend on nature and proper care of the patient for a cure. Doctor Billimoria was the leading T.B. specialist, and his diagnosis was immediately accepted. He left after pocketing an enormous fee of Rs. 75, which was almost a whole month's salary for my father.

My father put me in the custody of one of my loving mothers, left immediately for his office, applied for leave and collected a set of free passes for travel by rail to the south of India, and came back in time to take me to the Victoria Terminus where we boarded a train for Madras — a Herculean effort indeed. I have no memory of the journey through Madras to Mayavaram, and then on to our village, Agaravallam. All that I know is that we had arrived, and when my grandmother heard the reason for our sudden arrival all the way from distant Bombay, she wept her heart out. I was installed on a cot under a neem tree as advised by Dr. Billimoria, and there I stayed for the next year and a half, except when it rained.

There was no treatment as such, and all that had been prescribed was fresh air, a lot of sunshine, and diet of bread and milk supplemented by a calcium preparation marketed by the well-known firm Sandoz. The difficult part was the bread, for it was not a readily available thing, and Brahmins never touched the stuff. Someone had to go daily to Mayavaram by bicycle to bring a loaf for me. I remember that Bakthu joined us there soon after, and was with me till I recovered completely. I was not allowed to get up at all for more than a year. I believe that this illness moulded me in many ways, and gave me the ability to bear pain, frustration and many other things as well. I did not lack for company, of course, but nevertheless it was a trying time. My grandparents were most concerned. My mother's sister, Suli, was also with me for a considerable part of the eighteen months that I was there.

I expect that nature favoured my recovery, for after some months I was allowed to eat rice mixed with buttermilk. The children of the house, augmented by many children from our neighbours' homes, were playing around me all day long, and this made it a little easier for me. The fever persisted for many months, and the thermometer was constantly with me. I remember that one evening there was a thunderstorm, and my temperature had to be taken. Suli was playing some music on an old gramophone of those days. I had the thermometer in my mouth, and was beating time to the music on a loaf of bread that I was hugging to my chest, for I was to eat a few slices as soon as the temperature had been recorded. Just then there was a tremendous clap of thunder, and I gave an extra strong beat on the loaf of bread, and in the process I bit the thermometer right through! It was filled with mercury, of course, and therefore there was commotion in the house, for mercury was a poison as everyone knew. They feared that I might have swallowed some of it. Someone was sent post haste on a bicycle to fetch the nearest doctor living six miles away at Mayavaram. The doctor promised to come early the next morning but only turned up some thirty-six hours after the event. In the meantime I was administered a strong dose of castor oil as a purgative, to flush out the mercury in case it had been swallowed. It eventually proved to be a case of 'much ado about nothing!'

I survived the eighteen months or so quite cheerfully, and with Bakthu and my youngest uncle Ayya to look after me, it became almost pleasant. When I was finally certified to be free of the disease, I had to learn to walk all over again — and in this my uncles Ayya and Bakthu helped me, holding me up and supporting me on either side as I tottered around on legs unable to bear even my puny weight of forty-five pounds. Eventually, after about a fortnight of tremendous exertion, I began to walk all by myself. Looking back upon that period, I now feel that there was an element of mind over matter which assisted me in regaining my health. I was very feeble, but I was alive! And that was what mattered to my family. Much was made of me, and I was pampered to such an extent that I nearly fell sick all over again, until my father came to rescue me from this excess of love and affection, as he labelled it rather uncharitably. Soon thereafter, we began preparing for our return, or rather to leave Agaravallam, for I do not remember whether we went back to Bombay. My next memory is of my life in Jubbulpore.

At the time we came to Jubbulpore, in the Central Provinces, as the state was then called, my father was in service with the Great Indian Peninsula Railways — G.I.P. for short — as an accountant. Though poorly paid, he had a palatial mansion for his official quarters, situated in some seven acres of land, consisting of a five acre front garden, and a back kitchen garden of around two acres. We had a gardener to look after the immense gardens, and he was a wholly contented person on a monthly salary of eight rupees, and a small out-house to live in. And on this princely sum he and his wife managed to exist quite comfortably.

The house itself was vast, containing three bedrooms, measuring no less than five hundred square feet each, all laid out in one row. There was a rear service section with the kitchen, store rooms, and bathrooms, while the frontage was a long verandah, six feet wide, running the entire length of the house. One had to walk about a hundred and fifty feet from the gate to the house. The house faced west, and on the left a high compound wall separated us from the railway workshop. The gate was on the northern side, and just outside the gate there was a railway hospital, in front of which was a large play ground. The ground was very rough and full of weeds and thorny bushes.

Appa was at that time paid only one hundred and twenty rupees per month as the accountant. Living was cheap in those days — the late thirties. I remember that Appa used to buy a bag of rice weighing eighty kilograms for eight rupees, and milk was available at some sixteen seers (thirty pints) per rupee! We three boys were provided with pyjama suits for the night made of imported Vyella flannel on my father's salary. It was therefore not surprising that our *mali* was able to manage on his salary of eight rupees.

Our vegetables were bought once a week at a big bazaar called the Gurandi which was open only on Sundays. We used to accompany our father to the bazaar, which was really vast. We would walk around it for an hour or more, selecting the freshest vegetables which were put into a large basket carried by a labourer. When our purchases were completed we would head back home on our bicycles, while the basket man walked with his load two miles or so to our home. I remember that our weekly vegetable bill rarely exceeded two rupees, and the labourer who carried the basket home was content to receive four annas — one fourth of a rupee — for his trouble. It is difficult to believe that we could buy potatoes for the price of twenty-four seers for one rupee, and tomatoes even cheaper than that. It was a veritable garden of Eden!

We brothers had imported bicycles, for there was then no manufacture in India. In fact most things were imported from England, and as India was then part of the British empire, I believe that such inflationary things as customs duties did not exist. My very first bicycle, a twenty inch Phillips bicycle, cost a mere eighteen rupees! Kothand's eighteen inch machine cost a couple of rupees less. But for my father even this was a large expense, but he loved to spend lavishly upon us. To put it in a nutshell we lived like princes, and nothing was ever denied to us.

Seena did not have a machine of his own for some years as he was too small to ride one. We had small wooden seats specially made to fit on to the cross bar of the bicycle, and I generally had to take Seena to school on my bike. I did not like this extra burden, and I remember that often when Seena afforded me the smallest excuse to do so, I would pinch him mercilessly. This meaningless cruelty ended when Seena eventually got his own vehicle. How much there is for one to regret in later life! If only our early years and our youth were illumined with the knowledge of things to come, would we behave so heartlessly towards those whom we love? Poor dear Seena! I have given you so much pain, and heaped so many indignities upon you that I wish you were here so that I could personally apologize to you. But alas! The cruel hand of death has snatched you away from our midst, denying me this

Down Memory Lane

opportunity. I pray that in some spiritual manner you may nevertheless feel my sorrow and forgive me. How much wisdom there is in the Christian precept which exhorts us to settle accounts each evening before going to bed! If we would but follow this excellent advice, we would not live to regret in our later years the thoughtless actions of the earlier years.

My father was keenly interested in gardening, and we spent an hour or more every morning in the garden with him. Whenever possible we repeated this in the evening too. We had a lovely garden full of enormous trees, mostly fruit bearing ones. I remember that adjacent to the wall of the railway workshop was the largest tree of all, a mango tree. There were many guava trees, yielding a variety of fruit with a brilliant green exterior, while inside it was a dark pink, most luscious to eat. But we had to compete with the enormous flocks of parrots which always managed to get to them first. The ground beneath the trees used to be littered with half eaten fruit. These half eaten fruit were the sweetest of the lot, for the parrots went unerringly for the sweetest.

There was a centrally located masonry tank which held about two thousand gallons of water. It was only four feet deep, and so even though it was meant for irrigating the garden, we used it as a swimming pool. Our fun was often spoilt by the presence, in the darker corners of the tank, of some of the most enormous toads that I have ever seen in my life. They were harmless, of course, but to our boyish imagination they looked like small dragons, and so we used to try to evict them before we got into the water ourselves. But they almost always got the better of us.

Our *mali* had a full day's work, as all the plants had to be watered daily. There were brick-lined irrigation channels criss-crossing the garden, but to many of the distant corners the water

The Early Years

had to be taken in watering cans fitted with spouts that delivered the water to the plants in the form of a gentle drizzle — very much like a shower bath. Seedlings had to be specially looked after too. But our *mali* was a steady, if morose, worker, and did his job faithfully. The front garden was full of fruit-bearing trees and flowering plants. We had an enormous number of rose and jasmine plants, including some very exotic varieties. For instance we had green roses in which the flower resembled curled-up leaves, and it was not easy to distinguish the leaf from the flower especially if the person did not expect to see a green rose. I think we had more than twenty different varieties of roses growing there. We also had one particular rose bush which flowered so profusely that often it was not possible to count the number of flowers on it.

As for jasmine, there were some bushes which yielded several pounds of blossoms daily during the flowering season. We used to sleep out in the garden during the summer months, as Jubbulpore was one of the hottest places where the day temperature could rise to 118°F, and that was really hot! Our beds would be strewn with fresh jasmine blossoms by our *mali*, and the nights were fragrant and cool. One of our childish bits of fun used to be to catch many of the fireflies, of which there were literally thousands all over the trees, giving a christmas tree effect, and to put them into the mosquito nets under which we slept. We would go to sleep watching the glowing on and off of the fire flies. It all had a fairy tale effect in those days.

My father liked variety in the garden, and so we had all sorts of flowering plants and shrubs, planted very systematically in separate flower beds of all shapes and sizes laid out very artistically. We had dahlias and my father grew some of the largest flowers that I have ever seen. I remember we measured one of the largest that grew in our garden, and it was a full eleven inches across! It had the pride of place in the garden for many weeks, and we had visitors coming in to see and admire it all the time. It is a pity that they only last for such a short while! All beauty seems to be so evanescent! One summer we had a giant of a sunflower which measured an unbelievable twelve-and-a-half inches across. We had larkspurs, geraniums in pots, nasturtiums, hollyhocks, and some of the most colourful zinnias that I have seen. In winter our garden was a riot of colour — and only in the tropics can one see such a riotous profusion of nature's beauty and variety.

We used to get seeds from Poona, from a then famous supplier of garden equipment, cuttings and seeds named Pestonjee P. Pocha & Sons. We would order them and receive them by post in tiny packets. My father would personally prepare the seed beds, sifting the soil with great care, adding the appropriate manure, and then putting in the seeds himself, all the time admonishing the mali and exhorting him to water them with care. We were always part of the scene, and in this manner we picked up a considerable acquaintance with plant life, as well as a smattering of botany. We had a large variety of ferns, and even today when I see them I feel nostalgically drawn back to those days in Jubbulpore — our happiest years by any standard.

It was in Jubbulpore too that we got our first acquaintance with the canine world. Our first pair of pups were of mixed origin, and were named Jack and Jill. Since even my father had never kept pets before, training them and house-breaking them was a tedious affair. My father had a rather volatile temper, and I am afraid that Jack and Jill suffered considerably under his stern training programme. I have seen him throw a pup twenty feet when it misbehaved! But they seemed not to suffer much, except that, being mongrels, they ran off howling with their tails between their legs. I was never comfortable when my father treated the dogs in this rather heartless manner, but

The Early Years

he insisted that training entailed discipline, and that a small dose of punishment would avoid the later need for larger doses. We of course tended to spoil them, and came to love dogs. We have always had dogs in the house since then, and I feel uncomfortable without them.

When one of the dogs died, we would decide not to keep pets again. It was always a big tragedy when a dog died — and since we have been having them all our lives from 1936 onwards we have lost a great many of them. Such an event would leave us all weeping, with my father too shedding sympathetic tears. The saddest part was the burial, for we believed in giving them a decent burial in our own garden. We hated to see the loved one put under the ground, but it was a demand of love, and we went through it bravely though very sadly. We had dogs of mixed breed in those days, but later on we managed to get purebred ones, though not necessarily with pedigrees, as that would have cost a great deal of money. We have had many breeds, describable and nondescript, but now my favourite breed is the Labrador, black or golden, for these dogs have a gentle manner, and a way with children which is most desirable in pets, especially in homes with growing children.

During those years we also had many parrots, for the green parrot is native to India. They had cages hanging out in the verandah, and some of them whistled away so delightfully that I suspected they did not know they were in captivity. They could be taught to speak too, but it took a great deal of time and patience, for the parrot has a way of listening with its head bent sideways, one side after the other, all the time moving from side to side on its perch, which could be quite aggravating. Generally a parrot would try to repeat what it had heard only to itself, as it were, then climb the bars of the cage rapidly up and down several times, look to see if someone was watching or not, and then try to repeat it again just as we were about to leave. But speak they could, though only a few words. In that part of the country parrots were generally taught to say the names of Lord Rama and his divine consort, Sita.

We had one particular parrot which came to us very young, and which my father personally trained. It was a baby parrot too young to feed itself, and so he would make pellets out of flour and keep them on his extended tongue, and for some strange reason the baby parrot would perch on his forefinger and feed itself off his tongue, pellet by pellet. It grew up very well, but of course we had to keep it away from the cats. So it had to be caged at night. It learnt to answer my whistle. Its cage door was always kept open during the day. When I returned from school, I would whistle to it from the gate of our house, and it would fly out to meet me and perch on my shoulder, and ride with me into the house. Bakthu used to train it too, and would let it fly and whistle it back to himself. One fine day it went up high into a mango tree, and failed to respond to his efforts to call it back. We speculated that it was afraid to come down from that height. Whatever may have been the reason, it kept flying from branch to branch, higher and higher, and by the evening it had flown right away. It never came back, and that worried us considerably for some days, as we had become quite attached to it.

Many years later a friend of mine in Bombay had an enormous parrot — not really a parrot, but more like a cockatoo — from some African country. That particular bird had trained itself to cough, blow its nose, and make gargling noises exactly as my friend did when brushing his teeth! It was a source of much amusement to his visitors, but embarrassed him considerably. I remember that when his wife was annoyed with him, she would go to the cockatoo and make it perform its act just to annoy him.

The Early Years

We had guinea pigs once, and they were fun, but they multiplied so fast that eventually we had to give them away, especially since they were ruining the shrubbery in the garden. And if they got into the vegetable patches in the rear garden, well, that was that. We got a large hare once, a strong fellow who kept galloping round and round the garden. Our dogs were quite friendly with it, but chase it they would — for dogs will be dogs! One day the poor hare injured itself while jumping over a rose bush. It must have been hurt by the thorns because it started to bleed. That particular day our water tank was dry, and so to keep it away from the dogs my father put the hare into it. The crows began to attack it, and we kept shooing them away. After the mid-day meal when we went to have a look at it, we found the poor thing covered, literally covered, with red ants. And that was the end of that pet.

The one pet that I would have loved to have was a horse. I have never ridden one, except once or twice during a holiday in Kashmir, but for some reason I have always loved horses, without ever having had an opportunity of getting really close to one. I have indulged in the rather childish fantasy of riding to work upon an Arab, throwing the reins to a waiting boy, and walking into my office in riding garb. But it was out of the question as horses have always been expensive animals to own, and their upkeep affordable only by the enormously rich persons. So that has remained a dream, based perhaps upon too much reading of the cowboy tales of the wild West during my boyhood!

We had quite a variety of pets, and I believe that we became lovers of animals and birds because of the experience of those days, which an understanding father, capable of looking ahead to the wider aspects of his children's education, thoughtfully provided. It also made for us a life of companionship, for my father was frequently away on his official work of inspecting the accounts of other stations, and then the animals and birds provided us with a certain form of companionship that proved invaluable, at least to me. Even much later in life, there have been lonely nights when I was profoundly grateful to hear the croaking of the toads and frogs around our garden in Madras — for they seemed to tell me, in their own fashion, "All is well. Sleep peacefully!" Thus was the gap that my mother left, the painful void in our lives, filled by animals and birds, and for doing it I am grateful not only to them but to my brilliant and loving father who had the genius for doing such a thing in the most natural way.

Bakthu was with us for some time, and then Appa sent him to Bombay to study radio technology. My middle maternal uncle, Viji, then came to stay with us for a brief period, as he put it, but it extended itself into many long months. Our household consisted of a cook, a gardener and his wife, and a maid servant. The cook who was with us then was an expert, and his name was Khosla if I remember it correctly. He was a real jack-of-all-trades, and had a proud arrogance to match it. His cooking was varied and delectable. Now when Viji came to Jubbulpore, he seems to have expressed some interest in the local beverages, and Khosla seems to have introduced him to bhang, mixed in a glass of milk, in what he considered to be a mild dose fit for a debutante. Viji partook of it with dire results. All this happened when we brothers were away in Agaravallam with our grandparents for our summer holidays.

Bhang is an intoxicant much used by the local people. Brahmins generally have no experience of intoxicants, though Viji was obviously not new to the field. However, the mix that Khosla produced for him seems to have been a rather strong one, and poor Viji went into some sort of delirium. The consequences were rather grave, for he could not sleep alone after a rather nightmarish experience he had. All the rooms of course had doors, but the doors of that house had glass panels fitted into the upper half — not transparent ones but translucent panes of ground glass. Now one night when he was in bed, Khosla had brought a pot of drinking water for him, and as he came to the other side of the closed door, Khosla's shadow appeared on the pane, and to Viji, who had just seen the movie Frankenstein, it appeared as if the monster stood there holding the decapitated head of a human being — and he let out a horrible scream and rushed to my father for help, blabbering about a monster which of course my father did not understand. After that Viji never slept alone, and had to have his cot next to my father's, so close as to be able to touch him.

My father had to nurse him back to mental health, and this took almost a year. Thank heavens that in those days there were no psychiatrists — mercifully for Viji the profession had not yet come into existence in India. Viji regained health, but in the process kept giving us all nightmares! Khosla had of course to be fired, and we lost an excellent cook who was also a general *factotum*. The problem was to find a suitable replacement. This was, for us, a recurrent problem, for after my mother passed away we had to depend on cooks for our food for most of our life. I do not remember ever having eaten anything cooked for me by my mother, for she passed away so early in my life. Cooks have been an inevitable part of our household till we brothers married, when the semblance of a normal family life was once again restored, in my case after the lapse of twenty-three years.

This memory of Viji's experience in Jubbulpore reminds me of an earlier one concerning two of my maternal uncles, Kasturi the eldest, and Viji again. This happened when Thatha and Pattiamma were living in Madras, in a house called *Dwaraka* in Mambalam. It was a very large house, with a sizable compound of its own. We were there too at the time, perhaps during one of our brief sojourns away from Bombay. This was before we went to Jubbulpore. One morning Kasturi bundled me into a car, along with Viji and some others, and we drove to a sea-side village named Kovalam, some twenty miles south of Madras. It was a brilliantly sunny day, and we reached Kovalam after about an hour's drive, at around ten o'clock in the morning. We stayed at the Salt Inspection Bungalow, my grandfather being then the Assistant Commissioner of Salt & Customs, the last post, and the highest one he held. And as I have stated earlier, he was the only Indian to have held that post till then.

The inspection bungalow faced a lovely little bay of the sea. There were small wavelets all over its surface. The whole surface of the bay sparkled, with each individual wavelet dancing brilliantly with the reflection of the sun, so that it looked as if it was an inverted sky shining with the glitter of a million brilliant stars. I was sitting watching the sea, and the occasional fish that jumped out and back into the sea. Meanwhile my uncles and their friends kept drinking something out of bottles, filling up their glasses again and again. They eventually stopped drinking whatever it was that they had been drinking and we had lunch right there. Then we all rested for some time, and finally left for home just before sunset.

It had not been a very enjoyable excursion for me, as I was the only boy there, and had to enjoy myself as best as I could. But it was a sign of my uncle's affection for me that I had been taken along, and I appreciated that very much. When we came home my grandmother wanted to know what had happened at Kovalam, and I gave her a graphic account of everything that had occurred including of course a mention of my surprise at the enormous thirst that my uncles and their friends had seemed to slake but with difficulty, they having to drink so much out of so many bottles!

The story must have got round to my Thatha that night, for the next morning my uncles were chastised in our presence for exposing an innocent young boy to their evil ways! My uncles very naturally resented my carrying tales, though I had not known that I had been in fact carrying any tales. But after my Thatha went to his office, I was cursed roundly, and they attempted to thrash me, but my Pattiamma saved me. My father had never beaten me even once, as far as I can remember, and no one else had ever dared to do so. I threatened to complain to my father about their attack on me, and my uncles stopped chasing me around the garden. I was very resentful of this gross injustice for some time, but wounds, even to the ego, heal very soon at that age, and soon all was forgotten.

Another episode comes to mind, as it also occurred at this time in Dwaraka. One day, at about five o'clock in the evening my uncle Ayya shouted out to me to go up to the first floor, saying that it was something urgent. We were not very far apart in age, and were therefore playmates too, and so I rushed upstairs. There was a large cot against the wall upon which were put all the rolled up beds, as it was the custom in those days. I did not see Ayya anywhere. So I called out to him. Suddenly one of the bed rolls fell off the cot, and from between the stacked rolls and the wall emerged a frightening figure, a skeleton all wrapped up in white. It was horrible, and I thought that I was seeing a ghost about which so many awful tales had been told at night before we went to bed. I let out a scream, and my grandmother rushed upstairs to see what was wrong.

The awful figure of the ghost then suddenly laughed, and I heard Ayya's voice telling me not to be a fool. It was he who had wrapped himself with bed sheets to resemble Frankenstein, as he told me, just to frighten me. He never thought that I would be so frightened, and called me a "cry baby" which I resented with all my being. I called him names, and would have been surely thrashed by him had not Pattiamma intervened. It was from that time that I began to be afraid of the dark, and of sleeping alone at nights. A trace of that fear is still with me to this day. It is a pity that grown-ups do not realise the potential danger in threatening children with punishment, and frightening them with ghosts and other such nonsense. The consequences of such behaviour on the sensitive minds of young and growing children can be tragic.

My father once confided to me how he had conquered his own fear. For me this was a great revelation, for to us he had always been the very personification of courage and fearlessness. All his life he had been living with his mother in single room tenements, and when he came to Jubbulpore, the big bungalow and the comparatively enormous grounds were too much for him. Of course we never knew that he felt afraid to be in such a large house. But he overcame his fears in a very daring way. He said that every night at midnight he would go out into the garden all alone, and wander around in the total darkness for an hour or more. I am sure that he had all the fears that a normal human being has — fear of being alone in the dark; fear of ghosts; fear of so many other things that a village life, with all its superstitions breeds — and yet by this technique which he evolved for himself, he managed to overcome all his fears at one stroke. That was the marvel of the whole thing. For, in later life, I have never known him to be afraid of anything whatsoever. In fact, if there was a snake around, he was the first out of the house with a stout stick to finish it off. If someone said that there was a thief around, again he was out hunting for him, leaving the others behind to marvel at his bravery, or to call him a fool!

I remember several occasions in later life when he went out single-handed to root out and destroy whatever it was that was threatening the life of others. He developed an extraordinary disregard of the dangers to life, and never let fear of life come between him and what had to be done. It is an amusing thing that when I crossed fifty myself, he would not permit me to change a bulb, or climb a ladder to get something done, saying, "Pachu, you are getting old. Let me attend to it. You go and relax." And climb the ladder, or change the bulb he would, though he was nearly a quarter of a century older than I am. It used to amuse me that on such occasions my wife Sulochana used to be somewhat annoyed at her husband being labelled an old man by his own father!

Sometimes his bravery caused us quite some concern. In later life, especially after he crossed seventy years of age, it became necessary for him to walk for exercise — and that was difficult for one who had never believed in such things. Whenever he could, he would walk within the house from end to end, for half an hour or so. But there were times when he was too busy during the day to take his constitutional, and then he got into the habit of opening his bathroom door at the rear of the house and taking a walk all by himself at night — sometimes even at midnight! In Madras this could have been extremely dangerous, for anyone could have observed his habit and sneaked in while he was out. The even greater danger was that he could have been assaulted before someone entered the house. My wife was especially worried by this nocturnal activity of his, and only my intervention could make him stop this sort of dangerous activity. He would tell me, "While I am alive no one can harm you. Don't be afraid. I am here to protect you all from all danger." This was a pointer to the fact that bravery too must perhaps be within limits, or controlled so that it does not get transformed into rashness.

It was also in Jubbulpore that we were first introduced to the fascinating world of books. My father ordered a set of *Books of Knowledge* from Calcutta, and they arrived after ten days or so. There was a great deal of excitement in opening the wooden packing case, and that was an education in itself! When we got the case opened, we were wonder-struck to find ten volumes of the most beautiful books, all superbly bound in leather and calico, with the title in gold lettering. It was fascinating. And the smell of the books, a mixture of paper, leather and printer's ink — that was yet another fascination. We could not have enough of the books, and my father had a difficult time to persuade us to put them down till the next morning, when he gave us another lesson in covering the books beautifully in brown kraft paper. He taught us that art, and it is with us even today. Those books were extremely expensive, the set of ten books costing two hundred and twenty rupees — around two month's salary for my father. The purchase was made possible because the company gave us installment payment terms, so that the payment was spread over thirty months.

They were reference volumes, and we benefited a great deal by having them to refer to frequently, for my father insisted that we use them with due care, so that the purchase was justified. That was the beginning of our modest library, for he went on adding books that were necessary and suitable for a good general education. My father was tremendously foresighted, and at great personal sacrifice he provided all things necessary for our education, and this enabled us to stay well ahead of the boys not merely of our age, but of even much older boys. It also stirred in me a passion for reading which has been with me all my life. Most persons do not realise the value of developing a reading habit. If this is not done early in one's life, it rarely develops later on. It is only as we grow older and lonelier that we realise what a boon books are, and how enormously they can help us to get through life while all the time adding to our little store of knowledge.

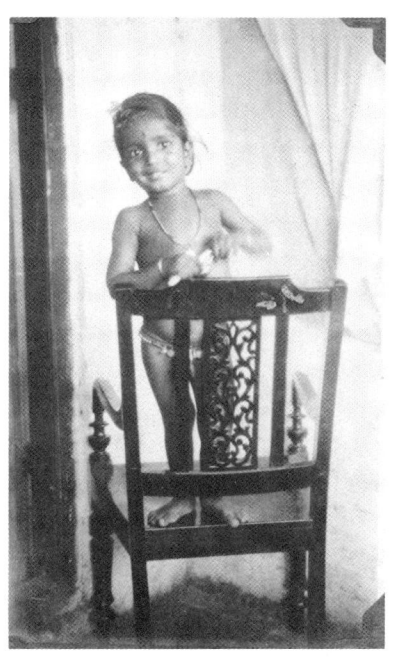

Parthasarathi - 1929

Parthasarathi - 1931

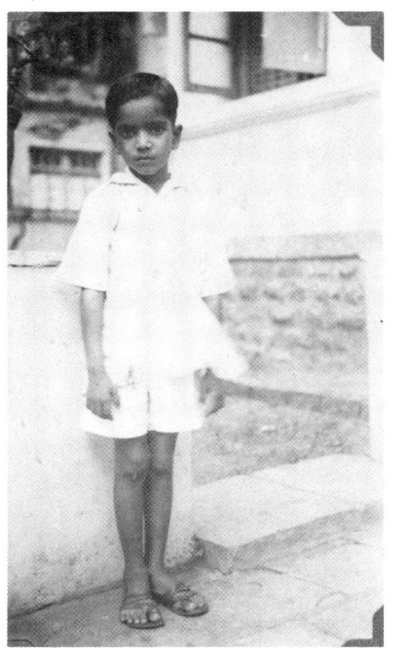

Parthasarathi - 1933

Parthasarathi - 1933

Parthasarathi,
having just recovered from intestinal
tuberculosis - 1934

Parthasarathi - 1935

The Early Years

I remember a rather tragic case of one of my father's colleagues, who collected books all his life with the intention of reading them after he was retired from service. At the age of fifty, just a few years before he was due for retirement, he became blind. It was awful for him not to have read all those books which he had loved and wanted to read, and which he had so painstakingly collected all his life. The even bigger tragedy for him personally was that a few years later he had to sell all those books! I know there are many persons, especially the rich ones, who buy expensive library editions which are used to adorn their drawing rooms, and are loftily called 'my library'. My father saw to it that we did not behave so loosely with books.

Books are considered holy in the Indian tradition, and are to be treated with respect. My father insisted that we treat books with respect, and we were strictly forbidden from placing an open book face down on the table, as well as from folding the corners of pages to mark the page. Books are not supposed to be dog-eared! We also participated in the annual worship of the goddess Saraswathi, when books were arranged before her picture in the morning after we had bathed, and prayers for her recited. Musical instruments too were kept there, for was she not also the goddess of music? That day reading was forbidden. Prayers were repeated again the next morning, and then we all had to sit down before the picture of the goddess and to read for some time, and to play the musical instruments.

This *puja* was especially important for the Brahmins, for they have been traditionally the caste supposed to act as ministers to kings, to be advisers, and to be priests officiating at all the sacrificial rituals often lasting many days, and called *yagnas*. Therefore knowledge was very important for the Brahmins, and they spent their childhood in learning to recite the *Vedas*, starting from the tender age of seven, going on for seven or eight years, during which period the average boy had to learn to recite by heart the selected *Vedas* for approximately three hours in the morning and a similar three hours in the evening, the recital of the *Yajur Veda* lasting, for instance, five or six days! Later on in my life, I too learnt a little part of the *Yajur Veda*, and know by personal experience the enormous mental effort required to memorize such vast chunks of material — and that too in Sanskrit!

For the more materially minded, there was the annual *Lakshmi Puja*, on which day the goddess Lakshmi was worshipped. This *puja* had more of colour in it, as women participated in it with more fervour, for Lakshmi is also associated with the *sumangali* concept, and with wealth and progeny — all dear to the hearts of women in India. The *sumangali* is a married woman, and it is the ardent desire of every married woman to die a *sumangali*, that is to die before her husband, so that she may leave this world as a *sumangali*! The *Lakshmi Puja* is also of the greatest importance to the business community, and their prayers are performed with great superficial fervour, and often at considerable expense. A peculiar feature of this *puja* is that many belonging to the business community indulge in hectic gambling on the night of the *puja*, as this particular goddess is also associated with luck, and by gambling they hope to attract her favours.

There are two more important *pujas* in the Hindu tradition, the *Vinayaka Puja*, and the *Kali Puja*. The former is celebrated at something of a community level in the state of Maharashtra, the celebration lasting ten days, with often enormous idols of the elephant god being kept in public worship where thousands of persons participate in the *puja*. Thereafter the idol is taken in joyful procession through the streets, with much frenzied dancing and revelry, and given a holy disposal by being worshipfully thrown into a river, a pond or the sea. The *Kali*

The Early Years

Puja, or the *Durga Puja* as it is also called, is an equally elaborate and expensive affair, largely confined to the Bengali community. In former times thousands of goats and buffaloes used to be slaughtered at the Kali temples all over the state of Bengal, but this gruesome tradition has been more or less eradicated.

Whereas the *Lakshmi* and *Saraswathi Pujas* were largely family affairs, celebrated at home, the *Vinayaka* and *Durga Pujas* have assumed the pattern of communal worship, as indicated earlier. This has often been the cause of communal disruption, as all those familiar with the Indian scene surely know. Such occasions have been used by interested persons or groups to disturb the communal harmony of the people, sometimes with disastrous consequences. It is my personal opinion that such public worship has promoted communal disharmony and hatred in India, and kept the flame of communal hatred alive, though decade after decade has passed with fervent appeals for brotherhood and peaceful co-existence. One wonders if there will ever be any change in this matter — but unfortunately the indications are for the worsening of matters, and not for their mitigation.

Those years in Jubbulpore were before India threw off the shackles of foreign rule. The British ruled India from England. They tried to maintain a minimum degree of communal harmony, but there were periodic upheavals of religious hatred generally resulting in violence, especially in what used to be cynically called 'violence-prone localities'. There were horrible stories of how innocent victims were murdered, even in broad daylight. Whenever such a horror gripped a locality all life came to a halt, and fear ruled the streets and the lanes unhindered. Schools and colleges would be closed, markets closed, milk supplies suspended, so that life became a difficult thing. Of course no one ventured outside the home, and the *goondas* had the town well nigh to themselves. Perhaps if the general population had come out to combat the *goondas*, such outbreaks of violence could have been aborted, but then fear rules the life not only of the individual, but of the whole community, and citizens were usually content to remain indoors allowing the violence and hatred to work themselves out — the few venturesome ones generally being the unfortunate victims, often losing their lives.

This communal disharmony and hatred came to its final and cataclysmic horror when India was split into two during the partition of the country. Tens of thousands of families left India to go to the newly created state of Pakistan, and similar tens of thousands of families left that country to cross the border into India. Homes and property were abandoned, and what little could be taken with them were carried as head loads, or loaded on to bullock carts or similar primitive vehicles, and taken with them as they fled helter skelter to the country of their choice. It was no doubt one of the largest of human exoduses in the world's history. And the cause was religious intolerance and strife, the fires of communal hatred fueled by the political machinery of the rulers of India who had been forced to relinquish their stranglehold upon a nation which had yielded them immense and incalculable wealth and power.

It is a sad and disastrous fact of life in India that the mixing of religion and politics — strange bedfellows by any standards — has made it impossible for the average Indian to live out his life of suffering and pain with even a minimum of peace or tranquillity because of this unholy marriage of these two potent forces. That after freedom such forces of disruption have, if anything, gained greater momentum and power is a sad commentary upon the forces governing a free India!

The Early Years

I remember an eerie experience that we had in our home one evening just after we all had returned from school. It was one of those days when Appa was away from Jubbulpore and I, for one, was feeling very lonely, and suffering from a deep melancholy. I was sitting out on our verandah, with one of our dogs contentedly asleep at my feet, gazing out over the garden. I was in a state of reverie, when something startled me into a state of awareness. I must have been in some sort of a semi-conscious state for this to have happened. I saw something very strange. It looked as if the water tank was on fire. Even the surface of the water in the tank appeared to be on fire! I looked up at the sky, and saw that the whole firmament was on fire too. The colour was of blood. It was as if everything had been blood-washed and was yet to dry. There was something eerie, something unnatural and terrifying about this experience. My brothers came out, and they too saw the same thing, as indeed our *mali* and his wife did. We rushed up to the gate, and saw many persons standing on the road and on the playgrounds, all gazing up to see this strange and terrifying phenomenon.

Knowing that we were alone, Nayudu mama came to see us all that evening as soon as he was free. He told us that the same blood red sky had been seen everywhere, and knowing that we might feel frightened by it, he had come to see that all was well with us. He added that according to the weighty opinion of the seers of Jubbulpore, this phenomenon indicated that the whole world was in for what they termed a blood bath. One morning the next week we came to know that World War II had begun in Europe! Little did we know about wars and peace, having lived a sheltered life so far. To us it was all a big joke, and much fun was made of some of the more pompous English boys who had already started boasting of their fathers being called up for active service soon! It was all fun for the children. Little did we realise that great changes were in store for all of us.

One of the unexpected results of the outbreak of the war was the disruption of our family life, and our separation for a few years from our beloved father. There was a general sense of curiosity in all as to how the war would affect us. It did not take us long to find out, for the government, for some mysterious reason known only to itself, decided to involve my father in it. He was selected for deputation out of the G.I.P. Railways for some years, and was soon relieved from his job. His services were placed at the disposal of the Government of India, and he was posted to Calcutta on deputation to the Directorate General of Munitions Productions — D.G.M.P. for short — since India, being part of the British Empire, had to get involved in the war effort.

As we could not live alone in Jubbulpore, my maternal grandmother was kind enough to come all the way from Agaravallam, and to stay with us until we were settled in — this process taking many months. She was severely diabetic, and had to be controlled in her diet. For her this was quite an impossibility, for she lacked the necessary will. I am afraid that I gave her a lot of unhappiness in rigidly controlling her intake, especially when she drank quantities of the delectable sugar cane juice of which she was very fond. I often treated her rudely, and with scant courtesy, and hurt her feelings too often so that now, after the passage of perhaps half a century, I feel sorrow and remorse for having denied the little pleasures and happiness that she could have had. I deeply regret having treated her as if she was my little sister. I am sure that she, with her immensely large heart, forgave me for all my lapses before she departed this world.

The Early Years

Since my father was to leave for Calcutta and had been relieved from the railways, we could not stay on in the big railway bungalow. Our life underwent its first major upheaval. A rented house was found in the city, and we had to move into one half of a building called the *Hawaghar* — the Hindi equivalent for observatory. All that it had by way of equipment to give it this pompous name were two contraptions, one an arrow-shaped one which indicated the wind direction — a wind vane, and the other a set of four cups mounted horizontally on the four arms of a cross, which rotated with the wind and served to indicate wind speed — a wind speed indicator. With this equipment the building rested on its laurels. One merit that it had was that the building was easy to locate.

We had a jolly time during the period of our stay at the *Hawaghar*. We had good neighbours, the family of the famous Hindi poet, Subhadra Kumari Chauhan. They lived in the other half of the building, the two sections being separated by a corrugated tin partition which, being full of large bolt holes, enabled us to peep into our neighbour's home, and to exchange a few words now and then. Mrs Subhadra Kumari's three sons, Ajai, Vijay and Ashok, were all students of our school, and that strengthened our friendship further. There was a little sister, the last of the family, called Mamta, but she was very bashful, and we did not see much of her except when she came into our field of vision when we peeped through the partition. In the India of those days boys and girls were generally not permitted to mix much.

As for Mrs. Chauhan herself, she was a famous Hindi poet, and we were somewhat in awe of her. She was a nice person, and often sent us some delicacy which she had prepared, and which she wanted to share with us. Mamta would generally bring it around, blushing and looking very pretty and demure, running off the moment she had delivered the dish to us. Of course my grandmother would reciprocate with some south Indian delicacy, and so it went on, exchange after exchange of delicious food strengthening our association, until we all became great friends. One consequence of this change of residence was that Nayudu mama's home was a greater distance away, and we could not visit them as frequently as in the earlier period. At the *Hawaghar* there was more company, for we were not enclosed within a huge compound, shut away from the rest of humanity, as we had been in the Railway bungalow.

Things improved even more when we shifted out of the *Hawaghar* into a house nearby, set in a row of houses. Here our neighbours to the left were a Maharashtrian family, the Borgaonkars. The father was aged forty-five years, the mother around thirty-eight or forty. They had seven daughters, the eldest of whom was older than I was by a couple of years. They desperately wanted a male child. Every time Aayee, as a mother is addressed in Marathi, conceived, they would perform a special *puja* called the *Satyanarayana Puja*, so that the gods would bless them with a male child. Alas! The gods did not listen, and even the seventh was a daughter. But on the eighth occasion nature seemed to smile on them, and a male child was born but, tragedy of tragedies, the child died a few weeks later. Their grief was terrible to behold. We were unable to console them.

The Borgaonkars and we had two adjoining homes, with a common open courtyard, the two houses being divided by a wall with a convenient door in it, so that we could go in and out of each other's house at will. It was as if we were all members of one family, and life was harmonious and joyful. Here too my grandmother accompanied us, leaving us some months later to go back to Agaravallam, as the call for her was insistent. I know that she would have preferred to stay longer

The Early Years

with us, but she was wanted at home, and she had to go with my uncle Ayya who came for her.

My father was still at Calcutta, and Nayudu mama was our official guardian. He handled our finances, though the money was in my physical possession. It had been like that for some years already. My training in handling and accounting for money began very early indeed. The money would come from my father in monthly remittances by money order. Bank transactions were very rare, all purchases having to be paid for in cash. My father had a bank account with the Allahabad Bank, and was one of the few to have one. Those were the days when even large sums of money were physically transferred from place to place, and it was quite safe to do so.

It was during my father's posting in Calcutta, in 1943, that I fell seriously ill, and had my third brush with death. I came back one evening from school with my face swollen up, and since I was feeling exhausted I went to bed for a brief rest. When I woke up again some four days had passed because I had become unconscious even as I had gone to bed. My father had, as we learnt later, fallen ill at almost precisely the same time in Calcutta in his office. He had felt giddy and vomited, and had to be taken to a nursing home. Nayudu mama was summoned to see me, and a doctor was called in who diagnosed my illness as uraemia, and the prognosis was 'condition critical'. A telegram was sent to my father and even though he himself was severely ill, he rushed to Jubbulpore, and had to stay with me for the next three months.

I cannot describe the patient love and attention that my father lavished on me during the first two weeks when my life hung in the balance. He was with me all the time, day and night. By accident he discovered that a famous doctor, who had been the state physician to the Maharaja of Travancore, was in

Jubbulpore. He went to him and requested him to examine me. Dewan Bahadur Dr. P.N. Lakshmanan, for that was his name, came and saw me, and told my father that there was no cure other than patient care. No urine had passed for more than a week. It was necessary to stimulate the kidneys again, and therefore he prescribed large quantities of fluid intake daily — fruit juices and the like — difficult for us to afford. I don't know how my father managed it all, but after a few days a few drops of blood were passed, and every one heaved a sigh of relief. Then slowly the quantity of blood increased, became paler and paler until, in some ten days time, it changed to urine. Only then did Dr. Lakshmanan say that now we could be optimistic about a cure. The eventual recovery took a little more than three long months.

Dr. Lakshmanan was a regular daily visitor, since he and Appa had become great friends. Dr. Lakshmanan was a Tamil scholar, and knew the *Ramayana* of Kamban by heart. He used to sit near my bed, with Appa near him, and go on reciting the Tamil *Ramayana* tirelessly from memory, and would generally stay for a couple of hours every day. He had a daughter living with him, and she or his wife would come to fetch him at lunch time. He was a grand old man already in his early seventies, but could look after himself perfectly well.

Finally, when I was pronounced normal again, he came on his last formal call and gave me a gentle pat on the back as a sign of his affection. My father did not know how to approach the rather delicate matter of his fees, but he managed to 'put the question' as we say. Dr. Lakshmanan replied with a gentle smile, "Rajagopalachari, your earnings for many years would not suffice to pay a bill if I should submit one. Nevertheless, since you insist, you may give me a cheque for a hundred rupees." And this my father did. Later on we discovered that he used to charge Rs. 64 per visit, and he had visited us almost daily for a period of three months! I do not know how we can ever repay the immense debt that we owe him, for there is no doubt that he gave me the gift of life. And how can that be ever repaid? I pray that his soul may find the everlasting peace that is the goal of most human lives.

It was during this particular illness that I developed a latent taste for music that I always had. I remember that I was generally whistling away gaily most of the time, and Appa used to admonish me for this ill-mannered habit. It was thought unmannerly to whistle especially in front of elders. During this long confinement to bed with nephritis, as the disease was diagnosed, Appa used to play my favourite records on one of those old gramophones which had a turntable, and which had to be laboriously wound up with a crank handle on one side. Then the record was put on, and the playing arm duly fitted with a new needle gently placed on the first groove of the record. Those records had a somewhat tinny sound, but the music was all that we heard, not having anything better to play them on, "even in England" as my Thatha used to remark. I used to whistle in accompaniment to the music, and that is how I developed my ability to whistle something recognizable.

Life in general was a great deal of fun. The total absence of any feminine presence in the home created a perceptible void, of course, but there was no way out of that situation. School was a great deal of fun, except when the summer came, and we had to go to school in the morning as the afternoon heat was too much to bear. During the summer months we had school from 7:30 A.M. to 10:30 A.M., and so we were always rushed for time. During the rest of the year school was from 9:00 A.M. to 3:30 P.M., followed by games or scout meetings. We had boxing, in the good old English tradition, and I had to participate whether I liked it or not. Training was quite arduous, and I disliked it heartily. It was worse in the boxing ring, because being a puny fellow, I was always battered around, though the referees saw to it that not much damage was inflicted upon weaklings such as myself.

There was the annual boxing event, the boxing championship with the team from the St. Aloysius School, the only other English medium school in Jubbulpore. They were called the Saintoos rather derogatorily! The championship bouts were held at night, commencing from around 8:00 P.M., and went on till midnight, depending upon the opposition put up by the Saintoos. We had all the rigmarole of the ring, and all the weights were represented, and it all had a very mystical and professional air to it, including quite a few battered noses and black eyes. I can remember only one occasion when a boy was actually knocked out! We were eager, if somewhat anxious, participants, because this was a great event, and the self-respect of all the CCBHS boys depended upon victory over the Saintoos.

There were sports and track events too, but the main event was the boxing championship. We had two large playgrounds in our school, and three levels of games and sports events went on throughout most of the year. Football was confined to the monsoon season — there being some mysterious connection with rain-soaked and soggy playgrounds and that game. Cricket was important, being a typically English game. It was played mainly during the summer months, commencing from spring. Then there was hockey, in which India was the world leader and the great Dhyan Chand its world renowned representative. I do not remember whether we ever had inter-school championship matches in sports and track events. In any case we never had such meetings with Indian school teams as far as I can remember. This was of course the well-known snobbery of the white man.

The Early Years

We had our own internal sports meets, and in these events the four houses participated with much ardour and heat. The four houses were named the Cullen, Darling, Chatterton and the Mendez houses, and all the school boys were assigned to one of them. I belonged to the Cullen House. I remember that when we joined CCBHS, on the first day at the prayer meeting when the whole school was gathered, I was asked by the boy next to me to what house I belonged. I answered that I came from the railway quarters. He repeated his question, "To which house do you belong?" And I repeated the same answer, for I knew of no other house. It was only a month or so later that I found out about the house system in such English schools. I managed to top the class in the first month of my school, and in one class conducted by Mr. Beatson the results had just been read out. He asked me, "Parthasarathi, to which house do you belong?" I answered that I did not know. He was surprised, but immediately assigned me to the house of which he was the head — the Cullen House. He did this because school performance also qualified for points which went to the credit of the house — and he grabbed the chance of putting me in his house, for the first rank added three points to the house!

I wonder whether he did not regret this later, because I never contributed to the house points in any other way. It was Mr. Beatson again who put me into the cricket team. It happened in a very funny way. I was watching a game played on the ground in the other school across the road. I was actually sitting on my bicycle with one foot on the ground, leaning over to the left. Suddenly a ball came whizzing straight at me. I instinctively put out my left hand and by the merest accident happened to catch it. Mr. Beatson who was very near me, seated on his shooting stick, watched me making this left-handed catch. Immediately he called me over to himself and asked me whether I was in the team. I answered that I was not.

He said, "Well, we will have to set that right," and a few days later I found out, to my surprise and dismay, that I had been given a place in the cricket 'B' team.

I was never any good at sports or track events — and that is an understatement. My shyness prevented me from doing anything physical properly, especially in the presence of others. I was a great guy in messing up things, and it did not take very long for me to be edged out of the team. I suffered similar disgrace in respect of other games and events too. I remember that in track events I was really awful. If the first boy completed the 440 yards in say two minutes, for example, I was sure to be unable to even complete the course. I was a total failure on the sports fields, and soon became a mere spectator, which I secretly enjoyed. Had it not been for my cursed shyness I would perhaps have done as well as the others, but then that was the stumbling block to all achievement.

This withdrawal from the world of games and sports made me a bookworm quite early in my life. Something had to fill the void, and the books did that with great effect. I have been a lover of books all my life, and if given a choice it is still the activity that has first preference with me. There is something amusing in this — a remark my wife Sulochana makes very often when she is exasperated with my buying more and more books. She often asks, with much acidity, "Why didn't you just marry a book?" I cannot say that I have lost much by not being able to participate in physical activity, for it turned me inwards and that has been a great blessing for my future life after leaving school. The only thing that I really enjoyed was my participation in the Boy Scouts' movement, in which I did quite well, qualifying for a few badges too.

We had a great many escapades, but one is deeply embedded in my memory. One day we three brothers, accompanied by some other boys, decided to go to the Bhera Ghat, some twelve miles away, to see the famed marble rocks. We had been there several times but decided to go all the same. Some ten of us left on bicycles, many of them rented ones, on a fine sunny morning at about eleven o'clock planning to be back home well before the evening. If I remember right we cut classes for half a day to do this. Everything was going as planned, and we arrived at the marble rocks after a fast ride of just an hour or so. Then our troubles started! The clear sky and the brilliant sunshine disappeared behind a forbidding bank of the darkest clouds, and it started pouring. We took shelter in the chowkidar's small and shabby cottage. It went on pouring cats and dogs for the next several hours, and the next thing we knew was that the bridge over the river Narmada, which we had crossed, had been flooded, and there was several feet of water flowing at a tremendous velocity over it.

It was obvious that had we tried to ride over the bridge, we would all have been washed away. There was no way out, since the only road was the one over that bridge. We had to stay the night in the chowkidar's cottage, and I remember that he very generously made chappatis for us without any vegetables to eat them with. It rained all evening, but fortunately stopped late in the evening. We were all completely miserable, for we had come without informing anyone about it. Neither our families nor our school masters knew anything about our foolish escapade. We did not know when the flood waters would recede sufficiently for us to venture crossing the bridge to get back home. Above all we were afraid of the punishment that certainly awaited all of us. Anyway, what cannot be cured must be endured, and endure it we did, in rain-soaked clothes and not-too-full bellies, shivering through the night. Fortunately for us, the rain waters had receded by the next morning, and the bridge was visible. And so we took our bicycles and drove back home — without taking the boat to see the marble rocks.

When we arrived home the next afternoon, we found Appa waiting for us. He was very relieved to see us, but this soon gave way to his anger. Fortunately for us his relief outweighed his anger, and so we all escaped without any corporal punishment on that occasion. Later on we learnt that they had known of our trip to Bhera Ghat because the owner of the shop which had rented out some of the bicycles had gone to our school and complained about their non-return!

A second such occasion surfaces to my memory, and that was going on a scout march which had perhaps been suddenly fixed up, and about which I could not inform my father. We were supposed to get back before dark, but something delayed us, and it was around midnight that we got back home. There I found Appa calmly waiting for us so that all of us could eat our dinner together. He never chastised us, but his waiting for us taught us never to be late again. My father taught us good manners and behaviour by such subtle means, and that training has lasted us all our lives.

We always went to our grandparents at Agaravallam for our annual holidays. It was a long train journey to Mayavaram via Madras. It also entailed a change of trains at Itarsi. We would normally leave around noon from Jubbulpore by the Bombay mail, reaching Itarsi at around 5:00 P.M. There we had to wait several hours till the Grand Trunk Express arrived from Delhi on its long journey to Madras. This train arrived around 10:30 P.M., and so we had nearly six hours to wait. It was a tedious wait as we were all three of us quite young and lacked the initiative to go out sight-seeing. So we wandered around on the platforms whiling away the time. We would buy *puris* and potatoes for a mere rupee, and in those days we were able to get at least two dozen *puris*, together with a generous helping of *aloo sabji*. We were often unable to eat it all, and gave away what was left. Things were really cheap in those days. As soon as the Grand Trunk Express arrived, we would board the train quite sleepily, since it was well past our usual bed time, and we were naturally bored and tired after having been on the station platform for five or more hours. There was never any problem in finding accommodation as we travelled on 1st class free passes, and there was reserved accommodation waiting for us. Those were orderly times when train travel was really very comfortable and trouble-free, and there was never any need to rush around frantically as has become necessary these days.

I remember that in those days there were four classes of accommodation available — 1st class, 2nd class, Inter class and then the 3rd class. The 1st class was for the rich and for the railway officers and their families, so that most 1st class coaches went nearly empty most of the time. I remember that on one occasion Appa had put us into a 1st class compartment at Jubbulpore. There was a bearded gentleman in it — and we were frightened of him. So at the next halt, Manikpur if I remember correctly, we got out of the 1st class coach and went into a 2nd class coach by which we travelled till Itarsi.

Eventually we would reach Madras the next afternoon, detrain at the Central station, and go by *jutka* to our periappa's home in Triplicane. We generally had sufficient time to bathe and to eat a meal, before leaving for the Egmore station early in the evening, from where the metre gauge trains to the south of India left. We travelled to Mayavaram generally by a train called the Boat Mail. It had this name because the train went straight to Talaimannar Pier from where the British officers could take a ship to go to England. Arriving at Mayavaram early in the morning the next day, we then had to complete the last six miles of our journey by bullock cart, reaching our village of Agaravallam around 10:00 A.M. Sometimes we would take a branch line train to Manganallur, and go from there the remaining three miles by bullock cart to Agaravallam. Quite a journey, but every bit of it was enjoyable, and we rarely felt tired or bored by the long journey.

Our grandparents were always delighted to have us with them, and I am sure that they would have kept us with them all their lives had our father only permitted it. They lavished their love and attention and care upon us. Our cousins, children of my mother's sister Suli, would also arrive at this time, along with my maternal uncle Kasturi's children, and the house was full. I remember that for the morning tiffin we were often thirty persons to be fed. All the children would be seated in two rows facing each other, and our Pattiamma would go around putting a dollop of curd rice into each outstretched hand, while Suli or Kamali followed, adding a little *sambhar* or a bit of pickle to the rice. The children ate their dollops and put out their hands once more, and so it went on for ten or twenty minutes, till the children had their bellies full. It was amazing what enormous appetites we had in those days! Truly enormous! I am convinced that had we been left alone to eat as we chose, none of us would have eaten even half of what we were able to put away when fed as a community with so much love and coaxing! In the mornings our breakfast was invariably the same curd rice, cooked tiffin being reserved for the afternoons. Those were jolly and carefree times, the like of which we shall not see again, in any case in my lifetime.

We would go to the river nearby for a bath. It was a branch of the famous river Cauvery, and was called the Veerachozhan. Rivers in that part of the country have water flowing in them only when the water is let out of the Mettur Dam, because all the water was meant for agriculture. Water was generally let out in the month of June or July, and the rivers flowed full well into November or December, by which time the north-east monsoon would set in. We were supposed to bathe in the river, but this generally took up several hours due to the horse play that we indulged in, especially because our youngest uncle Ayya would be there to egg us on to all the possible devilry that he could think up on each occasion.

Sometimes his devilry got us into difficulties, and not infrequently into dangerous, situations. I remember one occasion when I could have possibly drowned in the river. It was quite shallow at the near bank, but on the far side where the river took a bend, the water was quite deep — perhaps twelve feet deep. Ayya once enticed some of us to the far bank, normally strictly forbidden to us, and then started ducking us under the river. There was a small whirlpool there, and since we never had any bathing dresses but went in with our *dhotis*, or whatever we had on, I was caught in the whirlpool, and would have perhaps drowned but for the careful attention of a stranger on the bank who shouted out a warning. Then an elder uncle swam to me and pulled me through to safety. After that for some time I was quite nervous of getting into the river, especially when Ayya was around.

Shallow though these rivers were, the water flowed in them so fast that there were generally one or two deaths by drowning every year. One of the other tributaries of the Cauvery had a very significant name. It was called the Kodamurutti. A *kodam* is a spherical vessel of brass or clay used to store water in. *Uruttal*, in Tamil, is to roll something. The combination — Kodamurutti — meant that the water flowed at such a velocity that it could roll away such vessels with ease! Romantic names those rivers had, reflecting vistas of ancient Tamil history too — as for instance our own Veerachozhan, which was named after one of the Chola kings known for his bravery.

Generally we would be back just in time for lunch — and did we have an appetite! We ate like wolves, and famished wolves at that. But there was always more than was needed, and in fact my Pattiamma was never happy with what we ate, wanting us to eat more and more. In India food has always been a panacea for all the troubles and travails of life, and mothers and grandmothers believed that eating solved all the problems of existence. This continues even into the present! I think we children generally had four meals every day! This was the regular thing, and apart from that there were always delicious things to be picked from the orchard, or plucked from the plants, or knocked down from the overburdened trees, and eaten. The mango season was a great temptation for then the green mangoes were there, waiting to be knocked down by a well-aimed stone, and then to be eaten with salt and chilli powder with enormous relish — a deadly combination which was exceedingly tasty but which made the eater sick very soon after. If one ate too much of the ripe fruit, then one developed a certain variety of sores or heat boils on the skin, and that took longer to heal. But who bothered with such considerations? Temptation was always hard to resist, and especially when it grew on trees which were there all around us.

We slept after lunch under the stern orders of Thatha, and we generally dared not disobey him. But how can the young on holiday sleep? He sat near us on his old easy chair made of canvas — a deck chair as it is called. But if he was inattentive even for a moment — and who could avoid a snooze on a hot afternoon after a hearty lunch? — off we went for some more fun before he could even notice that we were missing, this time to the verdant mango groves or coconut groves behind the house. The scope for fun and mischief was literally unlimited. Often there would be quarrels between us — and I am sorry to say that it was our uncles Ayya and Viji who would deliber-

The Early Years

ately create them, and then egg us on out of a sense of fun all their own. We would fly at each other, and there would be hell to pay for some time before those very same uncles stepped in to sort out the quarrel, playing the peace makers! An example of pinching the baby and rocking the cradle!

We would come back home thoroughly exhausted after the afternoon quota of devilry was over, and demand tiffin from our patient grandmother. Tiffin was always available in one form or the other. There were delectable items which were made once a week and stored for use, and there were items which were made as and when necessary for instant consumption. To the former category belonged such delicacies as *murukku, thattai* and *thenkuzhal* — of which I am inordinately fond even today. And to the latter category belonged such mouth-watering and very filling and tasty dishes as *dosa, iddli, oothappam* etc. We ate with enormous appetites, and I am amazed at the quantity of foodstuffs that were cooked by my Pattiamma and the other ladies of the household every day. Cooking seemed to go on almost all the time, for there were things to be made to be stored for future use when there was time to do so.

Dinner was generally mixed rice — that is *sambhar* rice or *puliyodarai,* a rice preparation with a lot of tamarind paste and chillies in it. The *pulikkachal* was made as a thick viscous paste soaking full of oil. *Pulikkachal* could be preserved for many days, or even weeks, and all that was necessary was to mix it well with cooked rice, and there you had ready made *puliyodarai,* which was served hot or cold as needed. Another such rice preparation was *thengai saadam,* or coconut rice, but this could not be preserved and had to be eaten soon after preparation. It was not so pungent as *puliyodarai.* Such rice dishes were supplemented with *appalam* or *vatthal,* vegetables dishes not being cooked for dinner, as a rule. As a matter of fact *vatthals, vadam* and *appalam* were all prepared on an annual basis and stored just to supplement the meal when vegetables were not cooked. But for us children dinner was more often just curd and rice eaten with pickles. It was rare to have a cooked meal for dinner unless we had guests.

Our holidays were periods of hectic activity for all in our village, even the labourers from our farms being kept busy with one chore or the other. We had enormous coconut groves, and some of the farm hands were recruited every morning to cut down the tender coconuts for our use, as we were fond of the coconut water which was not merely tasty but very cooling in the hot summer too. Our home was a large rambling brick structure, and the brick walls were not plastered. The house had just the ground floor, and was tiled with country tiles which housed an unimaginable number of guests — scorpions! Even snakes were known to take refuge in the roof, especially if the house had been constructed using bamboo poles to serve as supports for the roof. On the outer surface the walls had holes in them which had been used to erect the scaffolding during construction of the house, but the holes had never been filled and built over.

One day we all had lovely guavas in our hands. They were ripe and a lovely, a shiny parrot green in colour. While I was about to eat it, I was called inside by someone. So I thrust my guava inside one of those holes in the wall, went in, finished whatever it was that I had to do, and came back to retrieve my fruit. I put my hand into a hole in the wall, seeing a green object there, grasped it and brought out my hand. I was horrified to find that I had a green snake in my hand, its head resembling my guava in shape, size and colour! There was consternation and horror on the faces of all near me. I shook the snake off, but it made matters worse because it wound itself around my

The Early Years

ankle. Just then a farm hand came, and with much presence of mind he released me from the snake and killed it.

My grandfather had extensive farm lands and there were truly enormous coconut and mango groves — so that there was no dearth of playing space for us. He also had a large herd of cattle numbering some 150 milch and draught animals. The number of farm hands exceeded fifty. There was therefore enormous scope for fun and mischief. There were occasions when we would just disappear under the influence of Ayya, and the elders had a hard time to locate us. On such occasions there was a great deal of chastisement and frowning all round, including from my uncles who had introduced us to the particular form of devilry for which we were being chastised. But all in all it was great fun, and we were always miserable when the time for us to return to school arrived.

Our departure could not be delayed, for at the other end waited a stern father who had been worried that we would have been spoilt by our grandparents. There were several letters from him instructing us not to extend our stay, sending us passes and making our rail reservations etc. Everything has to end, and so did our holidays. I believe that the sorrow of our grandparents far exceeded ours when the time came for us to part company. Pattiamma would bid us a weepy farewell, saying that she did not know whether we would ever meet again, for she was getting old! One of our uncles would accompany us to Mayavaram to put us safely on the train, and so we went back to Jubbulpore, again and again for many years, after the most enchanting holidays that boys could have.

It was a dreary life that we led when my father was away. I do not know what we would have done without him. He was certainly a strict disciplinarian but all his discipline was tempered with a great deal of love, so that we always understood that his demands from us were for our good — but that did not prevent our feeling annoyed and rebellious on those occasions. To harden us and to make us self-dependent, he insisted that we sleep in three corners of one of the three bedrooms — the end one adjacent to the workshop compound wall. They were enormous rooms indeed, and we all felt very much alone, as if we were separated by enormous distances. But we never disobeyed Appa, and somehow existed through the night, sleeping fitfully. We had that room to ourselves, while he slept in the third bedroom, so that a whole room separated his bedroom from ours. But when he was there we were comforted by the thought that so long as he was there nothing could possibly go wrong with us.

We were definitely ill at ease when he was absent from home. After sunset our psychic situation definitely worsened. We had only a cook to keep us company, and as we were afraid of being alone, we generally tagged along behind him from room to room as he went about his work.

Once my youngest brother, Seena, had a miraculous escape from death. As we were sleeping, the roof came crashing down in his corner of the room, and just missed falling on him by perhaps a tenth of an inch. The bungalow was roofed with a sloping roof, built of teak wood rafters covered with Mangalore tiles. Under the roof there was an artificial ceiling of canvas duck, over which the rats had a merry time, running helter skelter, hither and thither, all night. The roof had obviously not been inspected for very many years. The house itself was without a doubt many decades old. The timbers of the roof had been quietly invaded by the all-pervasive white ants which had bored into them, progressively weakening them. Eventually nothing but the outer shell of the timber was left, the inside having been eaten away almost entirely. On that fateful night the rafters were unable to bear the weight of the tiles any

The Early Years

longer, and the roof came crashing down just before midnight. My father heard the crash and rushed into our room. He expected the worst, no doubt, and was visibly moved, and his eyes were moist. When he found Seena safe and sound his relief was almost palpable. We had to temporarily shift to other accomodation — I believe we moved into the Railway Rest House — so that the entire roof could be relaid. It took the Railway administration several months to lay a new roof in the very same style as the old one. The house looked really lovely, and it was now sound enough for the next hundred years — as one of the Anglo Indian engineers from the Railways put it.

So many things happened during our seven years life in Jubbulpore — most of them happy and wonderful. My father had a contented life, far away from the centre of things, as far as his work was concerned. Further, he had a wonderful place to live in, a large garden which he delighted to tend, happy children, excellent friends, and a good environment at work. Generally therefore he was very relaxed and happy. He was admired by one and all, and was a sort of guide, philosopher and friend to most of the south Indian community, and to a large number of his friends and colleagues. He was greatly admired for being such a presentable widower, and yet so stern and rigid in his decision not to marry again. He was a really handsome and attractive person, and for him to sternly deny himself was a matter of not only astonishment, but of a sort of wonder. There was a tendency, especially among the younger set, to look upon him as some sort of budding saint, and they venerated him.

Appa used to travel on inspection duties over the whole Jubbulpore Division of the G.I.P.Railway. He was entitled to what is called a saloon — a special coach with bedrooms, bathrooms and a kitchen with a small place for the cook. There were several classes of saloons, starting with the one allotted to the General Manager which was a full length coach, hauled by express and mail trains, to the smallest one mounted on a bogie with just four wheels, such as the one allotted to officers of the level of my father. These small saloons were attached only to goods trains since they were too light, and would have gone off the rails had they been attached to the fast trains.

I once accompanied Appa on an inspection tour. We had a saloon to ourselves. It had only one bedroom and a sitting room. The goods trains were excruciatingly slow ones. They would often stop at each and every station, and often be shunted onto a loop line to let faster passenger trains pass. They, I mean such goods trains, often took eight hours to cover a hundred miles! We would have food cooked on board the train, buying vegetables, kerosene oil, milk, rice and everything else that we needed in the local shops of the stations through which we passed. The station staff on all the stations were very respectful and helpful. We took on, with the foresight born out of my father's previous experience, a considerable load of books to read on what eventually became a tedious journey. It was nice to feel special in some intangible way, and to be pampered by the railway staff wherever we alighted. The four day trip was wonderful, and a special experience which was never repeated, for soon after that inspection tour my father was transferred to Calcutta on deputation.

Appa used to play tennis at the Railway club. We also had a badminton court at home where we would often play in the evenings. Tennis enabled a life-long friendship to develop with a railway clerk named E.N. Nayudu, who was an expert tennis player, and was something of an unofficial coach to all who aspired to play the game. Being my father's assistant at the office, Nayudu mama, as we addressed him, was a frequent visitor at our home, initially on matters concerning the office, but later merely to visit us socially. He was a genial person, very sympathetic and helpful at all times. He had a very fat wife, a most loving person who mothered us whenever we visited their home in the city, near a cinema house known as the Plaza Talkies! They had two sons and two daughters. The elder daughter was aged fifteen, and was named Sharada, and because of her age (!) we were unable to become really close to her. The second daughter was named Sushila, and was very fat indeed. She was also somewhat mentally retarded, and poor Nayudu mama was always anguished about her, calling her 'my Susie' whenever he referred to her. She had her own ideas of play, and blundered around like a baby elephant somewhat drunk. We all loved her, but kept a wary eye on her since she was prone to embrace those whom she liked!

The boys were called Papa and Chotu — and it was not till very many years later that we learnt that their names were Rama Rao Nayudu and Lakshmana Rao Nayudu. We became quite close and intimate with that family, and they visited us fairly often, the boys coming to play cricket and hockey with us on the enormous playground in front of our bungalow. We used to play hockey with a palm frond from which the leafy parts had been removed, and as the solid part had a curve at one end, it was not a bad substitute for a hockey stick. I remember that we also used to play cricket using a six inch wide wooden plank for a bat, with bricks stacked up at one end to represent the wicket. We played with a wicket at only one end of the pitch, since there were never more than six or seven of us to play. There were no teams, but it was each for himself! There was quite a bit of drama, and somewhat more of tension when disputes arose, because none of us really knew the rules of the game. The bigger boys generally tried to dominate the younger ones, and intimidate them into accepting everything that they said.

Further, there were no clearly marked field boundaries, and the one who umpired the game was often the target of bitter attack when his judgement came under question. And since it was always one of the smaller boys who was chosen to umpire — for reasons that have remained mysterious to this day — and since he was as ignorant as the rest of us about the rules he had to interpret, it all tended to be terribly arbitrary! What would start off as a harmonious attempt to play a few hours would often deteriorate into a mild fracas within the first fifteen minutes or so. Thereafter it would get hotter and hotter until, in a burst of general indignation and mutual recrimination, the game would come to a very abrupt end! It was all great fun, because the acrimony rarely lasted more than a quarter of an hour — the time taken to rush home and slake our thirsts, and to complain to which ever of the grown up persons was present and willing to listen to us. Immediately after that there we were, discussing what to play next, as if nothing at all had happened, and off we would run to play the next game with fresh enthusiasm.

Such times when we had boys to play with were rather rare. My father was rather averse to our having frequent company because he thought there were greater chances of our being spoilt. For the same reason we were only very rarely permitted to visit friends, the exception being the family of Nayudu mama, but because of the distance that too was quite rare. Therefore in the main our days were quite lonely, and we were generally mooning around the house trying to find something to do that would keep us occupied for a fair bit of time. We had the magnificent *Books of Knowledge* of course, but how long can one study the books of reference, for heaven's sake? It was thus that I was led to the avid reading of the comics of those days, and to this day I remember with considerable nostalgia the larger-than-life figures of the heroes of those

The Early Years

comics such as *Rockfist Rogan, R.A.F.* I have read almost everything published till 1943 in the Sexton Blake series. Sherlock Holmes was also around. Mystery stories were read with very great avidity but with apprehension, even in the day time, because of the certain impact that it would have upon my night's sleep. I had a tree house where much of the reading went on, assisted by the mechanical consumption of roasted ground nuts or by a pocket full of sweets.

We were allowed to see one or two cinemas a month — a cinema being a movie — and we generally preferred to see good English movies as the cinema theatres in the Cantonment area were much better maintained, since they were patronized by the Englishmen and their families. Air conditioning was unknown in those days, and all the available comfort was in the form of well upholstered seats and the provision of a large number of fans. My favourite series was the Tarzan series, featuring the well-known Olympic swimming champion Johnny Weissmuller as Tarzan. I used to be thrilled by his films. My favourite actress was Ingrid Bergman, whom I think of as one of the all-time greats. I still feel that there was no better actress than her, but that of course is my personal opinion. I remember seeing her act in several fine movies which I still remember — *Gaslight*, with Charles Boyer starring opposite her, for instance — which made a tremendous impression on me. Another great actress was Greer Garson. Vivien Leigh was another actress who was extremely popular in those days. One of the films which impressed me very much was *Mutiny on the Bounty* starring Charles Laughton as Captain Bligh, a remarkable movie of those times. He turned in a really great performance in *The Hunchback of Notre Dame*.

Other favourites were Deborah Kerr, Clark Gable, Cary Grant, Gary Cooper and Gregory Peck. Later came movies such as *Bathing Beauty*, starring Esther Williams, introducing a shift in the whole business, bringing in the female form for cinematic exploitation, and in that class of movies several stars and superstars emerged — Marilyn Monroe, Jane Russell and others, with Marilyn the undisputed queen of them all.

I used to see horror movies too, though always in the company of my schoolmates. My father did not approve of our seeing such films, and so we generally saw one or two when Appa was away on tour — a wrong time to see them of course — but then, 'boys will be boys' as the saying goes! Such occasions were few, because there were not many horror movies around then, and if there was one it had to coincide with my father's absence. I remember going to see a picture called *The Cat and the Canary.* I do not remember who were the actors. No doubt it was not important as the theme was such a powerful one that the picture itself made an awful impression, at least upon us six or seven boys, all aged around thirteen. There were some scenes that really frightened the whole audience. One scene for instance showed a young girl in bed, an old fashioned one with an ornamental head board. As she is dozing preparatory to deep sleep, a figure sheathed from head to foot in black enters her bedroom surreptitiously, goes between the wall and the head board of her bed, and extends a hand, a cat's paw really, over her head, and strangles her. He was the cat! Many of the English ladies present let out hysterical shrieks 'which chilled us to the bone', as the saying goes.

When the movie ended, we all set out upon our bicycles very bravely to go to our respective homes. For some distance we were all together, but then one by one we had to go our separate ways, and 'there lay the rub' to misquote Shakespeare, for as each one had to go his way, there was fear of having to ride alone. I remember that three of the boys finally drove home to our place to sleep there — which not only made them extremely happy, but made me even more happy! This picture

The Early Years

continued to haunt my sleep for many years, and I realised the unwisdom of seeing such horror movies when they made such a powerful impression upon me. But they have a fascination, together with ghost stories especially when told at night, which is hard to resist.

Cinema houses were quite rare in the smaller towns, and did not exist at all in the villages of India. For one thing villages had no electricity. Also the population of the average Indian village was never big enough to justify a cinema theatre on a permanent basis. Even the larger towns with population around 50,000 usually had only one cinema house of a permanent nature, but this was generally supplemented by what were called 'touring talkies' which were generally very large tents capable of seating up to 300 or more individuals, and had a screen at one end and the projection equipment at the other. These tents were generally erected on a large playground with much fanfare and beating of drums. They would remain in one location for several months, and even longer if the audience lasted.

The cheapest seating was on the ground in front of the screen — on river sand liberally spread on the ground. This class of seating, called the *tharai* class cost half an anna — just 1/32 of a rupee! Then there was the bench class, where the viewers sat upon plain wooden benches without backs to them. They were extremely uncomfortable, but reasonably cheap at an anna per head. The highest priced was the chair class at two annas per head. One must remember that at the time about which I am now writing, one could buy say a pound of potatoes for half an anna, and two pints of milk for a whole anna!

I remember that in Mayavaram we saw a famous movie of those times called *Sivakavi* starring M.K. Thyagaraja Bhagavathar, the movie idol of those times. He was a musician of great popularity. In those days there was no playback dubbing, and so musicians often acted in films. But he was perhaps the greatest of the tribe. The tent in which this film was shown for almost a year was just across the street from our home. All that we had to do was to lie down on the raised platform on the front verandah after dinner, and we could see the movie from behind the screen. It seemed to make no difference whatever to our enjoyment whether we saw it from the front or from behind the screen! In any case we rarely saw the movie right through, for we would doze off and on, waking up to listen to the music of our choice with which the film was liberally sprinkled. I think we must have seen that movie in this fashion at least a couple of dozen times, and only on the first occasion we paid to enter the touring talkies and see it in the usual manner!

There is something which people have always found to be amusing, but which I see as something very profound, as reflecting the simple faith that a simple people had. The *Ramayana*, the famous epic, used to be shown as a lengthy serial running for approximately four hours a day for some eighteen days! It was patronised by most of the population of the towns and surrounding villages. and especially by all the devoted people. This epic has always been tremendously popular with the people of India throughout the ages. Just a couple of years ago a television serial of the *Ramayana* consisting of some seventy episodes, each episode lasting a half hour, kept viewers glued to their TV sets every Sunday morning — and the popularity of that serial can be gauged by the fact that it was officially reported that even meetings of the Cabinet had to be rescheduled as otherwise the Cabinet Ministers were absent! But in those earlier days the religious fervour and enthusiasm were far greater, if anything. The elderly persons attending the film show were generally equipped with all the paraphernalia necessary for ritual *puja*, and whenever Lord

The Early Years

Rama or his Divine consort, Sita, appeared on the screen, they would burn incense and light a lump of camphor, and then prostrate before the deity on the screen!

We were members of the Boy Scouts movement, and that was great fun too. I enjoyed the weekly evening meetings which provided a different atmosphere. There was a different sort of companionship, a spirit of camaraderie, and that was very exhilarating to us. We derived a different sort of education, such as learning the fundamentals of the art of survival. And it was stimulating to learn such arts as the tying of a great variety of knots, learning to send semaphore and light signals using the Morse code, learning to tie quite an extraordinary variety of bandages, to make crutches and stretchers from almost nothing, and so on.

It was an education that was not only enjoyable but very necessary too. It is sad that such education has not been made compulsory, as it would have benefited a large number of the youth of this country who have perished in rivers and forests because they could not swim nor could they find their direction, because they did not know which was north. Such basic survival training is very definitely necessary, and the sooner it is made compulsory, the better it will be for all concerned.

I remember that I participated quite capably in the training schemes, and the signalling part of it was very attractive to me. I enjoyed learning the Morse code, and it was easy for me to master it and to get the Signallers badge, one among several others which I qualified for. I remember one occasion when we had the annual proficiency tests, and especially the signals tests. It was the lamp signalling test that was going on. We had to sit two at a time, back to back, the scout under test facing the signaller's lamp winking away furiously about two hundred yards away. The scout being tested had to read the signal alphabet by alphabet, and say it out loud to the one at the back who wrote it down. I had passed my own test very capably, and it was my turn to take down the dictation of another boy who was being tested. The surprising thing was that I could read the signals with my back to the distant lamp merely by seeing the winking of the lamp reflected upon the grass in front of me! As I have said, I enjoyed signalling, though semaphore signalling, using flags was somewhat more difficult to master.

Attendance at the annual Scout camps was compulsory. Such camps provided us with an opportunity of testing our knowledge under actual test conditions. It was sometimes extremely difficult to recall all that we had learnt when we were faced with trying field situations, because we tended to get agitated and flustered. I suppose that that was the whole point, or the sole aim, of arranging for these camps. It proved to us very dramatically indeed that it was not enough to know something. It was also necessary to be able to use that knowledge at the appropriate time, and 'there lies the rub' — this time to quote Shakespeare more accurately. The camp fires were thoroughly enjoyable, and as each boy had to take part in something or the other — songs, dances, miming etc. — it helped most of them to get over their innate shyness, and to become better adjusted individuals.

Shyness has always been a major problem for me. I have always been a shy person, and I have not been able to get over it even now. It has tended to isolate me from others, or rather it has compelled me to isolate myself from all outgoing activities, and to sit all by myself, brooding in some corner, unwanted by all, as I stupidly thought. I have never been able to understand how and when this started. As far as I know it has always plagued me, causing me enormous embarrassment and extreme loneliness throughout my life. It has made a decent social life virtually impossible, because with this trait, or

The Early Years

blemish, I could not make any friends. The result has been that I can count the friends I have had on the fingers of one hand! This is by no means an exaggeration.

It has also led to my failure in many interviews and viva voce tests, where I would become tongue-tied, and be unable to answer even the simplest of questions. It was not for lack of the correct answer. Certainly not! I was considered a fairly intelligent boy in school, and even better thought of in college. So that was not the problem at all, It was the cursed problem of my shyness preventing me from opening my mouth — for there I would stand with an asinine expression on my face, perspiring away the few precious minutes allotted to me. This dogged me well into the fourth decade of my life, after which I was able to gain a certain degree of control over it, so that though it was still there, I was nevertheless able to ensure that it did not render me impotent! As far as I know, only my aunt Gouri has ever penetrated sufficiently into my psyche to know that my shyness was still there even when I had turned 40 years of age! She told me on one occasion, "Pachu! You have not lost your shyness even now, and I find that a most charming thing in you!"

All in all those early years slipped past very rapidly, and before one was aware of it one had grown up, in the Indian sense or context, where one has to be capable of handling adult responsibilities even as one enters one's teens. The transition from childhood to the adult stage is direct in the majority of families, very much like the abrupt shift from day to night in the Tropics, there being no long evening in between. Youth is the privilege of the well endowed, and their prerogative. The middle and lower middle classes are by and large denied this. For the poor classes which, at least in those times, made up perhaps ninety-four of the total population of this vast country, even children were compelled to handle what should normally have been adult duties and responsibilities. It is very common even today to see children of eight and nine going long distances to the village tank, or to a common village well, to bring home water for cooking and drinking. Little girls were expected to help the mother with all sorts of chores in the home, including looking after the even younger babies, of which there has always been an abundant profusion in India.

My life can hardly be described as having been so oppressed in my boyhood. Quite to the contrary we led a sheltered life, filled with the genuine and unstinted love of all our relations and the families of my father's close and intimate friends, of whom there were many. Except for the tragedy of losing our mother at a tender age, we really had nothing else about which one could complain. My father pampered us, provided us with all the comforts that his by-no-means large income could provide, lavished affection upon us, gave us an excellent education, and in all ways saw to it that we never lacked for anything in our lives. As I have said again and again, he was both father and mother to us. He was our guide in all the possible ways of life. He was also a teacher, even though in those days teachers taught fairly well at school, and except for home work — that bug bear of growing children everywhere in the world — not much was needed at home by way of parental instruction. And a friend he most certainly was. While he was a stern disciplinarian, and could mete out painful punishment when the occasion demanded it, nevertheless he was the best friend I ever had throughout my life.

I do not think we would have amounted to much in life had we not had him as our father. There were certainly many occasions when we were very resentful of his actions. Do children exist anywhere in this world who have never even once felt resentment against their parents? I do not think such a thing is possible, or has ever been possible. I have seen from the experience of my later life that, especially in the Occidental world, rebellion against parental authority, and hatred for the parents, is something so deep that it is frightening. It is my experience that such a strong emotion of hatred for parents has gone very deep into the psyche, and is carried into adult life, often up to the very end. It has caused psychological havoc in innumerable persons that I have come across. Thank heavens that this phenomenon is perhaps almost totally lacking in this country and in this culture. The early cultural and behavioural training that a child receives has a great deal to do with this happy circumstance. But the most important is parental love, of which there has always been a super-abundance in Indian life.

From left: Srinivasan, Parthasarathi, and Kothandaraman dressed in school uniforms, Jobalpur - 1937

VI

The Pleasures of School Education

The Pleasures of School Education

My education seems to have commenced only when I was first admitted into a school in Jubbulpore. I am unable to recall any earlier formal schooling. It was in the year 1937 that my brother Kothand and I entered the Christ Church Boys' High School. I was admitted directly into the third standard. In those days the educational system functioned in a quite relaxed manner. There were no admission tests prior to admission. Nor was a transfer certificate from the previous school requested. In any case, since I had no prior schooling, no transfer certificate could have been available. Very logically, I thought, I was admitted into the class appropriate to my age. So there was no hassle, as the Americans would have put it.

The Christ Church Boys' High School was popularly known as CCBHS. The medium of instruction was English, and I am grateful that my father chose that school for us. It was more expensive than the several Hindi medium schools that were available. Nevertheless he chose that school, and to that initial step we owe our comparatively good education — the best that was then available. It represented a monetary sacrifice for my father, but it yielded the best results that he wanted for us. It was an English public school, and the majority of the boys were from the English families. There were many Anglo Indians — that is boys of mixed parentage, one parent being Indian, the other English. As the years rolled by there were more and more Indian boys, but when we joined it there were not so many. As was, and perhaps still is, the custom, we had to have school uniforms and all the regulation attire. We wore khaki half pants and shirts, a green tie, and black shoes and stockings at all times. We also had to wear the variety of hat called the solar topee. The initial expenditure to outfit us was fairly heavy.

The second language was Hindi. Most of the boys inevitably mispronounced it. It was the Hindi of the ruling classes. We had not learnt any Hindi till then, of course. But having lived for some years in Bombay we could speak some Hindi, but it was quite a peculiar Hindi as spoken in Bombay, without any respect for gender or grammar. We knew enough of the language to manage in school, but it was not enough to appear for an examination, for instance. Fortunately we had an excellent, if somewhat disorganized and irregular, Hindi teacher. His name was R.P. Guru. Therefore quite naturally he was addressed as Guruji by one and all. He was an easy going sort of person, and was certainly not the strictest of teachers. I saw him as being rather vague in his methods, and the impression persists that he did not prepare for his classes as he should have done. Perhaps the senior staff could not supervise his lessons because they did not themselves know enough Hindi to be able to criticize his work.

Among the Indian boys there was a general feeling that Guruji tended to favour the English boys, and was unfair and discriminatory in marking the answer papers. But he was a friendly person all the same, and quite easy to get along with. Very many years after I had passed out of that school, as a matter of fact some thirty years after that, I had an opportunity to visit Jubbulpore again. I went to the school and, hearing that Guruji was still there, I sent in my visiting card — for I was by then a senior executive in a leading firm. Within minutes he came out of class to meet me, and I felt honoured indeed for such an affectionate reception. I was doubtful whether he remembered me, and I told him so. My visiting card was in the name of P. Rajagopalachari, whereas in school I had always been known as P.R. Chari. He smiled affectionately, and said, "How can I ever forget one of the best students that has ever passed through this school? I knew it was Parthasarathi as soon as I received your card. I have given the boys a holiday, hoping that you will be free to have a cup of tea with this old fellow, and perhaps to accompany me home."

I was moved that he still remembered me, and felt ashamed for all the misgivings that we had harboured about him. Anyway, all that was in the past. I had been waiting for him in the Head Master's room, a place which we generally shunned when I had been a student there. A call from the Head Master to his office generally meant trouble. The minimum to be expected out of a visit to him was a stern chastisement, the maximum punishment for serious misbehaviour being a stroke or two with the cane that was still hanging behind the Head Master's chair! But gone was the apprehension of those days, and I actually sat with a great deal of nonchalance, one leg crossed over the other, because the peon, seeing me drive into the school in a car, had been very impressed and taken me direct to the Head Master's room!

During my days there as a student, the room used to appear to be quite forbidding, but now it seemed to be a rather ill maintained and musty room, and looked very small indeed. Guruji gave me a cup of very sugary tea, and then suggested that I take a walk around the school. I accompanied him on a 'grand tour' of the school. It appeared so ridiculously small — whereas it used to look so truly enormous! Even the playgrounds looked so tiny, I just couldn't believe that I was looking at the same place. It is really amazing how things seem to contract as we grow older and older. Time seems to have the same effect upon us as the cake that Alice ate in her Wonderland. Do we grow larger, or do things grow smaller? I wonder whether any one can give a satisfactory answer to this question.

To many this question might very well seem childish — and it was perhaps in a retrospective mood that I asked myself this question. I was seeing the whole thing in two different time frames, and that is always a confusing thing to do. This whole problem of the size of things seems to me to be a matter of scale — I really don't know how to put my ideas into words. But those who have seen the same thing after a lapse of several decades must surely have felt the wonder and the fascination of the time-space distortion that I am talking about, and will perhaps understand what I am trying to say here. On the one hand it appears to be extremely childish. On the other there are some vague intrusions — I have no better expression for it than intrusions — from the subconscious which seems to say, "Try to figure out for yourself what is happening, or has really happened." The intimations are there, but alas! there is no answer, either intellectual or intuitive.

I made the asinine mistake of thinking that things appeared smaller because I had grown bigger — assuming it to be merely a physical phenomenon. But then why didn't my father appear smaller? No answer! The answer could be that it is all a matter of psychological growth, and perhaps that is a large part of the answer. But when one thinks of the fact that some persons seem to grow larger and larger, while others seem to do the opposite, then there is now a new sort of confusion. Whatever it may be, the whole place looked as if it had contracted uniformly. And that was rather tragic when I remembered the impact that it had upon me in my student days. The toilets were at one corner of the playgrounds, and when one was in a hurry, the distance from the classrooms to the toilets seemed to be an enormous one. If one waited too long to ask for permission to leave the classroom, it could lead to embarrassing consequences! But now it all looked so shrunken that it was almost an embarrass-

The Pleasures of School Education

ment to admit to oneself that one had really been a student there. And even Guruji looked so small!

Anyway it was my old school, and I was an 'old boy', and therefore I dutifully went round the whole place, but I suspect that Guruji could sense my disappointment, for he began to justify the fact that the school had not been enlarged, and so on. I asked him about the other teachers from my time, and it made me sad when he told me that none of them were there. I shouldn't have expected anything different, of course. I realised that even the fact that Guruji was still there was a matter of good fortune, but still I couldn't get over the disappointment.

When I had entered the school for the very first time, way back in 1937, there had been a great deal of confusion. For one thing, even though we could speak English quite well, we had to get used to the Britisher's way of saying and pronouncing things. It was a matter of correcting the conversational part of the language. Then there was the problem of the slang used, the cuss words, and the outright vulgarity on the playground during the games periods, and especially after school hours. We had not yet been introduced to the peculiarly pungent vocabulary of the British brand of English — and therefore the free use of four letter words — even in class — was shocking. Even more shocking was the free and repeated use of such words on the football field by the priest of our church — for the school had its own Protestant church. He was part of the faculty, being the sports master after school, while during hours he taught us Geography. On Sundays he delivered his sermons from the pulpit in a very sonorous voice, but in class he was free with such salacious language, and would throw the duster, which he kept ever ready in his right hand, with commendable aim at the boy who couldn't answer his question! Guruji informed me during our walk that he had committed suicide following a love affair with a student from the Christ Church Girls' High School just across the road.

I remember that one English boy, a classmate of Kothandu's, used to visit us fairly frequently. All of a sudden he stopped coming, because our cook Sundaram did not like him. One morning while all three of us were working in the garden with our father, turning over the soil under some bushes of Jasmine, my father asked us, "Why doesn't your friend Pound come here any more?" And instantly Seena answered, "Because if he comes here Sundaram will .... him!" Kothandu and I were shocked at the use of the word by Seena, but Appa, with his usual tact, just said, "Where did you pick up that word, Seena? It is a vulgar word and you should never use it again." Appa had that ability to turn a social disaster into a lesson! But that was the language used at school because it was thought to be the thing to do, and made one feel very manly. I was certain that many of the boys who used those words did not know their meaning, for then they wouldn't have used them at all. We ourselves owe our knowledge of the meaning of those words to the dubious education into those mysteries we received from an uncle of ours many years later.

Generally the teachers were quite concerned that we should all learn to behave and to speak like the gentlemen that we were assumed to be. The curriculum was designed for that. But then the Britishers of those days were mostly army officers, and the language that they used was generally of the coarser variety. Some of our teachers took real pains to make us learn the English language well. There was Mr. David Beatson who was our English teacher. He had one leg shorter than the other, and therefore walked with a marked limp. He was also the warden of the hostel, and had an enormous Alsatian that was allowed to run around everywhere without any restraint. He was always finding an opportunity to teach

The Pleasures of School Education

us. I remember one occasion when one of the boys stood up in class to ask for permission to go out. Mr. Beatson asked, "Yes, what do you want?" The boy said, "Can I go to the bathroom please?" The answer from Mr. Beatson was, "Yes. Of course you can." The boy had reached the door of the classroom when Mr. Beatson stopped him and asked him, "Boy, where are you going?" The boy answered, "Sir, you said I can go to the bathroom." Mr. Beatson answered back, "Of course you can go. God has given you two legs, and you can walk. But you **may** not." In such unobtrusive ways he taught us the importance of using the most appropriate word so that language became something elegant. Mr. Beatson had 'passed on' as Guruji delicately put it.

Our school had the distinction of having a science laboratory! Only a few schools had one in those days, this facility being restricted mostly to the English medium schools. There were no separate labs for physics and chemistry — it was all one. This was a very great advantage that the students of CCBHS enjoyed, and the difference in the final product was therefore very considerable. We were taught science by one Mr. P.N. Verma, a short and thin person, with a slight stoop and an aquiline nose which resembled the beak of a parrot. The boys promptly dubbed him *poppat* which is the Hindi name for a parrot! And he was always referred to by this name. I have seen some of the more rebellious boys calling out "*Poppat, Poppat,*" even in class when his back was turned to the students. Such silly misbehaviour was rampant in the class of some of the teachers who were not quite popular with the students. Mr. Verma did not rate very high for popularity since he had his own favourites, and gave them high marks. He too was partial to the English boys, and in his case the allegation was true — it was too blatant for anyone to mistake it.

Down Memory Lane

In our school each class had its own classroom, and the students did not have to move out of their class. The teachers would go from class to class to teach. There were nine classrooms, one for each of the standards, as the classes were called. The first and second standards had their classrooms in a small building across the street. All the others were housed in the main building, together with an assembly hall for prayers and so forth. The science classes alone were held in a separate classroom adjoining the laboratory, and so Mr. Verma enjoyed a rather dubious dignity from his isolation.

A small incident made me dislike Mr. Verma very much indeed. One day we were talking in front of his classroom about something, I don't remember what. It concerned the expression of opinions, and I said there had been unanimous opinion on it. He asked me how unanimous was spelt, and I spelt it out for him. He became quite angry, and shouted at me, saying, "You are ignorant. Don't use words which you cannot even spell." I quietly asked him what was the correct spelling, and he spelt it out for me — A N O N Y M O U S! I was amazed, and I made the mistake of telling him that he was wrong, and that anonymous and unanimous were two separate and distinct words having totally different meanings. He was annoyed, of course, and berated me in front of a bunch of boys for ignorance coupled with impertinence. He gave me some extra homework 'as a small punishment for your impertinence' as he put it.

I was naturally furious with him, because I knew that I was right. I looked the two words up in the pocket Oxford dictionary I had at home, and was elated to find confirmation that I had been right. And then I made the second, and in his eyes unforgivable, mistake of taking the dictionary with me to school the next morning and showing him the two words in the dictionary. It was in class with all the thirty-two boys present, and of course they all knew what had happened. There was a demand from the boys for clarification, and the dictionary was surreptitiously passed around from hand to hand under the desks. Mr. Verma pretended not to see anything. When the dictionary had made its rounds, there was a loud bray from one of the boys at the rear, and a cry of "*Poppat, Poppat,* can you speak English?" The whole thing was really ridiculous, and Mr. Verma could easily have passed the whole incident off as a joke, but he never forgave me for it, and took up a vendetta against me, giving me as low marks as he dared. But I was perhaps too good in his subject for him to do me any real harm — the only damage being a sense of hurt which still smoulders in me. I have never been able to forget this silly little episode from my Christ Church days.

The strange thing is that after many years he again entered our lives. We were back in Bombay, and it must have been the year 1947 or 1948, when Appa ran into him accidentally at a railway station, and brought him home. He of course recognized us, for we had spent some six or seven years together at the CCBHS. If I remember correctly I had just graduated out of the Benares Hindu University, and had acquired the social stature appropriate to that distinction. To be a graduate was a very respectable thing in those days. Mr. Verma appeared suitably impressed, and that annoyed me quite a bit for I felt as if he thought that I was quite incapable of acquiring a college degree. I tried to snub him but he was too wily a person to fall into such traps set by unskilled hands such as mine. Anyway, he reentered our lives and played quite a part in it later. It was strange that of all the teachers of those days it was Mr. Verma who came into our lives again!

Life at CCBHS was an enjoyable thing indeed. We enjoyed the prestige of being in the best school in perhaps the whole of the Central Provinces, as the state was then called. The school was located at a distance of about a mile and a half from our home. We often had to walk the distance, and on the way we passed through a colony of smaller Railway quarters. In those days all the quarters had only dry sanitation. Water closets were still more or less unknown in India. The bathrooms were provided with commodes, which were only stools which had holes in them, with a pot let into the hole which acted as the receptacle for human wastes. One sat upon the commode when necessary. These pots were periodically removed by the sanitary workers to be cleaned out, washed and replaced in the bathroom. This work was the lot of a particular class of persons. We used to meet a frail old man whose job this demeaning work was. His face had become permanently set into a grimace of disgust from trying to avoid the stink from the pots which he had to clean. He generally had one pot in each of his hands, held gingerly away from his body.

He was obviously a devotee of Lord Rama, as we discovered. Simultaneously he had a hatred for Lord Krishna. We used to tease him by shouting out, "*Radhe Shyam*!" and he would come at us like a bull charging its enemy. As he neared us, we would shout out, "*Sita Ram*!", and he would abruptly stop, setting the stinking contents of the pots in his hands splashing around dangerously, and putting them on the ground, he would break out into a beatific smile and say, "*Sita Ram Kaho! Sita Ram kaho*!" which meant "Yes, say Sita Ram." As he walked a few steps away from us, we would shout out again, "*Radhe Shyam! Radhe Shyam*!" And again he would lunge at us in fierce attack, until we stopped him with a cry of "*Sita Ram, Sita Ram.*" This game could go on for hours if one had wanted it to. The poor fellow never seemed to realise that he was being baited by boys perhaps fifty years younger than he was. He also never gave up! Such is religious bigotry, and the depths to which it can sink into one's psyche.

From left: Srinivasan, Parthasarathi, and Kothandaraman dressed in scout uniforms - 1938

From left: Parthasarathi, Kothandaraman, and Srinivasan with dog, Jackie - 1939

The Pleasures of School Education

I remember a story I heard from my Master many years later. It concerned bigotry of this very same sort. According to my Master it was from the *Ramayana* or the *Mahabharata*. According to the story the period of Lord Rama's avatar had come to an end. *Kali Yuga* had come, and it was the time of Lord Krishna. There was a great devotee of Lord Rama, a bear by the name of Jambuvan, who was still alive, living in a cave in the mountains. Lord Krishna set out to meet the devotees of the Lord, and came upon Jambuvan sitting in his cave, with his head bowed in prayer reciting the divine name "Rama, Rama!" When Lord Krishna entered the cave, Jambuvan perceived his shadow, looked up and saw him at the cave entrance. He was a bigot. He had no love for Lord Krishna, and thought of him as a profligate, a magician, a trickster, and so on. He told Lord Krishna, "Please leave me alone. I have no desire for your company." Lord Krishna smiled his enchanting smile, and requested Jambuvan to spare him a few moments, but Jambuvan only repeated his demand to be left alone. Suddenly he heard the beloved voice of Lord Rama saying, "Look at me Jambuvan." He looked up and saw his beloved Lord, and fell at his feet in adoration. Again he heard the voice, which now said, "Look at me now!" And there he saw Lord Krishna again. He was disgusted and dismayed, and moved away from the feet of the Lord. Then once again he heard Lord Rama's voice ordering him to look up and see him, and there he stood, resplendent and glorious to behold. As Jambuvan stooped to touch the divine feet of his Lord, the form changed again and behold, there was Lord Krishna once again. Jambuvan was confused and prayed for clarification. Then Lord Rama's form appeared for the last time before him and said, "I am the same. I was Rama, and now my form has changed and I am in the form that you detest. Know that the divine is ever the same, though the name and the form can change at His will. Don't make the serious mistake of differentiating between us because of your bigotry." Then Jambuvan fell at His feet, begged for His mercy, and prayed for liberation. It is tragic that such bigotry has never ended, being passed on from generation to generation.

My name underwent a rather drastic change at school. I had been named Parthasarathi and, as is usual in South India, the father's name was written before the given name. Thus my name was R. Parthasarathi. This was the name under which I was admitted into the CCBHS. I bought a set of class textbooks, and they were all marked with my name on the front page. Some months after I had joined the school, I was called to the clerk's office, where I was asked what the 'R' in my name stood for. I explained that it stood for Rajagopalachari, my father's name. He asked for my surname. I explained that in South India we had no surname, but used the father's name as our first name. He re-entered my name as Parthasarathi R. which, for some clerical reason, was later changed to Parthasarathi Rajagopalachari. This was subsequently contracted to P. Rajagopalachari — and then, mercifully for the last time, it was contracted to P.R. Chari. I have been known by this name throughout my life. A few individuals have always affectionately addressed me as Parthasarathi, my given name. At home I have always been called Pachu.

This change of name has resulted in several humiliating situations which served to expose my timidity. My textbooks were taken by my class master for checking. He forgot to return them, and being nervous of approaching him for their return, I bought a new set of books. Some months later the teacher discovered the books in his *almirah*. He saw the name R. Parthasarathi on the fly leaf, and so asked me whether they were mine. Instead of answering that this was so, I timidly said they were not mine! He said,"That is funny! I thought that you

The Pleasures of School Education

were named Parthasarathi. But if you say these books are not yours then that's that!" I felt extremely foolish, but it was too late to retract, and to claim the books as mine. Many years later I discovered the books still lying there in his *almirah*, and felt quite ashamed for my foolish timidity which, sad to say, was still very much part of my character. It is sad to have to record that there was virtually no change in me till I, some three decades later, came to the holy feet of my spiritual Master. But that is another story!

The school years passed swiftly, though during those years time seemed to almost stand still. Days passed, seemingly in interminable succession. The only relieving feature was our holidays, for which all of us waited with the greatest longing and impatience. There were welcome occasions when the heavy rains made it impossible to go to school — and that was great fun. Anything which seems to come unannounced as a sort of gift is always more welcome than the routine gifts. Jubbulpore had extremes of climate, exceedingly hot in the summer, very cold in the winter, and with very heavy rains during the monsoon. During the peak summer months we had school from 7:30 A.M. till 10:30 A.M. or thereabouts — so that virtually it was no more than half a day of schooling. Nevertheless all the 'portions' — as the prescribed material for study during a school year was called — were covered during those days. But human nature being what it has always been, the very bountiful nature of those apparent holidays became something of a bore, for we could not stir out in the burning heat, nor would friends come to us to play. So all that we could do was to sweat it out at home, lacking the energy and the inclination even to complete our homework.

The monsoon season was not only difficult but expensive too, for often my father had to call for a *tonga* — a horse drawn vehicle — for us to go to school in. Needless to say we all got very wet during the drive, and we often had to return home because the school had been closed on account of the enormous downpour. Jubbulpore had between sixty and eighty inches of rain each year! Hectic and wonderful days, those were, full of fun. One of our fun-filled ways of passing the time was to make small boats out of half shells of walnuts, put a blob of candle wax at the bottom, set a match stick vertically in the wax as a mast for a sail made of a small triangle of paper, and sail those boats by putting them upon the surface of the water in our tank, and then blowing them about. Often we brothers would make several of them and indulge in what we imagined were the great sea battles of the British navy!

Our leisure hours were largely restricted to the home because our father did not approve of our going out too much. We had a large playground just outside our gate which we used to play cricket and hockey upon, though we rarely had more than half a dozen boys to play with. We were a timid lot, and adventure was something not in our spirit. In fact adventure is almost totally absent from the Indian mind. It is actually shunned as something risky, and therefore to be avoided assiduously. All adventurous undertakings were forbidden by the elders. India has such an enormously long coast line, and so many rivers too, but few are the ones who can swim, or have ever even got into the sea. The only occasions appear to be the holy days when a dip is prescribed by the scriptures, and on those sad and dreary days when the ashes of the dead have to be immersed in the waters of a river or the sea.

I remember going from Haltugaon to Dhubri, or somewhere else in Assam, by car with my uncle Bhadran. We were driven by my uncle's driver Rhompong. On the way we stopped on the bank of the mighty river, the Brahmaputra, which was extremely wide at that spot — the other bank not being visible to our naked eyes. Chitya told us that it was

The Pleasures of School Education

perhaps three miles wide there! Rhompong wanted to have a bath in the river — *snan*, as he said in his broken Hindi — and my uncle agreed to stop the car there for a few minutes. Rhompong got out of the car, walked sedately to the river a few yards away from us, muttered a few words of prayer, took off his cap and sprinkled a few drops of water upon his head, solemnly replaced his cap with a satisfied look upon his face, and got back into the car. We asked him why he hadn't bathed in the river. He replied with a puzzled look, "It is over. Did you not see me bathing?"

The Himalayas to the north should have called to the adventurous spirit of the Indians, but I have rarely heard of anyone going to climb them. The Himalayas have no doubt beckoned to the spirit of the Hindu mystic throughout the aeons of Indian history, and many thousands have responded to this most ancient and undeniable inner call, but they responded out of an inner yearning for the quest of life, and not because of any urge for adventure. For the merely mundane pleasure of climbing them the great and mighty Himalayas seemed to have had very little appeal until recent times. The Indian psyche has shunned all such temptations of the flesh for the merely mundane and worldly achievements.

Children, and even grown up boys and girls, were generally not allowed to climb trees or to go out in the dark. It is symptomatic of this lack of spirit for adventure that when we have coconut trees in our gardens, and the ripe nuts have to be plucked, professionals are employed to do the job! As a matter of fact, there is very little that the average Indian can do by himself if it involves physical effort beyond stretching his limbs. Even going for walks are thought of as something very funny, and somehow foreign! Of course things have changed a great deal since then, and now we have all sorts of games and sports involving strenuous effort, and even potentially dangerous activities such as mountaineering. Today, as I write this in 1992, things have changed so dramatically that girls are now to be seen out-performing boys in many fields! This is a very welcome change indeed, and deserves to be supported wholeheartedly by society.

At school we had necessarily to participate in some, at least, of the sports and games, which I, for one, did quite reluctantly. Scouting was the only activity that I enjoyed, and in which I willingly took part. But I must confess that I was never able to get over my cursed shyness and stretch myself to my full capacity in any endeavour. I almost always ended up as a mediocre fellow in all things — except in my studies. I became something of a bookworm for lack of anything else to do. I was unable to really participate in any vigorous physical activity because of my poor eyesight which I have inherited from my dear mother, and therefore I was drawn to the reading habit. Thus I was quite at home with books from quite a young age. I enjoyed reading, and this habit has kept me company throughout my life. It has been a blessing for one not inclined to socialization, or to activities involving the need to go out of the home. The early acquisition of this very desirable habit — a pleasure in my case — helped me enormously with my studies.

I managed to stay within the top three positions in my class. I never slipped below third rank while at CCBHS. In fact I quite often managed to reach the top rank. Otherwise I generally succeeded in retaining the second place. The boy generally acknowledged to be the best in my class was Samuel Brown, generally addressed as Sammy. Melville Champ and I gave him a run for his money, and kept him busy in his efforts to retain the top position in our class. We three developed an easy and intimate friendship, though there was naturally some friendly rivalry between us. We spent a great deal of time

The Pleasures of School Education

together though I don't remember that we visited each other's homes except on very special occasions. That sort of mixing was not a general thing, especially where English boys were concerned. Relationships with the Anglo Indian boys could be both easier, and often more difficult too. The social life of those times tended to be inhibiting, and did not provide for free mixing, which was largely confined to the school environment.

Champ and Brown were my best friends, followed closely by a Sikh boy named Sarbjit Singh. Sarbjit was a giant of a boy, quite double the size of the smallest boy in our class — a blundering giant of quite an enormous strength, but gentle as a child. None of these three boys were keen sportsmen, but they all managed to do reasonably well in whatever they participated. I was the only one almost totally without capacity in games and sports — much to my chagrin. The sportsman of the school was a boy one year my junior. He was a Malayalee boy called Kenneth Currion, and he took all the first prizes in the 100 yards, the 220 and the 440 yards running races. He was also the permanent champion in high jump, and in the pole vault events. I couldn't run for my life, though I did manage a rather weak performance in high jumping! I do not remember that my brothers were much better than I was, but that is perhaps only the self-defensive aspect of my memory!

It is strange that after I passed out of CCBHS, after passing the Senior Cambridge examination in December 1943, I have had no contact with anyone from my school days. A close friend was Pratap Singh who, I discovered, was a medical practitioner in Nagpur, but the only letter I wrote to him many years later did not evoke any response from him. Much is made of friendship, but I suppose that this is the experience shared by many, or perhaps by even most, that as we move on in life, old friendships seem to drop off without our even noticing them, though there may be some anguish at the moment of parting. Promises are made to each other, but alas! — only to be broken. When I read Plato's dialogue titled *Lysis*, I was struck with all that he had to say, but my only conclusion, after a lifetime of experience which has already measured sixty-five years, is that friendship is really a great thing, but only as long as friends are physically together. Few are the friendships that endure the test of separation over long spans of time. They are so rare that I can mention only one such friend, but that must come in its proper place, later on in this narrative.

We managed to learn pretty much all that was offered to us at school. My father's supplementary efforts added greatly to our growing store, often exceeding the requirements of the school curriculum. Kothand and I generally managed to be on the right side of our teachers, but Seena often ran into trouble both at school, as well as at home with my father, for Seena was very active and volatile, and totally fearless. He easily got into scrapes, and earned a name as a rambunctious fellow at school. Some teachers were quite uncomfortable with him. He often got into hot waters with my father, and occasionally had to suffer corporeal punishment on occasion. But nothing curbed his spirit of mischief and adventure, and he sailed through life with a mischievous grin always on his face. He was an average student, and never made the mistake of developing an ambition for scholastic honours, but was content to pass on from class to class, treating education as some sort of necessary and unavoidable evil, which one learnt to enjoy if one possibly could.

At school there were a few highlights of the year, such as the annual sports events restricted to the inter-house sports meets which created a lot of enthusiasm, and the demand for special practise sessions as a convenient way of reducing the class hours. Then there were inter-school events, often hotly contested, capable of generating considerable heat during the meetings. The finale was of course the annual events between CCBHS and the Saintoos. This was a climax, much looked forward to, since every boy in the school wanted to gain a victory over them. The boxing events were the culmination — an often hectic and bloody evening altogether! The morning after the boxing events our boys generally came with bloody noses and black eyes, but with wide grins all over their young faces, happy that they had roughed it out, victory and defeat having been forgotten in the fray for survival, as it often appeared a matter of life and death to them. Life was a good thing, and enjoyable if one but cared to enjoy it as it comes from minute to minute, without worrying about how to change it and to try to sculpt it according to one's tastes or inclinations.

During lunch break we would eat our sandwiches in a small area adjacent to the school office, secluded from curious eyes by a tall hedge around it. We generally ate standing up, as we were eager to finish and to run off to play. One day our Head Master, Mr. M. Doutre, saw us, and admonished us saying that one should always sit and eat! "Eating while standing is not healthy," he told us. This is supported by the Hindu tradition, as I later discovered. Of course, at home one always ate sitting on the floor. We had no dining tables and other such modern conveniences in those days.

When I became a senior boy after passing out of the VIth standard, I got into the habit of going to a sweetmeat seller just outside our school gate, and buying one anna's worth of the delectable sweet he sold. This was made out of roasted groundnuts embedded in sugar or jaggery, and was called *chikki*. This sells today at perhaps one hundred rupees per kilo, but in those days it was hardly a rupee per kilo — and we generally bought a small square piece weighing perhaps five grams, for one anna, which is the equivalent of six paise in modern coinage. None could indulge in this dessert everyday of course. Few could afford it. Our pocket money — a purely English indulgence, as my father called it! — was only four annas per month! Unfortunately for me, the sweetmeat seller very cannily offered us credit. I began to buy on credit when I had run through my pocket money. One month end I was horrified to find that I owed the old fellow all of half a rupee! I had nightmares for several days when I thought of the old fellow following me home to ask my father for the money. I then did a shameful thing. I picked the pocket of my father for a coin, and what came out was a half rupee coin, which saved the situation, at least for that month. Did it end there? I am ashamed to say that it did not. I had to resort to infrequent dips into my father's coat pockets, and one day when I realised that I owed the old seller a whole rupee, I stopped eating his sweetmeat.

It is funny how easy it is to acquire such shameful habits when we are young. I have no doubt that Appa knew of the occasional raids upon his own meagre resources, but he never spoke about it — and thus I avoided the excruciating disgrace of being found out. But there is one's conscience, after all, and one has to be able to look it squarely in the face, and for that one needs, above all else, a clean heart. I had to wait some twenty-five years before I received spiritual instruction from my Master, but these foundations for a moral existence were laid early in life, and therefore I am happy that my moral education began in a healthy way with petty thievery, which I was able to soon overcome. I am grateful to my father for providing me this opportunity for, had he ever hauled me up, I might have rebelled against his authority, and gone on doing the very same thing.

This was not the only temptation. There was another fellow who had a wooden trolley made of planks mounted on bicycle wheels — called *thela* in Hindi — with a carpenters' plane mounted upon it. His raw materials were several bottles of coloured syrup — sugar boiled in water, and coloured variously — and a huge block of ice. He sold what he called ice fruit. This was made by breaking off a suitable piece of ice, and planing it on the plane, collecting the ice shavings with his left hand held under the plane. Thereafter he would put a thin stick some six inches long through the powdery mass of ice, and then mould it into a tight ball around the stick. The final, and very showy, action was to spray some syrup upon it. It was now ready to be offered to the customer with a flourish! One bought it, and sucked at the syrup as long as it was there. Then if one was in good standing with that fellow, one could approach him, albeit timidly and with some trepidation, for a further spraying of his syrup. When that was finished, one ate the ice. This delicacy — for it was delicious especially in the hot summer days, though it tended to cause one to purge — cost but a mere anna. But this was not a round-the-year delicacy unlike the *chikki*, and so did not feature in my life as a major temptation!

There was yet another delicacy of which the boys bought often, from yet another vendor. It was dried mango pulp, named *aamsat* in Hindi. It was possible to make it only during the mango season, from say May to the end of July, or thereabouts. A woven bamboo mat was spread out in the hot sun, and mango juice poured over it to a thickness of about a quarter of an inch. It dried quite rapidly under the burning summer sun of central India, where it was quite normal for the temperature to go up to 110° F, and occasionally to exceed it too! As the juice dried, more juice was poured upon the dry layer, and this went on until the dried slab was about half an inch or more thick. It was allowed to dry for a few days more to get it quite dry, and then cut up into salable slabs of approximately six inches by four inches. The slabs had the cross woven pattern of the mat on one side, of course.

Those were the good old days before packaging technology had invaded the scene, and so the slabs were sold in their naked condition, as it were. Such a slab sold for a mere quarter of a rupee. The slabs varied in colour from a golden honey to an almost dark black. The light coloured ones were also soft to the touch, and quite sticky, being made of the more exotic varieties of the fruit. They were usually marginally more expensive. The black slabs were dry and leathery to the touch, and not sticky. They were made from the popular local variety called the *langda*.

Life was full of sweets, sunshine and fun, but there was always the haunting loneliness during the long nights, and all the time when my father was away on tour. This could not be avoided, and so I lived a life which swung from one extreme of joy and happiness to the other extreme of loneliness, fear and sorrow. I think that it was during this period that I developed the knack of sleeping deeply however much I may have been troubled in mind or body. This was also the time when I trained myself to draw some solace, some sense of comfort, from the barking of a dog, or from the croaking of the frogs and toads in our garden tank. However frightened or lonely I might be, a dog's bark set me right, at least temporarily, until I fell asleep. The croaking of a frog seemed to say, "All is well, dear one. Sleep well. We are here to keep you company." This trick works even now, and when I am lonely, a streak or flash of lightning or the croaking of a frog gladdens my heart in some mysterious manner — un-understandable but welcome.

It is amusing to recall the buried memory of a nearby flour mill which worked almost all day throughout the year. It made a very agreeable sound, and kept going plup, plup, plup all the delightful day long. There were days when I was alone at home, perhaps because I was ill and did not go to school. Lying in bed with a favourite book, this plup-plup-plup kept me com-

The Pleasures of School Education

pany, and made life acceptable. Even now when I hear a similar sound, there is a feeling of nostalgia, and the longing for those days of innocence which, alas, will never return. Of such compensations is life really made. The children of India are by and large from poor families. They are brought up in simple and down-to-earth fashion. Toys were largely unknown in those days. The children therefore learnt to do with what was available around them, and we all picked up these tricks of adaptation, and that ability, that habit, has stood us well in our adult life too.

Education is certainly not restricted to, or available only in, schools and colleges. This has been my experience, growing into the strongest possible conviction, for I learnt only a few facts about a certain number of subjects at school. It was no doubt essential, but life itself taught me how to live — whether successfully and purposefully or not, only the end of my life will testify to with certainty. Life is the great school, and schools and colleges and academies are but the school rooms of that greatest of all schools — life itself! If one is able to realise this early in life, then one's life will be a life of continuing education, free of the ideas of success and failure, joy and sorrow, happiness and unhappiness, and all such dualities of existence to which human life is subject.

As long as one is grounded between these dualities, life can only be miserable, and a living torment. But if we allow life to be a school through which each and every one of us must pass, so that the lessons that life has to teach are absorbed, then that life becomes a purposeful life, one oriented towards the goal of evolution, and such a one becomes Nature's Child. Nature lavishes her gifts upon such a person, and that brings about the culminating miracle of the truly educational process — a Prodigy of Nature!

From left: Srinivasan, R. Kasturi, Parthasarathi, Kothandaraman
1945

VII

Growing Up in Calcutta

Growing Up in Calcutta

With our move to Calcutta I entered the adult stage, because by then I was well into my sixteenth year. I had passed out very creditably from the Christ Church Boys' High School at Jubbulpore, getting a 1st division, with an 'A' in all the subjects. The school year in Jubbulpore ended in December, and as soon as I arrived in Calcutta I went to the St. Xavier's college for admission which I easily secured, being admitted into the first year Intermediate Science class. Here we made one mistake which cost me one whole academic year! We did not know that a Senior Cambridge student could have started his college classes in the first year course in December itself, going on to the second year in July. We waited till June to enter the first year class, and this of course cost me that one year. It was too late to do anything about it.

My college life went on quite smoothly without much excitement. I missed the genuine intimacy and the easy familiarity of school relationships. In college the life of the student was more seriously structured, and there was not much time, either, to play with others. There also developed the idea of a rather rigid hierarchy which did not permit free friendships as had been possible among school boys, to which I had been accustomed in Jubbulpore. And further, the need to commute from the Lake area to Park Street daily took up so much time that there was really no time for friendship. I also missed the free and frank relationship between the teacher and the student that had been prevalent at school. In college there was a formality that forbade such freedom, and we saw the teachers — lecturers as they were called — only in class. It is significant that I cannot remember the name of even one of my lecturers from my college days at Calcutta!

Our classroom resembled a small stadium, with tier upon tier of seats, and could seat around 180 students at a time. The benches in our classroom were long ones, and could seat ten boys per bench. There were three such benches in each row of seats. I don't really remember how many we were in class, but I believe it was in excess of eighty or ninety boys and girls — for here it was co-educational. There were still many colleges which were colleges exclusively for women, but more and more of the higher educational institutions were becoming co-educational in nature. Even today there are women's colleges all over India — and they are filled to capacity.

The only lecturer I can remember is the one who taught us physics. As soon as he entered the classroom, he would go through the rolls to mark those absent. He went row by row, calling out, "1 to 10", and the first boy in that row would have to call out the number of the students absent. Then he would say, "11 to 20" and the first boy present in that row had to call out the numbers of those absent in his row, and so on up to the last row. There was always some tension before he arrived, for one did not know who would be the first boy in each row — for often boys would slip in just before the roll call. This lecturer did not know the name of even one student, and even when we met outside class he would address the student only by his roll number! A very peculiar person indeed.

He had a squint, and therefore always appeared to be looking upwards. This was a most disconcerting habit, for no one knew where he was really looking, as we found out very soon! When he appeared to be looking to his right towards the ceiling, he would most unexpectedly call out to a boy on his far left in the very first row to ask him a difficult question.

Naturally the boy had been inattentive, thinking that the lecturer's attention was not on him — and would flounder for a reply. This particular lecturer used to race through his lectures, never stopping to ask whether the boys had understood what he was teaching. He was supposed to have been a brilliant student, and went through his class like wildfire, using advanced equations, without taking the trouble to lay a foundation for the boys not so strong in mathematics, among whom I was of course one.

I have found this to be a general feature with all brilliant lecturers. Those who had themselves plodded through their own education seemed to remember that there were weaker boys to be taught too. They were kinder in that they laid a very firm, proper and easy-to-follow foundation to their subjects as they went on, so that even the dullest boy could follow them. I wonder when school and college authorities will realise that the most brilliant are not necessarily the best teachers, and arrange to recruit faculty members more carefully to ascertain who can really teach well. This must be done if education is to be truly of benefit to the least endowed, as well as to the well endowed boys.

Under the present system, schools and colleges vie with each other to get the cream of the students as well as the best available talent to man their faculties. I consider this system dreadfully wasteful of human potential, because the not so well endowed are thrown out upon the refuse heap of humanity, as it were. This has serious repercussions, for it breeds, and has already bred, a new caste-ism, separating human beings into classes, and adding steadily to the lower sections of the population. There is no advantage in having an elite class if more and more of the population are to be relegated to a section which cannot even aspire to, or afford, education and therefore end up as poorer and poorer people. Today education — good education — has become dreadfully expensive, and the whole business of education has assumed the nature of a club for the elite. So-called democratic governments pretend that they provide the poorer classes with education — and offer free education too — but that facility to the poor is in a deplorable state, and deserves to be scrapped.

It would appear that there is no way of scrapping the elite institutions which cater only to the brilliant, nor would scrapping them be desirable. At the same time society must somehow ensure that all sections of the population benefit from social schemes, of which education is no doubt at least as important as health. My growing conviction has been that there should be a different set up altogether, under which the not so intellectually well endowed can be taught in special schools and junior colleges, merging the students all together in higher institutions of learning, so that at the culminating level all are at one level, more or less.

The present system in India by which there are reserved seats for all categories of the population has only served to dilute everything, so that schools and colleges are only churning out batch after batch of mediocre stuff. This is at least one reason — and an important reason in my opinion — for the so-called brain drain. Why should it be a matter of wonder if promising students run away to the USA for higher education? What is India doing for them? The political system of reserved seats in schools and colleges, as well as reserved posts for employment has brought this great country down to such a miserable level that it is now officially declared to be the ninetieth or the ninety-first in the list of countries of this world. A very sad state of affairs indeed — for which the sole responsibility rests with the powers that have governed the destiny of the people of this ancient land.

Usually I would leave home by around 8:00 A.M. to go to college, walk approximately one mile to a bus stop near the lakes, and wait for the right bus to take me to Park street, a distance of about seven miles. Generally it was easy to find a place in the bus when going in the morning, but it was a different story altogether coming back in the evening. Then the buses came overflowing with twice or more the capacity of the bus, persons hanging from every possible hand-hold that was available. It was a real feat to even get on to the bus — rarely ever could one actually get into it! Even to get on to it one had to position oneself with great foresight, wait for the bus, run as it appeared around a curve in the road, out-running all the other aspirants, and jump on to the moving bus — for it never stopped — often holding on for dear life to the outstretched hand of one already in the bus. The buses stopped only when women had to get in or out of the bus, which fact, or need, was intimated to the driver of the bus by a loud shout of *zenana hai* by the conductor — meaning that there was a woman to be attended to! But passengers helped each other all the time, and though there was always the risk that one could fall out of a moving bus, this rarely happened.

The attitude of passengers has always been something very funny to me, especially when travelling by train. Train travel has always been an affair of crowds and dust and discomfort of all sorts, predictable or otherwise. One needed to be very agile, strong, and determined to get into a train as it steamed in to the platform, for there were always huge crowds waiting to get in. Those inside the train would resist the efforts of those trying to get in with considerable vigour and force, but if one was intrepid enough to push one's way in somehow, then he was not only welcomed by the others but he himself became one of the 'insiders' as it were, and immediately started resisting the efforts of those still on the platform who were trying their luck! This rapid change of sides was always something that amazed me.

Many had to be pushed in through the windows, with an equally enthusiastic opposition from inside trying their hardest to keep the intruder out — but once he was in then it was tea-time for all! Of course there was always the odd person who took all this too seriously, and then tempers would flare but, mercifully, only briefly. All this was extremely exciting to watch, but I was always a little nervous about train travel, since I have always lacked both the will and the strength necessary to indulge in such gymnastics. Fortunately for us we were entitled to travel First Class since my father was a Railway officer, and this helped us considerably. In those days first class compartments were generally empty, for paying passengers were few and far between. Also no one ever dared to get into a class for which he had no ticket, which is so common nowadays.

One of the best things that happened to me in Calcutta was the physical training that my father enticed me into. I had been a puny fellow when I left Jubbulpore, weighing perhaps eighty-four pounds, and being just below the five feet mark in height. I remember that on the rather rare occasions when we had a medical examination in school, my chest expansion upon deep inhalation was literally zero! The doctor examining me would charitably mark it as one inch, fearing no doubt that no one would believe him if he turned in a report showing zero inches expansion. I was always the target of the boys mischief, and had my hat knocked off my head and booted around more times than anyone else. It was humiliating, of course, but there was hardly anything I could have done about it.

Knowing all this Appa joined the *Bajrang Vyayamghar* situated about a mile from our house, and took me along to be admitted too. The director of the institute was one Mr. Krishna Kali Banerjee, and I was terribly impressed with his muscular physique, sculptured to resemble one of those marble statues of the Greek gods and goddesses that one sees in museums everywhere. He had the most impressive forearms that I have ever seen — and when he flexed the muscle, one could not put a pin through it. He exhibited this to me the very first time that we met, and that made me determine to build my own body into something resembling his. Ambition indeed! But then without it this adventure would not have lasted at all, for my father left body building after a couple of weeks, his sole purpose having been to get me into it!

I bought the usual paraphernalia necessary, and started buying copies of *Health & Strength*, a monthly magazine which featured lovely glossy pictures of the famous bodies of the world, Mr. Universe title-holders and lesser fry, all with superbly sculptured bodies glistening with well-oiled musculature. This became a passion with me, and thanks to the passionate nature of the approach I developed a decent body, and grew to be five feet eleven inches tall, and achieved a body weight of about 144 lbs, all within one year. The truly unbelievable development was the broadening of the chest, and the perhaps incredible expansion of six inches that became possible. Progress indeed! I was the star pupil of Krishnaka, as he was affectionately called, and for some time I was exhibited by him to new entrants to demonstrate the possibilities the courses offered in his *vyayamshala*, as a gymnasium is called in Hindi. But he spoiled the whole thing, for me, by showing a photograph of myself as I had been when I joined his institute! I started to eat enormously, much to the annoyance of an aunt of mine, who kept making derogatory remarks until one day my father told her off.

It was all great fun, and I have spent many secret minutes admiring my body in front of a mirror behind closed doors. Since full length mirrors were not available in those days — for it was thought extremely indecent to look at one's own body — I had to assume some very funny and awkward postures to see myself, but alas! I was never happy with what I saw. It is a strange thing that I have never been happy with myself in any way. I have always had a dislike of my body. I disliked my mind. In fact I have never had anything in myself that I was able to admire or to even tolerate. This aspect has not changed at all with the passage of the years. One can even say, if it makes any sense to say so, that I was shy of myself. I do not know how else to put this.

There is another funny thing about myself that may be of interest for those interested in analyzing such idiosyncratic phenomena. I have always felt very old — that is, I have always felt that I was a very old man, and this feeling was there even when I was eight or nine years old. I do not of course know the reason for this, but it has ever been so. This has inevitably created an unbridgeable distance between other youngsters and myself, adding to my isolation. I can say that I have had no more than perhaps three or four friends in my life! It has also had the intriguing consequence, in later life, that I have developed friendship with men substantially older than I am. In fact such older persons have been real friends, young friends of my age being few. I suspect that this has been so for the important reason that since I always felt myself to be an old man, it was impossible to be *en rapport* with members of the younger set, the exceptions being certain friends who had attained a degree of maturity that perhaps made them, too, seem old to me!

Anyway, this has been so during the early years, and I have no doubt that it caused my father much worry since I was always hanging around the house with nowhere to go to, and none to meet. This developed in me the habit of going for long walks all by myself, and such walks have become a definite part of my daily existence. I have therefore generally been something of a loner, in contrast to my two younger brothers who were more gregarious by nature. I have no doubt that they enjoyed life among friends, and were happy to do so, whereas I developed into something of a recluse. All this was to change later, due to the influence of a person who was instrumental in changing my life totally — of which more later.

During the years at Calcutta I was in the unfortunate situation of being unable to get on with fellows of my age as well as with persons of older age. In essence I was therefore becoming lonelier and lonelier, withdrawing into myself more and more to such an extent that Appa and Bhadran Chitya became often perturbed, thinking that I was developing into a recluse. Of course their worry must have been that I would become a bit of a misogynist and refuse to marry later. I was never able to mix with girls, and indeed till I was married I had virtually no contact with the fair sex. This was a result of having neither a mother nor sisters at home, thus being compelled to grow up in a totally male environment. Because of my painful shyness I avoided any association with women, becoming totally tongue-tied in their presence. My companion was generally Bakthu, my youngest paternal uncle, who had a special fondness for me, and with whom I used to go for long walks practically every day. He and I got on very well together, and we were the best of friends all along. My father had very little time for us, but with Bakthu and Chitti living with us I had no problem.

It was in Calcutta that the first of Bakthu's two sons, Chakrapani, was born in 1943. He was sixteen years my junior, and I have carried that child around a great deal, for he was dear to all of us. When he was old enough to crawl around, I would put him down on the floor and walk away a few feet from him and wiggle my toes — and he would come at me like a roaring lion cub, and grab my toes with his budding teeth. It was enormous fun having a baby at home to play with, and of course Chakra was petted and spoilt to an enormous extent, but such love does no harm either to the child or to those who adore a child at home. A home without a child in it is like a room without a lamp in it — a dark and dreary place which is fit to be shunned. A couple of years later Ranga, the second child was born, also in Calcutta. We did not have much time with him as by then the family was getting ready to be scattered again, which of course we did not know.

It was war time, and there were occasional air raid sirens, and a general sense of unease prevailed. Rationing was in force, and I had the task of going to the ration shops to buy the weekly rations for the family — rice, sugar and other provisions covered by the rationing rules. I liked this chore because I was given a certain sum of money, and I was allowed a sort of unofficial commission on the total purchase, also pocketing the small change at the end, thus augmenting my monthly pocket money. This caused great annoyance to my aunts, for they would have no doubt liked a little money to spend themselves! The war effort cost India a great deal in terms of human misery as well as in monetary terms. As the war spread, India was dragged into it more and more, and eventually things became quite difficult though India had no direct part to play in the war, being inimical to none. But it was the price extracted for the sin of being a part of the British Empire! Life became more and more expensive, and that was the first dose of substantial inflation that we suffered, from which there was never any recovery.

Life became tougher and tougher, and there was unease and fear everywhere. Families began to be split up as male members of the families were transferred from place to place — essentially in the munitions department. Finally, when the scare of Calcutta being bombed by the Japanese forces came to a critical level, there was mass evacuation, and then it was heart-rending to watch the misery of the women and children at the railway station when they were packed into the available trains, leaving their men folk behind. My family was not spared such separation, though we children were not affected. Only women and young children were sent out of Calcutta, as being members of the vulnerable section of the population. For India and the Indians this whole thing of a war and evacuation was all very bewildering, never having been involved in this sort of mass bloody violence before. Rationing had been bad enough! And now separation of families! What was the world coming to? This was the general cry of anguish among the people.

Though my own family managed to elude separation for some time, nevertheless we had to move out, for my college education at Calcutta ended, I finished with St. Xavier's College, having passed the Intermediate Science examination with a first class. My brothers were very happy in the Calcutta Boys' School, where an extremely effective and humane Head Master, Mr. Clifford Hicks, almost succeeded in converting Kothandu to Christianity. For some time there was some sub-surface tension in the family, since Kothandu had presumably told Appa of his intention to become a Christian. The problem was resolved by a wise approach by my father, and Kothandu was 'saved', though in a sense quite different to the Christian sense!

Christianity, or rather the life of Jesus, the Christ, has always had a fascination for Kothandu and myself. I do not know what exactly attracted Kothandu to it, but for me it was the love and compassion that Christ exhibited towards all human beings throughout his life on earth. The Hindu religion does not appear to have these blessed qualities, since the doctrine of karma would appear to condemn a person to work out his karma, suffering or enjoying whatever the accumulation of past lives brings in its wake. On the surface the doctrine of karma seems to be heartless, and to exclude the possibility of being forgiven for one's past thoughts and actions. The very definite ideas of compassion and love that Jesus offered, and the merciful nature of his life towards all, had a very definite attraction to those who were perhaps frightened by the karma theory.

It is not therefore surprising that Christianity has flourished in India, the religion attracting large numbers of converts to itself. The presence of Christianity in India can only be explained by these ideas translated into practice by the offer of free education, free medical services, and even help in obtaining jobs etc. Hinduism has certainly not succeeded in offering basic amenities of life to its adherents but, by and large, the people do not seem to have bothered about this lack, attributing such lacks even from religion itself, no doubt, to that very same doctrine of karma! But notwithstanding this appeal of the church, there was the tremendous financial support of the British government, as well as of charitable organizations throughout the world which explains the expansion of the church in India. Truly enormous resources have been made available to the church, to the exclusion of other religions, and so Christianity has gained a very definite presence on the sub-continent. It is a pity that until the advent of certain organizations, which attempted to rid Hinduism of its ritualistic cant and to work for the temporal relief of the Hindus, such assistance was not made available to the purely Hindu organizations. But it has never been sufficient, merely scratching the surface; but something is better than nothing, and I have nothing but praise for such organizations that came into existence just before the advent of that great personality, Swami Vivekananda, on the Indian scene.

Having said all that, one must also appreciate the real teaching behind the *Sanatana Dharma*, loosely called Hinduism. I really do not know whether this is so, but to my understanding there has not existed any provision for the absolution of sins in this religion. One is responsible for one's thoughts and actions, and if they form impressions, or leave residues behind, then one has to work off the effect of such residual impressions either in this very life, or in the next. There is thus a responsibility cast upon the individual to work off the effects of his own life, whereas other religions would appear to depend, perhaps even solely if my understanding is correct, on absolution being granted by a priest or authorised representative of the religion. I do not think very many persons desiring to be pardoned for their deeds have had any real faith in the capacity or the authority of the priests to grant them such pardon, and herein lies one at least of the reasons for the break down of religious faith.

The *Sanatana Dharma* has recognised that the ultimate authority for the granting of such a pardon is one's own self. Either that, or the living of one's life in such a way that the effects of the past are worked off to such an extent that there is automatic redemption, which the Hindus call *mukti*, or liberation. The priests have not had any power or authority to grant a pardon, though there developed the idea of prayers being offered for that purpose — and thus entered the ritualistic mode of worship. This was certainly not a desirable development, but that is what would have appeared to have happened. But notwithstanding this, there has been the idea of Divine Grace, and the possibility of invoking it for the purpose of attaining *mukti*. This has been a rather exclusive feature of the

Sanatana Dharma, as I understand it, though I may be wrong, not being a scholar of the religion. There exists Vedic authority for saying that only he achieves whom He desires to bless in such a fashion. To my mind there seem to be therefore two possible approaches to attain liberation: either by one's own effort, life after life, trying to work off the effect of the past upon one's life, or throwing oneself upon His mercy and appealing for His Grace to redeem one from the thraldom of the temporal existence.

During the two years we lived in Calcutta I became a little familiar with the life and teachings of Shri Ramakrishna, the Paramahamsa, and his world-famous disciple, Swami Vivekananda. I may say that the foundation for my spiritual thirst, such as it has been, was laid in Calcutta by getting into contact with the Ramakrishna Mission's teaching, and by reading their literature. I did not do anything practical about it, but the first glimmer of my thirst appeared out of the darkness of temporal existence, and that was a very valuable insight into what had to be done in the future. There was neither the desire to do anything about it, nor the time to do it in. Nevertheless the foundation came into being, and I am grateful for that. It was from this timid and tentative contact with the holier aspect of the Hindu religion that I began to understand the need for a guru to guide one's life in the spiritual realm; but as I have said, I had neither the time nor the inclination right then. It was only two decades or so later that the real cry from inside manifested itself, and the Master appeared before me.

Life at Calcutta was lived, inevitably, at a much faster pace. Calcutta is the largest city in India, and the British empire had its commercial base or foundation there, after its humble beginning in Madras with the establishment of the East India Company there. Jubbulpore was, on the contrary, a small town, tucked away in central India, and had no particular importance of its own. Life in Jubbulpore had been essentially a quiet and predictable affair, there being little difference from one day to the next. Calcutta hummed with life, being the commercial centre of India. It also teemed with the largest population in India, both in numbers as well as in density of population. In comparison, Jubbulpore was a small place. The climate was also totally different. Jubbulpore had a continental type of climate, with extremes of dry heat and an even drier cold, whereas Calcutta was humid and hot, the winters being quite balmy. The ways of life in those two places were naturally quite different.

The local language, Bengali, was naturally quite new to us. We had to make an effort to learn at least something of it to enable us to manage the little things, the daily routine chores, such as buying vegetables and so on. It was not a difficult matter, really, except for our lethargy in learning something new. Bengalis, as the natives of the state of Bengal are called, are very proud of their language, and expect others to learn it. At the time we were living in Calcutta, if a Bengali were to be approached for advice, or even for directions when searching for an address, he would reply promptly, and be most helpful, if the request were made in Bengali. But if the question were to be asked in say English, often a haughty stare was all the answer that one got. A very closed community, the Bengalis were. I hope that things have changed since then.

But whatever may be the attitude of the Bengalis, their language is a beautiful one, with a very rich literature, ennobled by the well-known works of authors like Bankim Chandra Chatterjee, Sarat Chandra Bose and of course the great Rabindranath Tagore, who won the Nobel prize for Literature. Tagore also established the University at Shantiniketan. A certain class of music is also there in the name of Tagore, called *Rabindra Sangeet*. Bengal has produced more than its share of the great sons of India. There have been very well-known and respected politicians such as Ashutosh Mukherjee — who was known as the *Tiger of Bengal* — Rashbehari Bose, Deshbandhu Chittaranjan Das and the world famous Netaji Subhash Chandra Bose. The last named had been selected for appointment to the prestigious Indian Civil Service, but decided to renounce it in favour of service to the nation. He made a name for himself as a great freedom fighter, later leading the Indian National Army — the I.N.A. as it came to be called. In the field of science one of the greatest names is that of Jagdish Chandra Bose whose fundamental researches in many fields are just becoming known to the world.

A great son of Bengal who inspired sweeping social changes against considerable opposition from the people was Ishwar Chandra Vidyasagar. He was responsible for trying to bring in widow remarriage, and he also standardized the Bengali alphabet, if my understanding is correct. Vidyasagar was inspired and motivated by the great Raja Ram Mohan Roy who was the moving spirit behind the Brahmo Samaj, of which I understand he was the founder. The Arya Samaj, an organization which has brought about great change in doing away with ritualistic aspects of the Hindu religion, and in simplifying the marriage ritual, for instance, was the creation of Maharishi Dayanand Saraswati. Shri Ramakrishna Paramahamsa had close connections with the reformist group, the *Brahmo Samaj*, through Keshub Chandra Sen. Shri Ramakrishna was perhaps able to mould the thinking of the reformers when necessary. It was through this organization that Narendra, as Swami Vivekananda was known before he took *sannyasa*, met Shri Ramakrishna — a meeting which changed the course of his life! Swami Vivekananda went on to preach the great message of his Master, and established the Shri Ramakrishna Mission and Math — an organization which has its branches in very many of the countries of the world today.

It is in the field of the transcendental human spirit that Bengal has produced its greatest personalities — Shri Ramakrishna Paramahamsa, and his world renowned disciple, Swami Vivekananda, as well as Shri Aurobindo, to name just a few. Ramakrishna Paramahamsa became a well-known figure because of the dedicated efforts taken by his disciple, Vivekananda, who preached the message of his Master throughout India, and in many countries of the world. Without his almost super-human efforts, Ramakrishna might not have achieved the fame that he has in fact achieved. Vivekananda was a truly great disciple of a truly great Master!

Shri Aurobindo began as a revolutionary, determined to liberate India from British rule, and had to spend some time in jail as a political prisoner of the British government. While in jail his life changed and he began to meditate, and he developed into something of a mystic. Later on, he dedicated his life to matters concerning the soul, and moved to Pondicherry to establish the Aurobindo Ashram there. Aurobindo has written many books on Indian yoga and allied subjects, and his book *Savithri* has been acclaimed as perhaps his greatest work, written not for the present but for the future! All his books are of gigantic size, heavy tomes not only in weight but in content too. When my interest in these matters was at a peak, I bought up many of his works, and I remember plodding through his *Life Divine*. I found it heavy going indeed! His tomes on yoga were attacked by me next, but with no better results. When I bought an abbreviated edition of his *Savithri* I fondly hoped that I would have better success with that work — but I had forgotten my weakness in the matter of poetry which I find very difficult to appreciate. Therefore that work of his has remained on my book shelf virtually unread.

Another great personality of Bengal whom I have forgotten to mention is Chaitanya Mahaprabhu. He was born at Nawadwip, and became very popular and very well-known. He preached his message of love of God in music and ecstatic dance — called *bhajans*. He is regarded as one of the great saints of the *bhakti* cult. Lord Krishna, the *Yuga Purusha* governing the present epoch, the *Kali Yuga*, is the greatest Personality who introduced the idea of *bhakti* — love for God — into India. The next great personality credited with the idea of *bhakti* as the predominant way to God is the southern *acharya*, Shri Ramanuja. In fact, according to my great Master, the chief personalities of the *bhakti* lineage following Lord Krishna himself, are Shri Ramanuja, Shri Chaitanya Mahaprabhu and Saint Kabir, in that chronological order.

Rabindranath Tagore called his state *Sonar Bangla* — which means 'golden Bengal'. But notwithstanding the fact that it has produced such great sons, the average population has remained a prejudiced and bigoted lot, sadly failing to benefit from the great literature, and the truly great spiritual writings and moral teachings of Swami Vivekananda. No prophet has ever been honoured in his own country — and this is proof of it, if any were needed!

I have been an ardent admirer of Vivekananda, and have read his works again and again since my college days in Calcutta, going to his books repeatedly for guidance as well as for inspiration over a period spanning very nearly five decades. I was drawn to that great figure ever since I visited the Belur Math in Calcutta for the first time, way back in the forties. I was influenced by his example to such an extent that I commenced the practice of *asanas* and *pranayama* without any guidance, on my own, and sort of graduated into meditation, also without any formal guidance. There have been many occasions when reading his books has moved me to tears.

Growing Up in Calcutta

I got into the habit of going to visit the Ramakrishna Math and there to sit in silent meditation amidst the clamour and din of their own ritualistic worship at the shrine of Shri Ramakrishna. Such visits to the Ramakrishna Math became something of a habit with me whenever I was troubled in my mind and needed the solace of deep meditation. It is something of a pity that the lay disciples were made to perform the traditional *puja* at the Paramahamsa's shrine, instead of being instructed to sit in silent meditation. I have found this system of ritualistic *puja* prevalent even in the Ramakrishna Maths outside India which I have visited. I understand that the *sannyasis* do meditation, but I have never been able to understand why the lay devotees are not permitted to meditate. This sort of discrimination is there, unfortunately, in most of such organizations which I have come across.

I did not think of either Ramakrishna or Vivekananda as my gurus — not at any time — because in my understanding a living guru was essential for one to follow, profit by, and to emulate. Nevertheless I owe a deep debt of gratitude to them for guiding my feet in the right direction, and for this service I am eternally grateful to those great souls who took birth in this ancient and noble land. For me, Vivekananda has been one of the greatest of India's sons throughout its long and hoary history, filled, as it is, with the noblest personalities of the highest spiritual achievements ever produced in this world of ours.

I deeply regret not having studied the Bengali language — for I had ample opportunity of learning it, and time enough and to spare too. My college studies did not take up all that time, and the environment was perfect — for where can one learn a language better than where it is spoken? Alas, that was not the only missed opportunity. I have an aptitude for learning languages, and I could have mastered several languages had I but decided to do so, and applied myself. But here again my deplorable shyness obstructed me, for I was too tongue-tied in the presence of others, and could not venture into words in another tongue. My shyness, in retrospect, has caused me such an enormous loss in so many ways that I could kick myself for it again and again. But there is no use in bewailing one's stupidity when it is too late to mend matters. What is most upsetting is the thought that the ability and the opportunity were both there — and I criminally wasted both!

There is surely some karmic reason for this awful shyness and reserve in me. Perhaps I was inhibited in a previous life from exhibiting my attributes! Or perhaps I was too exhibitionistic, and have to pay the price in this life. Who can unravel the mysterious ways in which our attitudes and mental make-up is created by ourselves? I do not subscribe to the theory that heredity explains these things. Physical attributes may be explained by the theory of heredity, but mental attributes? I think not. In any case there is hardly any use in analyzing the reason for it, the fact being that I lost much of my capital — by way of potential achievements — due to shyness which very considerably stunted my growth.

I have always been deeply interested in music, but my shyness prevented me from trying to learn the sarod to which I was drawn. It is an instrument which has enthralled me, and in Calcutta instruction would have been easily available. But here too I missed the bus, whereas my younger brother Kothandu began to learn the sitar, though I must say that he never exhibited any great interest or aptitude for music. It was only later in Bombay that my father dragged me to a flute master of the Carnatic tradition of south India to learn to play the bamboo flute, and I am grateful to Appa for taking that step, as otherwise I would never have gone to a teacher all by myself.

Growing Up in Calcutta

We lived in a fairly large and roomy house located on the Raja Basanta Roy Road, very near both the Lake market and the lakes. The landlord occupied the first floor, while we rented the ground floor which had two small entrances. My maternal uncle Kasturi, his wife Kamali and daughters Vathsala and Vaidehi lived with us. Later on Bakthu and Chitti joined us, after which Kasturi and family moved out. We had a boy named Bhagwan to help us in the house — but he was useful only for the most ordinary jobs such as sweeping the floor, washing the cooking vessels, the clothes, the bathrooms and so on. His Hindi was of the Bihar variety. He spoke no other language. Kamali, on the other hand, knew no Hindi at all, and was just attempting to pick up a few words here and there. Their attempts at conversation were extremely funny, and on occasion devastatingly hilarious.

I remember one occasion vividly. I came back from college a bit early, around lunch time, and heard Kamali shouting at Bhagwan in an angry voice. I went in through the open door, and found Bhagwan with a bucket full of water, his posture indicating that he was about to empty its contents upon my aunt! I asked him what he was trying to do. He said that Kamali had told him three times that her stomach was on fire, and therefore he wanted to pour a bucket of water on her to put it out! I asked Kamali to repeat what she had said, and she told me that all she had said was that she was hungry! Unfortunately, she had used the Hindi word for fire — *aag* — instead of the correct word for hunger, *bhook*! And this had caused the comic episode to occur. Bhagwan was of course not to be blamed for anything other than his extreme stupidity. I told Kamali to make sure that she only used words which she knew, to avoid the recurrence of such comic situations. Such situations were almost a daily occurrence, but though they were comic, my father was concerned because there was always the possibility of a troublesome, and possibly a dangerous, situation developing, given the ignorance of the one and the stupidity of the other.

Kasturi had a job in the Central Excise department of the government, and was a busy and disgruntled man. He could have been happy, and made his family happy too, but he had a permanent grouse against almost everything. Poor Kamali! She had to bear a great deal of abuse, silent but visible because of the effects it produced upon her. Theirs had been a love marriage, a very rare thing in the India of the twenties, but the marriage was a total disaster. She suffered all her life, first at the hands of her husband, and later at the hands of her son. Her only support has been her daughter Vathsala, and son-in-law A.V. Rangarajan, who have supported her throughout. Rangarajan went to the U.S.A. soon after his marriage, and settled there, and so was not available, of course, but nevertheless they helped Kamali a lot.

Raja Basanta Roy Road was a fairly long road, and had a great number of houses built upon it; but the numbering of the houses was just terrible, and a total mess. The Calcutta Corporation, we were told, assigned house numbers sequentially as the houses were built, but since houses were never built adjacent to each other, but came up here and there according to who built where, it was virtually impossible to locate a house by knowing the street number. Innumerable were the inquirers who stopped at our house to know where a particular number was located. The house next to ours had the number 135, whereas ours was 47A! One day Appa and I set out armed with a large sheet of paper and a pencil, and drew a map of our road, and marked in all the houses upon it, leaving blank spaces for vacant plots, marking in the numbers as we went on. In this way we ended up with a map with numbers marked upon it, and this was a great help to all who wanted to locate an address.

Growing Up in Calcutta

We displayed the map prominently on the outside wall where it could be easily seen from the road.

Sad to say, Calcutta continues to be a nightmare even today, things not having improved even a mite, in spite of the passage of half a century since I was a student there. The Calcutta of those days had a charm all its own, and people were attracted to it. The streets were hosed down every morning with water from hydrants located everywhere. There were parks and gardens all over the city, and the streets were lined with tall shade trees. Then of course there were the lakes, and the river Hoogly passed right through Calcutta. The Botanical Gardens are perhaps the largest of any in India. Then there were the Eden Gardens where the cricket matches of those days used to be played. The enormous open area known as the *maidan* was a boon to all, and enabled a great many football and other games to be played all at the same time. A very scenic and attractive city to live in, with no water shortage, a reliable electricity supply, a good tram service, and an efficient if overcrowded bus service.

I remember that Calcutta had the best ice cream sold on the streets — Magnolia Ice Cream — the memory of which makes the mouth water even today. We three brothers were very fond of it, and sometimes when we went for a walk around the lakes, we were allowed to have one each. On one occasion we pestered our father for more, and he, in a fit of exasperation, gave me a five rupee note and asked us to eat as much as we could. I regret to say that we could not eat more than three and a half rupees worth of the utterly delicious stuff — and at that we were quite sick! Today one small serving of a good ice cream could cost a minimum of three or four rupees.

Calcutta has been justly famous for a delicious sweet called *rosogolla*. *Rajbhog* was another, and a third sweet not so sweet was the *sandesh*. They are still enjoyed as sweets peculiarly Bengali in nature. Today they are available almost everywhere in India, but in those days they were available only in that state. All in all, life passed pleasantly during my two years stay there.

It was while we were at Calcutta that uncle Bhadran was married in Kollengode. He was serving as Assistant Conservator of Forests in Assam then, and returned to Shillong via Calcutta with my aunt Gouri. I remember that she brought us a gift, one shirt each which we never wore, for the colour was terrible — a thick white chalk stripe on a background of violent purple! I remember that our chitti, Shakuntala, was very indignant about this. My father was annoyed when we refused to wear the shirt, for he felt that we should have been grateful for what we received. I believe that the shirts eventually 'disappeared' to the satisfaction of all of us.

An important development was our introduction to homoeopathy. In Calcutta there was a very large number of homoeopathic physicians. We had as our neighbour Shri G.V. Pillai, and he was a dedicated homoeopath. He helped us very much, and was responsible for my father taking interest in it. Years later, I too started studying the books, especially Dr. Kent's *Materia Medica*, and the very well written and useful book, *The Domestic Physician*, by Dr. Hering. I remember that when my son Krishna was born, there were occasions when homoeopathy helped enormously, and seemingly miraculously. I remember one occasion, an evening in our Wenden Avenue home in Bombay, when the baby was screaming with his knees drawn up to his chin. Sulochana was in tears. Appa studied his books for a few minutes, and then put one globule of medicine on the baby's lips. Instantly, and I mean instantly, the baby was asleep. Where children are concerned it is perhaps the most effective system of treatment. We owe a lot to this science, and in fact enormous medical bills were avoided by domestic treatment of almost all ailments.

Life was a wellspring of happiness, and passed off peacefully enough, notwithstanding the second World War which inevitably broke up families due to the need for evacuation. The greater horror was the Bengal famine — a man-made disaster without parallel in India's history. Millions are reported to have died of starvation during that ugly and miserable period, and one could well believe it when one saw the dead bodies being removed every morning, even from the streets of Calcutta. But before these horrors turned everything topsy-turvy, the family was all together and it was a time of joy, happiness and expansion in every sense.

The only thing that marred our happiness was a burglary in the house. Thieves broke in through an empty room adjoining an external courtyard. The tall windows were protected by nothing more than widely spaced vertical bars of iron. The house was a fairly old one, and the window bars had been rusted through due to exposure to rain. These had been easily pulled apart to provide access into the room. Strangely enough it was the only unoccupied room in the whole house, and all our boxes were stored in that room. We were all blissfully asleep in the other rooms, and even though the thieves must have made some noise to gain entry into that room, we none of us were aware that anything had gone wrong till the next morning when we were awakened by our neighbour, a retired Indian civil service officer, who told us that there was a large number of trunks lying in the adjoining empty plot of land. We said they could not possibly be ours!

Appa was however curious and went out to inspect them, and found to his consternation that every one of the twenty-one trunks and suitcases were ours. They had all been broken open and thoroughly ransacked, and jewelry and other valuables taken away, leaving saris and men's clothes strewn around all over the place. A police complaint was automatically filed, though none of us really expected anything to come out of it. Surprisingly, about two months later, a gold-topped baton belonging to my grandfather, which had been in Kasturi's possession, was found in the servant's room of our I.C.S. neighbour. The police naturally went to him to make an enquiry, and to search the servant's quarters. Our neighbour became very indignant, and said that we 'foreigners' were causing him annoyance by having the police call upon him, and was this the way of showing our gratitude to him for having drawn our attention to the burglary a few months earlier? A strange and wholly un-neighbourly attitude, but that was the way of the people there. Unfortunately his outburst brought the enquiry to an end, for after all he was an I.C.S. officer, though retired from service!

This annoying episode, which robbed my chitti of most of her jewelry, came at the fag end of our stay in Calcutta, and left a rather sour taste in the mouth. All in all our stay there of nearly three years duration had been a happy and fruitful one, and so we left Calcutta with happy memories of our life there. Calcutta has left a deep impression upon my heart, and the period of my life lived there has no doubt produced, or caused, fundamental changes in my own life — especially in bringing about the turn that my life took towards spirituality.

Parthasarathi
Bombay - 1948

Parthasarathi, dressed in
military cadet uniform - 1948

VIII

Life Beside the Ganges at Benares

Life Beside the Ganges at Benares

I had moved to Bombay after finishing with my education in Calcutta, and there I received a telegram from an intimate classmate of mine named Samarapungavan to inform me that I had passed the Intermediate Science examination with a 1st class. I applied to the Benares Hindu University for admission to do a Bachelor's degree course in Science. I secured it easily. Benares was famous for its chemistry courses, and I had chosen to take a bachelor's degree in that subject. In south India there were generally three subjects, one of which was treated as the major, the other being subsidiaries. In the B.H.U. all subjects had the same importance. I took chemistry, physics, and geology along with biology. Though only three subjects were prescribed I chose to do four since I had a desire to go for a medical education after completing the bachelor's degree. Therefore I included biology. I had a keen interest in the geological and other earth sciences, which led me to take it up.

The day came for me to leave for Benares, and I was put on the train at the Victoria Terminus station by Appa. I was armed with a first class pass permitting free travel, and a hundred rupees for expenses, including admission fees and hostel charges upon arrival at the B.H.U. as the Benares Hindu University was known throughout India. Travel was comfortable in those days, and very safe too. First class passengers were greatly respected, and that was an advantage in itself. I travelled by the Calcutta Mail, a famous train of those days, which ran from the Ballard Pier in Bombay, carrying passengers who had arrived by steamer from England, all the way to distant Calcutta. I got off at Moghalsarai junction after a journey of about twenty-four hours, and changed to another train to go to Kashi from where I took a cycle rickshaw to the university — a six mile ride, if I remember rightly. It was a good thing that we were accustomed to travelling alone by train from an early age — which was rather unusual in the India of those days.

The distance from the main gate of the B.H.U. to my hostel, the Broacha Hostel, was over a mile! I was overawed by the campus. After the cramped St. Xavier's College campus in Calcutta, this was truly enormous. I was perhaps one of the first students to arrive. There was only one other boy standing on the verandah, holding on to a wire strung between two pillars, presumably for drying washed clothes. He hung on to that wire as if his life depended upon it. He was quite obviously very lonely and homesick. I was too shy to approach him, but went and stood next to him. He turned and greeted me, and I discovered that he was a south Indian, but one who had spent most of his life in Calcutta, and knew very little Tamil. His name was Krishnamurthy, and he spoke Bengali fluently, as if it was his mother tongue! Because we were the first two to meet there on the verandah of the Hostel, we became very good and intimate friends. It was a good beginning, and augured well for the next two years that I would have to spend there.

We both looked for and located the hostel warden and got our accommodation allotted. Since we were third year students, we were allotted double rooms. Krishnamurthy and I could not stay together, for it was B.H.U. policy to mix the first and third year students, while allotting single rooms to the second and fourth year boys as they had to study hard for their finals in the Inter Science and Bachelor of Science classes respectively. I had a room on the first floor facing the road, whereas Krishnamurthy was given a room in the rear wing far away from me — a good five minutes walk. Initially there was

Life Besides the Ganges at Benares

the desire to move closer to each other, but as time passed this desire vanished!

Mr. Madan Mohan Malaviya had established the university by collecting money from all over India. There were many Rajas and Maharajas in India, and large donations were available to the right man, and Mr. Malaviya was such a person. Shri Malaviya was the first vice-chancellor of the B.H.U. When I entered the B.H.U., Dr. Sarvapalli Radhakrishnan was the vice-chancellor. The university was situated on a large property of about twenty-five square kilometers, and was on the left bank of the Ganges. On the other side of the river nestled the palace of the Raja of Benares.

After I had moved my steel trunk and my bed to room No. 63, which was to be my home for the next one year, I went out to buy a cup of tea for myself, and discovered that I had to walk to the university main gate as the college messes were not yet operative. In fact the students had to get together and organize the messes, and that took up the next two days. Anyway I walked the mile to the gate, had the delicious experience of buying tea and drinking it out of a clay cup called a *kulhad*, and then walked back to my hostel, all the while being overtaken by students arriving on rickshaws — some of whom were obviously senior students in the final Inter and Bachelors' classes, because they were exchanging jokes and badinage from rickshaw to rickshaw.

When I came back and went up to my room, I found a young fellow gazing away into infinity, with unshed tears glittering in his eyes. I accosted him and discovered that he was my roommate, a young boy named Narasimhan, whose father was a chemist on one of the railways. The college administration had paired us on the theory, perhaps, that two south Indians would hit it off better than an odd pair! Very considerate of them, to be sure, but totally unnecessary as far as I was concerned. Nevertheless it was nice to know that the authorities had consideration for the happiness of the new inmates, and that they were willing to do their best for us.

There were 360 rooms in my hostel, which was built as three sides of a square, with the hollow side to the rear. The central hollow square accommodated the bathrooms and showers. The latrines were located, to my dismay, almost half a mile further to the rear, some thirty-two of them all in one row. At night it was difficult to go there all by oneself! There was only one weak lamp hanging from a tall lamp post right behind the hostel, and another equally weak one near the row of latrines, and no light at all in between. The latrines were dry ones. By night boys were generally nervous of going alone to the distant latrines, and if they did not get someone to accompany them, I am sorry to say that they used the shower rooms as latrines, much to the annoyance and disgust of those who went in for a shower the next morning. The first boy generally found a filthy bathroom, and as I had been trained to wake up early and to bathe immediately, I generally had this misfortune.

I had arrived on a Friday evening, and was well in time to register early before the crowd started coming in. The older boys took it easy, being familiar with the routine and the place. Classes commenced only the next Monday, so we new boys had a full weekend to familiarize ourselves with each other as well as with our new home. It was amazing how quickly friendships developed. Our warden, Dr. Nand Lal Singh, was also my physics lecturer. A short and rather rotund person, he was very kind and took considerable trouble to help us with all that had to be done. He lived in the hostel. He helped us to get organized and to form ourselves into messes. The college authorities provided only the accommodation — a kitchen-cum-dining area not more than 400 sq. ft. in extent, with a fire place at the end where the maharaj, as cooks are called in that region, sat and prepared the meals. We were just thirty or so to a mess, and the system was to divide the expenses at the end of each month among the members. There were fifteen such messes all located at the rear of the hostel.

We had a committee to manage the affairs of the mess, and I found myself selected to manage the finances and to keep accounts. Another was in charge of purchases. There was no such thing as a menu, because the food was simple and monotonously regular — chapattis with a dry vegetable and dal, day in and day out! But the food was delicious since it was freshly prepared and served hot. One assistant cook prepared the wheat dough, while a second rolled it out, and the chief cook grilled it on an open fire, and served it straight from the fire, throwing each chapatti expertly to the students seated in a rough semicircle around him. The boys brought their own *desi ghee*, a clarified butter not quite boiled free of water, which they applied on the chapatti before eating it. Pickles were also personal property, though there was a great deal of swapping of these delicacies between the students.

No tea or coffee was served in the messes. In fact coffee was virtually unknown in the northern parts of India in those days. We had two solid meals a day, and for that we paid, on an average, sixty rupees a month. On Sundays we had only the midday meal, which was generally a feast with sweets and other delectable preparations. We fasted on Sunday nights. This was to permit the cooks to have a half day off every week. On Sundays it was usual to invite friends for lunch — and so boys moved around from hostel to hostel. The size of the monthly bill depended on the Sunday menu, as well as on how many guests one entertained. The Sunday feast was solid fare, and often some of the boys had difficulty in getting up from the table to walk back to the hostel. One of my friends, Dargar by name, could polish off two dozen chappatis, several helpings of vegetable, half a kilo of *dahi*, and anything else that was available. Often things would get so serious that in some messes servings were restricted to what was called 'measured meals' to keep the monthly bills down, for the boys who had elephantine appetites were a handful while many boys with average and poor appetites paid for them!

On Sundays it was customary to go into the city, take in a movie, stop at a place called Lanka for some delicious *lassi* and then return to our hostels. *Lassi* is a delicious and filling drink made from *dahi* — curds — and a large *kulhad* full of creamy *lassi* could be had for just two annas! Notwithstanding the feast in the morning, we were generally hungry by the evening, and *lassi* was the only affordable way of assuaging it. *Samosas* were delicious, and depending upon the state of our finances, we indulged in them with gusto. *Samosas* and *lassi* became our regular indulgence. But it was all so cheap when one compares the then prevailing prices with today's prices — for instance two large *samosas* and a large *kulhad* of *lassi* cost only four annas, or one quarter of a rupee. Today the same thing costs not less than five rupees — twenty times as much!

The main gate was locked at 9:00 P.M. sharp, and if one came in late, it meant a great deal of trouble. Therefore the return journey had necessarily to be by rickshaw, or another peculiar horse-drawn conveyance called the *ekka*. It was a vehicle meant for one, but generally three or four could be seated in it with reasonable comfort. On occasion even eight or nine could be seen hanging on for dear life! A Sunday excursion generally cost us, on an average, a rupee and a half! But it was a strain upon our student's meagre allowance, and on some Sundays we were compelled to remain in the hostel, envying the others who still had some money in their pockets.

Life Besides the Ganges at Benares

Appa used to send me one hundred rupees each month. It came by money order through the post office. Bank accounts were a rare thing, and I don't remember there having been a bank within the University campus. It was a princely sum I received, considering the fact that students from less well endowed families had to make do with sixty rupees per month. In my mess we ate well, and so the average monthly mess bill was around seventy rupees! That did not leave a great deal for other expenses. And for my father it was still something of a strain, and one had to be prudent. I never managed to save anything while I stayed in Benares.

The postman who served the neighbouring hostel, the Birla hostel, and our Broacha hostel was a portly person, very short and very stout, but always beaming with good health and goodwill. He knew every student by name. As soon as he arrived we would crowd around him — for who was not anxious to receive news from home? He would look over the crowd, and call out the name of each one who had something in the post, and that boy would push his way through the crowd of students to him to receive it. If it was a money order, Parmanand dispensed it with a flourish, giving money orders priority over letters. When the boy had signed the receipt, Parmanand would hand over the money after deducting his own cut — generally half a rupee for a hundred rupees! No one protested at this 'taxation at source', for Parmanand was such a jolly fellow, and so sympathetic when one received nothing, that protest was out of the question. He actually seemed to suffer when a boy had waited two or three weeks for a letter from home, and there was still nothing in the post for him!

Parmanand became something of a god-father to us. He would watch our faces anxiously as we opened and read our letters on the spot, and ask if all were well at home. He was a sympathetic, and at the same time an astute, fellow, and soon learnt most of the details of our young lives — to this extent that sometimes he appeared to know the contents of the letters in advance of their even being opened! On the days when he didn't turn up there was general desolation. We missed him terribly — and in some way we came to have much affection for him as one who sympathized with us in our loneliness and distress, and helped to bring cheer into our lives.

There was a gymnasium attached to our college, and I began to make use of it, having become accustomed to a daily work-out in Calcutta — but this did not last long. The reason was that I became interested in military service and applied to join the University Officers' Training Corps — the U.O.T.C. as it was generally called. There was a rigorous and difficult physical test, or rather a series of them, and I wondered how I would pass them. One had to jump over a six foot wall, with a round top, smooth as a bald pate, after jumping across a four feet wide ditch just in front of it. One had to jump across the ditch, hold on to the smooth and slippery top of the wall, and go over it. Not easy for one unused to activities requiring at least an average physical agility. I managed it, much to my surprise. Then there were several tests like climbing over obstacles, jumping, crossing over from one tree to another using a rope, and things like that. The final test was to run one mile in six minutes. I have never run a mile in my life, nor even half a mile, for that matter, and that is the truth! But when I saw the seventy or eighty boys lined up at the starting line, I also joined in, and once again to my surprise and joy, I did it. I have never attempted to run a mile again!

I was admitted into the 1st U.P. Battalion, U.O.T.C., I.T.F., as a cadet, and was ordered to draw my equipment from the battalion stores. I was given two pairs of the regulation khaki uniform, a pair of ankle length military boots, called ammunition boots, and a belt, cross belt and puttees all made of webbing. The boots proved a little difficult as I have big feet, but they eventually managed to find a pair which fit. There was also the Lee Enfield 303 rifle with bayonet, but we were allowed to draw weapons from the battalion armoury only just before each parade. I was assigned to the 'D' Company, which had a Major M.C. Pandey commanding it, and a Lieutenant I.C. Pandey as second-in-command. They were assisted by a Company Sergeant Major, and a Company Quarter Master Sergeant. There were sergeants in charge of each of the four platoons. These sergeants were in turn assisted by three corporals and three lance corporals per platoon. Quite an impressive set up indeed, and I was extremely happy to be part of it — a wing of the British Army.

The battalion was commanded by a Brigadier of the British army. He was a British officer of the regular army. I never learnt his name, for we saw this exalted personage only once a year, and then too only from a distance, and that was on the day of the annual parade when the whole battalion paraded as one unit. He had a stentorian voice which was rather hoarse, and he used to pull out his commands — Attennnnnnnnnnnnnn Shun!! for instance. When the parade had formed on the enormous parade ground, the battalion had to present arms. The command was given by the colonel who commanded our four companies of the battalion. The colonel pulled out his commands for such a long time that we had difficulty in responding to it, since we were not used to his commands, as he too was present only for the annual parades. The four companies had difficulty in co-ordinating their response. He would bellow out, "For general saluuuuuuuuuuute........ pre-seeeeeeeeeeeeeeeeeeennnnt arms!" It was a great deal of fun, and I enjoyed the life enormously.

But of course a great deal of rigorous training went into all this. We had to attend weekly parade every Saturday, which began at 7:00 A.M., and finished only at sunset, leaving most of us totally exhausted. The British army believed in marching, and we did miles and miles of it.

Once we went on a route march in Benares itself, going twenty miles one morning, laying camp, doing fatiguing exercises throughout the day in awful terrain under a blistering summer sun, sleeping under the most uncomfortable conditions, and marching back twenty miles the next day to our base. We were made to stand at attention for about half an hour at 5:00 A.M. while the officers were studying the route maps. Now it appears very easy, but I can say from personal experience that it is one of the most difficult things to do. Three cadets fainted right there, falling like trees struck down by lightning! The officers had perhaps forgotten that we were standing in formation.

Then we stepped out briskly to commence our long march. We had been warned to carry full water bottles, but some of the careless ones had failed to heed this warning. When one of them was thirsty, another offered him his bottle. "Stop that!" bellowed our sergeant. "Fall out!" was his next order, and both the cadets fell out of the marching order. "What were you doing?" was the question he addressed to the one who had offered his water bottle to the other one who had forgotten to fill up his own. The answer was obvious, of course. He was sharply reprimanded, and ordered never to do such a thing again. The offender was told, "My son, it is a serious fault to go on the field without water in your bottle. You shall have no water till we make camp. I may appear cruel, but this may save your life when you are really on a battlefield."

When we set out from our base, I had been mildly surprised to see an empty military lorry following us. Now I understood why it was there at all. The erring cadets fell into their marching positions again, looking crestfallen. The march continued, and after some twenty minutes, the one who had been denied water fainted even as he was marching and fell down. The column halted briefly while he was carried to the truck which had been following us, and dumped into it. This happened again and again several times, and we finally ended up with nearly a dozen cadets in it. Of course we all felt that our officers had been cruel without necessity, and were unhappy about it, but one cannot deny the value of the lesson that all of us learnt that day.

The army is a hard taskmaster, but it teaches for life, and its lessons are rarely forgotten. We had an uneventful camp, with a lot of creeping and crawling through dense bushes to do in the course of the exercises, and returned to the hostel the next day without further incident. We returned on a Saturday evening at about 5:00 P.M., but it was only at 6:30 P.M. that we finished cleaning the weapons and depositing them in the armoury. I came back to my room and fell upon my bed with my boots on, dressed in the cadet's uniform, and must have fallen asleep immediately! When I woke up, it was Monday afternoon! I had slept for more than forty-five hours continuously.

We had to be dressed impeccably with boots polished to a mirror finish, belts and webbing greened freshly, etc. Any slipshod preparation invoked the wrath of the sergeant, after we had been fired by the corporal. The weapons drill was great fun but very tiring. We had to fire on the range, and the Lee Enfield 303 has a kick like a mule. In the beginning one tended to hold the rifle loosely to one's shoulder, and if one did that, the recoil was like the impact from a battering ram. We were repeatedly warned to hold the rifle well pressed to the shoulder, but when one had fired twenty or more rounds, one's shoulder tended to disagree with this suggestion. Then we suffered all the more. Once I fired 200 rounds on the range, and I came back to the hostel with my right shoulder terribly bruised, and almost dislocated. Yet, notwithstanding all this, it was tremendous fun. In spite of my wearing spectacles, I became one of the best shots in the four companies. I did best at the 200 yards range, but at 400 yards my vision let me down, though even at that range I did better than most of the others.

The culminating event each year was the annual camp, held in the winter at Allahabad. It was dreadfully cold, of course, the temperature often falling to freezing point. We had one bogie reserved for our use on the night train, and all the 140 of us had to be accommodated in it. Major M.C. Pandey and Lt. I.C. Pandey of course had reserved berths in the 1st class coach. There was a rigid pecking order, naturally, as is to be expected in such a severely and rigidly structured hierarchy. Therefore all the benches were occupied by the CSM, the CQMS, the sergeants, the corporals and the lance corporals. We cadets had to sleep under the wooden benches of the third class coach, and in that bitter cold we were truly miserable. We boarded the train at eleven o'clock at night, shivering in our totally inadequate army issue pullovers. We suffered all night, and reached Naini, a station near Allahabad, at five o'clock next morning.

As soon as we alighted, we had to load our kit onto the one military lorry that was there, and then we were served hot tea and two biscuits each. On that breakfast we commenced to march to our camp site about eleven miles away, toting our rifles in the hand, bayonets suspended from the belt, and our back packs full and heavy on our backs. The regulation attire also demanded a full water bottle suspended from the belt. We generally reached our camp site three hours later, and immediately began to put up the tents, unload the baggage, and to make everything ship-shape. Those who were assigned cooking duties went to the cooking area to shoulder that work. The others drew rifles and set out on field march, or for certain exercises involving attack and defence, and so on.

Since the ground was very wet with the overnight dew, our uniforms were soaked through during such manoeuvres, as we had to crawl about on our bellies to get into position, after which we were generally running like mad, screaming like banshees at the top of our voices. We would generally return from these exercises at 12:30 P.M., but the day was not yet over. We had to clean our weapons, return them to the armoury, wash up and then go to the dining tents where we had our lunch by approximately 1:30 P.M. The poor fellows on cooking duty never ate their lunch before 3:00 P.M. Fortunately for us, the whole battalion shared in the cooking, and so none of us had to do it more than once during the fifteen days camp. It was exhausting but also exhilarating, and the fifteen days passed swiftly. We had the whole afternoon free, and there were cultural programmes in the evenings. We were allowed 'gate passes' once a week. Some did go to Allahabad, but there was no fun in it unless one had something to buy. Also since one had to be back before 9:00 P.M., there was not much one could do out of the camp.

The culminating experience was the 'guard mounting' which was taken by groups selected for the purpose. It was an honour to be selected for it, and I was overjoyed when I found myself being selected during the first year. We were separately trained for the guard duty, and of course this meant that we spent an additional three hours every day, apart from the daily parade. So I had virtually no free afternoons, being on the parade ground, being honed to perfection in all that a guard patrol was supposed to do. As I was the tallest, I was the key man in the guard patrol, and had to give the appropriate but inaudible signals that ensured perfect co-ordination from the dozen of us. The long awaited day came for us to go on guard duty — a twenty-four hour stint of duty. The ceremonial handing over of the guard and the taking over by the next guard was the most colourful spectacle. We were dressed to kill, as the saying goes, all spit-and-polish, and our major expressed full satisfaction with our turnout. That was a good beginning — and well begun is half done, as the old saw goes! Everything went off to perfection in the changing-of-the-guard ceremonial. As key man I performed exceedingly well, fumbling only once, but the guard group behaved with exemplary discipline, having been thoroughly trained for the job.

We assumed guard duty at 4:00 P.M. The ceremony was witnessed by the brigadier himself. It was British army ceremonial drilled to perfection, and the brigadier assured the company commander that he was pleased. All were envious, and for the rest of the evening we were strutting about like peacocks! Very arrogant and very proud, wallowing in the envious looks of all who witnessed our performance. That night we went somewhat berserk — challenging every leaf fall, as it were! We were no doubt supposed to challenge everything that approached the armoury which we were guarding. But as I said, we went crazy with the new-found authority, and challenged all noises, until one of the senior officers came around midnight to ask us to reduce our enthusiasm, assuring us that there was really no danger of anyone attacking the installation! As a consequence of our perfect performance, most of us were promoted, and I was awarded the rank of lance corporal the very next morning.

It was a sort of victory procession from Allahabad back to Benares for our guard group, and the immense satisfaction and pleasure that we all felt because of the promotions that we had earned, kept us aglow for a month thereafter. It was a great day when I asked the company tailor to put on the one stripe on the sleeve of my uniform that my rank entitled me to. It was even greater when I was occasionally ordered to take charge of my 'D' Company during parade. I was still shy, and so did not bellow out the orders as most of the others could, but it was all quite acceptable, and my officers commended me upon my achievement.

Benares Hindu University opened another avenue for me, that of social service! Our hostel had a committee, and this was constituted by a democratic process of election, all the hostel inmates having votes. For no reason at all I decided to stand for election, and filed my nomination papers, wanting all the time to immediately withdraw them in case I should be elected. "Fat chance of my being elected," I thought to myself, "with all the seniors there to attract the votes of the boys." I thought that I was being rather uncharacteristically egotistic in thinking that I had any chance of such a thing happening. The election day came, succeeding fifteen days of hectic electioneering which included walls emblazoned with appeals for votes, speeches of exhortation, laying bare the speaker's soul in an attempt to win votes, special parties to chosen 'key persons' who were thought to have the ability to sway the opinion of the boys, and private dialogue with all and sundry seeking to give heart felt assurances of service to the inmates of Broacha Hostel! This was my first — and unfortunately by no means the last — exposure to the democratic process practised in India!

I suppose that this was the very first occasion that I saw my own name splashed in large letters upon the walls of the hostel, and it made me rather uncomfortable to see it so blatantly publicized. But I had supporters who planned my election campaign, and one did not let down one's supporters! So I had to tolerate this blatant display of one's own ego — though I personally detested the vulgar publicity. The college walls were not permitted to be thus adorned, and strangely enough that gave me a twinge of disappointment. The only complaint that Dr. Nand Lal Singh, my warden, voiced was that I had a name which was not only far too long, but also so difficult to pronounce. This criticism was not quite fair, for there were north Indian boys with equally long names, some of them quite difficult to pronounce, at least for south Indians. But that is the way of all prejudice, that things are generally irrational.

Astonishingly, I seemed to gain in popularity. My shyness and my newness to the university had not been conducive to the development of any intimacy except with one or two of my classmates. But my shyness seems to have been perhaps mistaken for humility — and if that was so, I must apologize to all those who deluded themselves under this misconception. Any way, my popularity did go up very speedily, but I was a bit nervous of this because the more popular I became, the more expenses I would later have to incur whether I won the election or not — and I had slim resources. Of course one had to remember that popularity alone never won any elections!

The campaign got noisier and noisier as the election drew near — and this was something that I detested. India has always been a very noisy country — nothing is celebrated, nor even mourned, without a great deal of noisome rituals. Elections, as I discovered at Benares, were perhaps the noisiest of all, for it involved large numbers of people. Why this should be so no one has been able to explain, but noise is regrettably very much a part of the Indian scene. On election day, which was around the middle of August, the noise level was horrible, though the warden tried to keep it down. It soon mounted to a crescendo! There was much running around — quite unnecessary I thought — and the polling began at 10:30 A.M. with much fanfare and shaking of hands all round — a sort of advance celebration of victory by the cocksure ones. The voting was over by lunch time. Lunch that afternoon was in a very excited state, and the maharaj in the mess had to put up with a great deal of nonsense aimed at no one in particular, but which seemed to home in on him as if he were the logical target. The day was of course a holiday, for these elections to the Hostel Unions were something held dear to the heart of the students.

The counting of votes commenced upstairs in the warden's rooms, at around 4:30 P.M. and ended by 6:30 P.M. All were excited to the point of exhaustion, and waited with bated breath for the results to be announced as the warden appeared from his room in his second floor apartment. Three names were announced, and I thought to myself, "Well, that's that." I had not made it after all. Nevertheless I waited as my supporters were there, waiting to see if the unlikely candidate they had supported would come in or not. When eight names had been announced I decided to retire beaten, and walked out of the office, and made my way downstairs to go back to my room. I went in and bolted the door as I did not want to face the shame of defeat in public. A few minutes later there was a great din, a noise of hundreds of feet rushing down the stairs, and it approached my wing. It was soon followed by a battering upon my door which threatened to break it down. I had to open it, and there stood a beaming crowd of over a hundred students, with a rather bedraggled garland, waiting to garland me.

I was informed by my exultant supporters that my name had been announced as an elected member of the Hostel Union Committee. It was the tenth name to be announced because the names were announced in alphabetical order! This was the first occasion when I found myself being garlanded amidst a large gathering. I was extraordinarily embarrassed by this business, and simultaneously moved to tears, and so tried to hide myself. But I found to my despair that victory has its own price to extract, and this price had to be paid. I was escorted downstairs to the lawns in front of the hostel, and all the dozen or so committee members were publicly applauded, and made much of. The inevitable *samosa* and *peda* — the latter a sweet made of milk — was called for in large quantities, followed by tea for all. This was merely the immediate celebration, of course. After dinner the real celebration followed in the way of a fireworks display, creating a great din for half the night, until the warden came down and put an end to the hilarious celebrations which were threatening to become riotous.

The very next morning we had the inaugural meeting of the newly elected committee, and I was given the portfolio of 'Secretary for Social & Religious Functions.' An old proverb says, "Coming events cast their shadows before them," and looking back upon my life from the present to that time nearly half a century ago, I have to agree with the truth of that old saying. There was something almost prophetic about that first public office that I held, almost entirely by accident. That initial meeting lasted a mere hour, most of the time being devoted to eating *samosas* and sipping very hot tea which almost burnt my tongue. I was informed of the calendar of my duties. I was expected to organize and celebrate *Rama Navami, Krishna Janmashtami, Divali* and *Holi*, apart from organizing two religious lectures during the year to be delivered on the hostel lawns under a specially erected *shamiana*. I had assumed that the College of Science would release funds for these celebrations, but I was informed that I had to show my mettle by collecting funds from the students of the university as well as from the public at large to finance the affairs I had to conduct!

This activity gave me a great deal of insight into the *Sanatana Dharma* of the Hindus. I had thought that I had received a fair amount of exposure during my sojourn in

Life Besides the Ganges at Benares

Calcutta, but that was a mistake. Here, at Benares I was exposed to the religion in depth, and I was astonished by the wisdom, the generosity, the greatness, the sheer beauty of the Vedic *Dharma*. There were three things that contributed to the broadening and simultaneous deepening of my appreciation. The first was the presence of the great philosopher, Dr. S. Radhakrishnan, who was then the Spalding Professor of Eastern Religions at Oxford. He came regularly to Benares, and delivered lectures on the Vedic and Upanishadic texts several times a year. His lectures were attended by people from all over the state, and I too was there. His Sanskrit was chaste, and his pronunciation truly magnificent. That is all that I can say about it. It was a great thing to sit and listen to that erudite man speaking in Sanskrit, and translating the difficult passages in his equally chaste English. The experience was often mesmeric!

I had been able to introduce myself to him as soon as I arrived in Benares. This was made possible by my father's boss on the railways who was Dr. Radhakrishnan's son-in-law. He kindly gave me a letter of introduction to the famous philosopher whom I visited a few days after my arrival. Rather surprisingly, he was sitting quite relaxed, and received me affectionately, patting the cushion by his side to offer me a seat next to himself. I was awed by his presence, and shyly proffered the letter I had brought. He read it and asked me, "Well young man, what can I do for you?" I answered that I was there to pay my respects to him, and that I had really nothing to ask of him. He looked at his secretary, and said, "There is at least one young man who has nothing to ask of me. This is a very special day. We must celebrate it. Please ask for something for this boy to eat, preferably some sweets. And some coffee of course. I am sure he is starving for it!" I was with him for more than an hour, and then left with his blessings, and with his parting advice that I should not hesitate to meet him if I ever needed anything. I am sorry to say that I never went to meet him again, for he was too busy, and I was far too young to socialize with him.

This brief personal contact with him made his lectures seem magical to me, and I am sure that I profited considerably from the exposure to his personality as well as to his lectures. During my stay at the university I cannot remember having missed even one of his famous lectures. His delivery was chaste and awe-inspiring. His diction perfect. But sometimes his way of speaking was such as to frighten the more timid ones, for he seemed to admonish those present for their ignorance and for their timidity. Also, he had scaled heights that were not for mere mortals to attempt! And therefore quite regrettably few people approached him. They lost a great deal by this aloofness. He was one person who, because of his greatness, prevented others from approaching him too closely — and that was a sad thing, as I realised many years later when I met my Master.

The second factor was the rigid requirement that every student present a paper on Hinduism before he was allowed to appear for his degree examination. This was law there, and there were no exceptions to it. One could not plead ignorance of the Sanskrit language, for instance, for there was a Sanskrit college within the campus, and anyone who gave this excuse could be sent there for basic instruction. This compelled me to attend another set of lectures that went on all the year round, once every fortnight. They were held on the eleventh day of each lunar fortnight, and if this day fell on a Sunday, it meant my having to find the time to attend it somehow, as I also had to attend the U.O.T.C. parade. I often arrived at these lectures straight from the parade ground in my uniform, making a great deal of noise with my muddy ammunition boots, but there was no help for it.

These lectures were more like formal classes in religion, and that was of great benefit, for this was what gave us basic instruction. I was able to combine the fundamental approach of these *Ekadasi* lectures with the visionary approach of Dr. Radhakrishnan's soaring, imaginative and ecstatic approach to the same subject. Therefore my paper, when I eventually presented it, was much appreciated, especially having regard to the fact that I totally lacked a knowledge of the Sanskrit language.

The third factor was of course the secretary's post, which brought me into contact with some eminent persons whose lectures I arranged, or rather tried to arrange. Not all were willing to oblige for, due to the paucity of funds, I generally had to request them to give free lectures, assuring them that their transportation to and fro would surely be paid. The fact that many pleaded other engagements gave me the opportunity of meeting many of them — and from this I benefited. I was able to arrange the two lectures during my junior year as was demanded by my election, and all the preparatory work that was involved made it necessary for me to read something of the subject matter so that I could introduce the speaker appropriately.

My work went on spasmodically for there was nothing that I had to do continuously. *Rama Navami* and *Janmashtami* celebrations went off very well. I was able to arrange special *kathas* on both these occasions, which was greatly appreciated by most of the boys. Of course it meant that musical recitation of the *Ramayana* — during *Rama Navami*, and the *Bhagavata* — during *Krishna Janmashtami* — went on all night, to the accompaniment of the *dholak*, a percussion instrument. It was all extremely noisy, of course, and kept most of us awake all night, but it was fun all the same. I was enormously pleased with myself for I discovered that my predecessors in office had never thought of the *katha* part of the celebrations, so that I gained a tentative reputation of being something of an innovator!

The *divali* celebration was something again. I had managed to amass quite a considerable amount of money, approaching Dr. Radhakrishnan's secretary himself for a donation. He fortunately remembered me from my earlier visit, and I got the magnificent sum of fifty rupees from that one source. It was really a large donation for, in those times, a single rupee could feed a man for four or five days. Finally I ended up with a total availability of two hundred and twenty five rupees to be spent for the *divali* celebration. There was enough for a truly gala celebration, with a great deal of fireworks, and massive quantities of *divali* sweets for distribution.

The culmination of my year's efforts was the *Holi* celebration. This was a rather delicate celebration, for it involved the preparation of an enormous bonfire to be burnt in the evening, symbolizing the burning up of all the bad things accumulated since the previous *Holi*. The delicate part of it was the illicit consumption of the drug *bhang* which was strictly forbidden by the university authorities. But there were persons whom nothing on earth could stop, and this was a problem to me, for I was responsible for the maintenance of a proper decorum on these occasions. I built an enormous pile of wood, for I had again accumulated more money than was needed, and the *Holi* bonfire was a real spectacle. My one year as Secretary for Social & Religious Functions thus went off very well indeed, and I was especially commended by my warden in his report about the students in the hostel.

Life Besides the Ganges at Benares

There was yet another influence, though by no means as powerful as the other three; nor did it pertain to the study of Hinduism. In the neighbouring hostel there lived a gentle Buddhist monk from Ceylon (as the country now known as Sri Lanka was then called). I never asked him what precisely he was doing in the B.H.U., but I had an impression that he was teaching Pali and perhaps something of the teachings of the Buddha. I don't think that he was on any faculty as such, and so perhaps he was himself a student of the University! Whatever he may have been he was an exceptionally kind man, and we became fast friends after an accidental meeting at one of Dr. Radhakrishnan's lectures. He introduced me to the teachings of Gautama, the Buddha, and we used to meet once or twice a month for long discussions. I learnt something of that great body of knowledge known now as Buddhism, and also learnt a few phrases in the Sinhalese language — though all that pertained to the language has remained behind in the past of half a century ago. He helped to make use of my spare time in profitable discussion, and for thus assisting me I am grateful to him. His name was Bhikku Sangaratna. I never had the pleasure of renewing our acquaintance after I left the B.H.U. in May 1948.

I benefited substantially from my stay in the Benares Hindu University as far as religious training and the acquisition of basic knowledge of Hinduism was concerned. I did not realise the benefit of this, until many years later when what I had to do made it essential that I possessed this knowledge and experience. How Nature prepares one in advance is not realised by human beings, and most of us waste our time in fretting and fuming against what we believe to be an adverse circumstance or perhaps even a malignant destiny. It is only in retrospect that the enormous wisdom of Nature, and its even greater patience in preparing us for our own evolution, is recognized and appreciated. I think that my two years stay in Benares contributed to my preparation, which enabled me to take my first, and very tentative, steps on the path of my spiritual evolution.

In such fashion Benares did play a definite role in my life, and the great tradition of its essential role in helping human beings achieve their goal is not a false tradition by any means. It was my greatest good fortune that I got the right guidance from the beginning, for otherwise I might have made the same mistake as millions have made through the ages of thinking that a bath in the Ganges was enough to achieve one's goal. I have bathed in the great river, of course, but not more than twice or thrice altogether. I went to the Hanuman Ghat for the first time soon after I arrived in Benares. I was not merely shocked by what I saw, but also deeply grieved, for the exhibition of greed, dishonesty, corruption, and chicanery of every sort I saw there nauseated me. I bathed in the river with the most pious sentiments, but the filthy state of the river deterred me from going there again. Thereafter I bathed in the university ghat, quite near the B.H.U., which being up river flowed much cleaner.

I think if one wants to see the Hindus at their worst, for mere superstition and fear and greed, one must go to Benares. Nowhere else can one see such perversion of the essentially great Hindu traditions, the traditions of the ancient *Vedas,* and the almost total corruption of the priests there. I suffered a direct experience myself as I was once walking down one of the narrow alleys of the city. There was a cow barring my path, and the lane being a mere four feet wide, all those passing that way were ducking under its belly to go on their way. I hesitated to do so, and just then a priest who was passing that way saw me. He no doubt recognised me for a newcomer to that ancient city. He came up to me and offered to help me perform the *go-daana,* or the offering of a cow to a priest to propitiate the gods and thus ensure one's future. I asked him where the cow was. He immediately pointed to the one blocking the path, took its tail in his hands, and asked me to hold it in my right hand. I asked him how much the ritual would cost. Without blinking an eye he said it would cost five thousand rupees — a princely sum at any time. Seeing my consternation he quickly reduced it to a thousand and again to five hundred. I berated him soundly for trying to make money out of a student, using a wandering cow for the purpose, and this encounter gave me the courage to duck under the cow's belly and go on my way.

Benares has everything — a magnificent temple to Lord Shiva; a great river with the most ancient traditions flowing through it; the sacred traditions of the Vedic lore practised here and there by those who yet retained some true piety; a great university, perhaps then the largest in India, along with unspeakable filth, corruption, human misery and vice, as well as fearsome violence of a hidden nature which whisked away many rich ones of whom nothing was heard again. But the rich and the beautiful would stream into Benares by every available means of transport, many pilgrims in their thousands also walking down from the very Himalayas to pray here. Many came even from the farthest south to die there, for was there not the hoary tradition, almost amounting to a divine promise, that all those who died there, or were even cremated there, would go to heaven?

I had the feeling that if one wanted to know the essence of India, one visit to Benares would suffice, for to my mind it epitomizes India. It is as if India has been pressed and the juice squeezed out, and that is Benares. The ancient Vedic lore, tradition and practice in all its divine purity is to be found there, though nowadays one has to search assiduously for it. The pure and mighty all-purifying river is there, though it itself badly needs purification now, and if people still bathe in it, it is only because of some remnant of a true faith, but more generally because of the darkest superstition, which makes them do so. Lord Shiva is supposed to reside in this ancient city, but today his temple is perhaps the acme of corruption, vice and misery, where the gullible and simple folk who come to worship are robbed mercilessly by well-fed priests sporting golden wristwatches and dressed in spotless silk *dhotis* and immaculately pressed silk *kurtas*.

The ashrams of many great *rishis* of former centuries are yet there lining the banks of the Ganga, but who is there now to reflect, even faintly, the spiritual glory and the divine wisdom of their ancient saintly occupants? Saint Kabir had lived there, and found his spiritual goal there too, under the spiritual umbrella of his Guru, Swami Ramananda — but today there is no Kabir there, only a sect bearing his name! Look where you will, it is the same tragic story of a former greatness destroyed by the filth and corruption of a decadent and selfish people; a former spiritual brilliance darkened almost to the point of extinction by the merely material aspirations of a self-seeking people; the piety of the sincere worshipper subdued by fear induced in him by a shallow and corrupt priesthood. The Ganga itself polluted to the point where a former river of mighty proportions and spiritual promise had been reduced to hardly anything more than a massive sewer. Benares made me weep for India, and made me shed secret tears again a second time when I visited that city again some thirty years later. That second visit left me in a state of shocked anguish, for true to its role of representing India, it now faithfully mirrored the decadence that had become a cancerous growth in the bowels of this great nation — the glory that was India had dimmed in its very heart, and held no promise of ever recovering that pristine purity, glory and the spiritual wealth that had been Bharat.

Life Besides the Ganges at Benares

It is a matter of divine mercy that later I came into personal contact with a modern savant who, in some measure, has brought reassurance, and perhaps renewed a promise, that Bharat is not yet dead, and that it shall once more awaken as if it had been a sleeping spiritual giant, and restore its people and the people of the world to right aspiration, right thought and to right action, thus showing them the way to the true goal of human life.

As far as my education went, there is nothing much to say since there were no outstanding events to impress themselves on my memory. The daily grind began at 5:30 A.M. when I got up and studied for an hour or so, while the milk was being boiled on an electric heater which was nothing more than a ceramic bed with the heating coils wound inside it. A very risky thing, on the whole, because the source of the electricity was quite perilous. The hostel rooms had just one light switch, and no plug points at all. We therefore improvised by drawing electricity from the switch by two copper wires, and connecting them to two nails hammered side by side into the wall where it was convenient to use without being obvious to a visitor, and without being easily accessible to an outstretched hand, for instance. From the heater the two leads had copper coins in them with a large hole in the middle, which we just hung on to the electrified nails on the walls, and then put the pan of milk upon the ring to boil. A truly hazardous enterprise, as I now realise, but something which most of the boys did as a matter of need. As soon as the milk was ready I prepared for myself a cup of Ovaltine, a beverage which I have not seen since 1950 or thereabouts. It was delicious, and I had it once every morning, and once again in the late evening before commencing the night watch.

After bathing one had to get ready for college, which lasted according to the subjects that one was studying. Some days were very full, and others not so. On an average I would say that I had no more than five hours of classes per day for six days a week. Not by any means a big burden to bear. We came to the hostel mess for lunch, of course, and then sometimes we went to sleep if the afternoon had what were felt to be boring subjects or boring lecturers. Some evenings I had to report to the parade ground for special parades or exercises, otherwise most evenings were free to do what one wished to do. The more studious ones went to the library — a fairly large one well stocked with approximately 100,000 volumes — while the sporty type went to the several playgrounds to play games of their choice. There were many peculiarly Indian games such as *khokho, kabaddi* and so on, the most peculiar, for me, being *malham*, if I have the name right!

There was also the gymnasium which attracted the ardent body builders, of which group I had been one too. It was fun to exercise for an hour or so, and then to admire one's body in the several mirrors conveniently placed for that very purpose. It took a fairly long time to critically examine every aspect of each muscle, and to view oneself from different angles. Very narcissistic, I thought! I had a friend and classmate, a boy from Maharashtra named Deshpande, who had a truly magnificent body, bulging with corded muscles. He oiled his fair body, and then it was a pleasure to see. But I think he derived more pleasure from looking at himself than others did — for he spent hours before the several mirrors, often missing classes too! It was intoxicating sometimes, and I finally decided to stop this involvement with one's own body which I felt to be very unhealthy. I missed my old friend Krishna Kali Banerjee, and so my visits to the gymnasium dwindled, and dropped off altogether within the first six weeks.

I started to visit the library, and there I found an elderly gentleman, the librarian of the university library, named Dr.

Life Besides the Ganges at Benares

S.R. Ranganathan. I went to meet him personally because my father referred to him in one of his letters as having been his teacher at the Presidency College in Madras. I went and introduced myself to this person, and the first thing he asked me was, "How is that fellow, your father?" I was rather annoyed at my father being referred to in this disrespectful manner, and gave him a somewhat abrupt reply. I formed a poor opinion of him at this meeting, but later I saw that I had been wrong, for he was a thorough gentleman, well-mannered and sympathetic with all. He was gentle, and helped me with the selection of what to read. I also found that he had a very high opinion of my father, whom he thought of as an outstanding pupil whom the vagaries of a capricious destiny had very nearly destroyed. He admired my father for his tremendous guts in fighting all odds, and rising to the position of Assistant Controller of Stores on the Central Railway, which position he held at that time. Dr. Ranganathan was the pioneer in library science in India, and deserves to be remembered for his substantial contribution to that science.

I am somewhat sad to recall that my reading habit suffered a bit because of my preoccupation with my class books. I was not able to make use of the enormous library which one particular student did with substantial rewards. He was a south Indian boy named Ramanujam. He came as a first year engineering student, and was housed in the neighbouring Limbdi Hostel. He was very obviously an orthodox Iyengar boy, as he still had his sacred tuft on the top of his head which he refused to shave off in spite of almost continuous jeering and humiliation by almost everyone in the university. He also adorned his forehead with the Vaishnava symbol, the *Thiruman Sreechurnam* as it is called in Tamil, while he went about his affairs calmly, always reading a book even when walking. He was one boy who was most often to be seen in the Library. He was not affected by a total lack of friends. He topped his class in the first year, and then all his classmates as well as most of his seniors fell all over him — and he emerged as something of a hero, and a mentor to many. His scholastic career was outstanding, and he went on to top his class every year of the five year course, emerging as the top engineering student of his year. Sad to say, I never got close to him because the engineering students were in quite a separate world of their own, and our meetings were restricted to the monthly meetings of the Tamil Sangham.

The Tamil Sangham was originally a society to censor Tamil literature as it was created by the authors and the poets of the times of the Chola and the Pandya kings — that is from about the second century A.D. Now it is an organization for the propagation of Tamil literature in its pure form, as well as for the preservation of the pure Tamil, or the *Chen Thamizh* as it is known. The correct word for that language is *Thamizh* and not Tamil. It is supposed to be the only language with the sound 'zh' which most non-Tamilians find it more or less impossible to pronounce. I have not found this sound present in any of the languages that I have come across. The Tamil people are quite jealous of this matter of the purity of their language, and often seem to go to absurd extremes to preserve it in the form in which it is said to have originated from its so-called divine source. Of course in this matter of preserving the purity of a language, the protagonists of Hindi too have gone to really absurd limits, and this seems to be the case with all languages except perhaps English.

I used to be a member of the Tamil Sangham in the B.H.U., and attended as many of its monthly meetings as I possibly could. This was not out of any sympathy with the ideals and objectives of the Sangham, but purely to try and learn something of my mother tongue if I possibly could. It is a sad fact that none of us three brothers knew how to read or write in Tamil. As a matter of fact most of the children living in the north of India spoke among themselves, and often with their parents too, in the local language. Instruction in the many tongues of India was not available in schools, which generally taught in English or the local language — only infrequently in both. Therefore since Appa had tried to impress upon us the need to be facile with our mother tongue, I joined the Sangham hoping that it would help me, but this did not really happen, since it had only classes in Tamil poetry and such like things.

The Tamil Sangham however attracted all the great persons from the south who were Tamil scholars, and I was able to meet many of them. A memorable event was the visit of Shri C. Rajagopalachari, a very prominent politician from the Madras Presidency of those days. I had to rush from my U.O.T.C. parade, and was in full uniform, my boots making a terrific racket on the cement floors. Rajaji, as he was called by one and all, was just about to begin his address to the students. Hearing the noise that my entry made, he looked at me and smiled, a smile of genuine welcome, and said in Tamil, "We need more people in uniform, with a sense of the real discipline that the army alone seems to give. I am glad to see you in uniform, and sorry that there is only you here from the outfit."

He then went on with his address in Tamil. I thought that he spoke with a sort of lisp, but I could understand everything he said. At the end of his one hour speech, he told us, "You have all come here to be educated. Go about your business with dedication, remembering that you are here for this purpose alone. Do not waste your time. The south Indian has a reputation for a high level of intellect — and rightly so! But do not become arrogant, for you have much to learn from these people. Learn all you can and get back home, ready to serve your country." Later on he was to become the last Governor

General of India, but at the time he visited the B.H.U., he was only a politician not much in favour, and perhaps not even a member of the Congress Working Committee. Of course I could be wrong in this, since I have never followed Indian politics even with remote interest. I do know that he did not see eye to eye with most of the others, and this set him apart in general, though he was highly respected by Gandhiji and other top Congress leaders. Rajaji edited the *Swarajya*, a political paper which published his views on men and matters periodically.

Another memorable visit was that of Lord Louis Mountbatten, who was the Viceroy and Governor General of India. He came to deliver the annual convocation address. Since his visit was in his official capacity, there was a great deal of pomp in receiving him. We of the 'D' Company of the U.O.T.C., had to welcome him with army ceremonial, and spent a fortnight drilling seriously for the purpose, and sprucing up our uniforms. I was already a lance corporal by then. We paraded before him and 'Presented Arms' after which he officially inspected the company. And then I found myself having to escort him to the dais. When I saluted as I left him there, he graciously shook hands with me, and asked, "Are you happy with life in the army, son? Do you intend making the army your career?" I stammered out a shy reply that I was considering doing so, backed one step, saluted him again, and returned to my post. This created a great deal of jealousy in all, for I had stolen the cake, or at least a big slice of it, as it were. Lord Mountbatten was a very handsome person, tall and lithe, and with the perfect manners of an educated Englishman belonging to the 'upper crust'. He endeared himself to all of us by his courteous charm, and this brief episode with him remains a cherished memory.

Parthasarathi, student at
Benares Hindu University - 1948

Parthasarathi with cricket team
Benares Hindu University - 1948

Life Besides the Ganges at Benares

The final memory is a most horrible one. It took place in 1948, when I was in my final B.Sc. class. One day there was a tremendous rush of students from all over the university campus, all of them running madly as if for dear life. I came out to the verandah, thinking that some calamity must have occurred to cause this — and it had. The news was that Mahatma Gandhi had been assassinated in New Delhi at the Birla House while he approached a waiting crowd to deliver his usual address. There had been enormous bloodshed in the Hindu-Muslim riots which had shattered the peace and robbed many innocent families belonging to both these religions of their loved and innocent ones. Gandhiji had gone on a fast-unto-death, and had just broken his fast after perhaps five or six days of total fasting at the Birla House.

The assassin had been arrested. He was said to belong to a rather militant political organization known as the Rashtriya Swayamsevak Sangh — the RSS for short. Strangely enough I had joined the B.H.U. wing of the RSS a month earlier, impressed by its insistence on discipline, and the way the meetings were conducted. I had left it a few days later after my friend Ahuja, who was, incidentally, my best friend at the B.H.U., as well as my classmate, had informed me that this organization had political ambitions. Ahuja too had been a member for those few days. Thank the heavens for that, for the target of the 3000 students that morning was the RSS office in the B.H.U. The office was raided, all the furniture set on fire, the records burnt, and the whole thing damaged beyond repair, as it appeared to me, for I too joined the crowd of students in this mad lust for revenge! The RSS did not recover from this vicious attack during the rest of my stay at Benares. The really serious members and the people behind it naturally laid low, for fear of reprisal, and I have no knowledge whether it ever managed to recover from that blow to its material existence and, more importantly, to its moral image in society.

There was a rush of the students to Allahabad, for the information was that Gandhiji's ashes were to be immersed in the Ganges, at the Triveni Sangam. That was perhaps the most arduous travel that I have ever undertaken, for the trains were packed full, people riding even on the roof of the carriages. I managed to grab the door handle and there I hung on for dear life for the duration of the entire journey lasting six very long and seemingly interminable hours. At Allahabad itself the streets were like rivers of humanity — and that is no exaggeration at all. I estimate that on that sad and dark day there must have been ten million or more persons packing Allahabad's streets to their utmost limits. We went where the crowds led us inexorably.

All of a sudden there was a heaving of the crowds, and one had to virtually fight for life not to be crushed to death within that pressing mob of people. There were shouts of grief, wails of sorrow, and there appeared a gun carriage with an urn draped with a flag. Sitting on the gun carriage were Pandit Jawaharlal Nehru, Sardar Vallabhai Patel and a host of other Congress members all of whom had been close to the departed Mahatma. Nehru was in tears, as were most of the others, and their visible emotional anguish was passed on to all of us. I don't believe that on that occasion there were any dry eyes in Allahabad. We tried to move to the place of the immersion, but that was totally futile. So we let the crowds pass on, and returned to the railway station hoping to get something to eat. But there was nothing at all to be had for all the shops and the hotels had been closed ever since Gandhiji's assassination. We went hungry, managed to board a train going strangely empty, and returned to Benares.

Life Besides the Ganges at Benares

During my first year, as I have related earlier, a young boy named Narasimhan was my roommate. He was a stickler for personal cleanliness, and carried things to an absurd length. He would wash his hands before going for lunch and dinner, and keeping his hands wet — for they might get soiled by the towel if he wiped them! — he would refuse to even lock the door. The strange thing was that he suffered from two attacks of the ringworm during the first year! The next year of course he had a room to himself as a senior boy, and I was free of his foibles.

The food was monotonous. We had chapattis, hot and appetizing, for every meal. There was the inevitable *dal* and *sabji*. The dal was all right — one needed protein, after all, and one got used to imbibing it in fairly large quantities. But the *sabji* was something else altogether. We had *lauki* — bottle gourd — and *taroi* — another variety of the gourd family, endlessly. For a change, on feast days, we had potatoes. When potatoes were served there was never enough of it, as we all gorged ourselves on it! *Lauki* was supposed to have gold in it, but we never found any, naturally, and most of us began to hate the stuff within a few days. The local boys however seemed to enjoy it! Each one to his taste! Very naturally we had to bring some variety into this monotony, and this was achieved by the use of pickles and *papad* brought from home. The *papads* were always in great danger of being literally devoured by other eager boys, since they had to be grilled on the fire of the cook. The pickles had to be shared too, and this all did with a certain good will in the beginning, but as supplies began to dwindle, the boys got into the habit of bringing their supplies in their own *katori* — a metal cup, leaving the pickle bottles safe in their rooms! They were then cursed cheerfully in the most colourful language for their selfishness — but the boys with their pickles never protested, being careful to protect their *katoris* from being grabbed by eager hands if they were in the least careless!

As for my education, it went on smoothly. I was fairly regular in attending my classes, and I believe that my lecturers were happy with my performance. I remember that on one occasion I was out with the boys on the streets to protest against something or the other, I can't remember what it was. We caught the eye of Dr. Nand Lal Singh who was on his way from the hostel to the college. He saw me, and coming up to me in that crowd, he said, "You are a boy of considerable promise. What are you doing among these hooligans? Get back to your class. Don't waste your time for you are here to study. The others may be rich enough to go on the streets, but I know that you are not." And I promptly did go back to my class.

At the end of the first year we had to wait seemingly interminably for our practical examinations, for all the laboratories were taken up by the seniors. The wait went on and on, and we were almost mad by the time they were freed for our examinations. It seemed awfully unfair since our exams lasted but three days! Anyway it was all mercifully over and we set out for home. During those three weeks of waiting, we used to tell stories in the long evenings. I remember that as the night wore on, the stories became different, and ghost stories took the field. We were all a frightened lot, and after an hour or two of ghost stories, some of the boys from the neighbouring hostels would have difficulty walking back to their hostels. Then very bravely some of us would walk them home, and have difficulty getting back to our own hostels!

Those were the days of real happiness, for we were waiting for our practicals and had nothing to study, really. So we had the long days to ourselves, and generally went out foraging in the large gardens that abounded. We were allowed to eat all that we could of the mangoes and the guavas, but we were strictly forbidden to take even a single fruit out of the garden. But boys, being dare devils at the best of times, would attempt to smuggle one or two out — it seemed to be a game of trying to outwit the watchman rather than to take fruit out. If we got caught, we had the very devil to pay!

Very soon the long-awaited day came, and we were saying goodbye to each other. Strangely enough there was much melancholy at the parting, and some wet eyes too. "There doesn't seem much point in going home after all," seemed to be the general feeling. But one had to return home, and so after a great deal of goodbyes, we got into our rickshaws in ones and twos and rode off to the railway station to catch our respective trains.

It was perhaps the end of May 1947, and I had holidays till the first week of July, when my college was due to reopen again. I took the train from Moghalsarai for Calcutta. The train journey was a long one, and it was made even longer by the several unscheduled halts that was imposed upon it. There was a halt at a particular station called Mokameh Ghat, if my memory serves me right, where the tracks were just by the bank of the river Ganges. As soon as the train stopped there, almost all the passengers got down and went to the river for a dip, for it was a holy river, and a dip in it was supposed to grant one the boon of liberation. The scheduled halt there was for a few minutes only, but the passengers kept it there sometimes for as much as half an hour. Trains nevertheless managed to get to their destinations on time, in those good old days, unlike now when almost everything runs or flies late.

We eventually reached Howrah, and I took a bus from there to the lakes and got home just when my father had left for office. My brothers were at school, and so the home was virtually deserted, with only my chitti there. My cousin Chakra was there, a baby of just over two years of age. He was a jumbo baby, and I had a great deal of joy carrying him around most of the time. I was a hefty fellow myself, and it was no great shakes carrying him even on my evening walks to the lakes. I used to have fun, wiggling my toes at him. When he saw me do that, he would charge at me like an enraged bull, and grip my right big toe with his toothless gums, and play with it. It was fun the way he came for that toe! I have no doubt that he remembers nothing of it.

It was fun to be home and to be pampered by all, and to eat luxuriously and hugely of our south Indian food. This was the period when I saw an enormous number of cinemas. There was no restriction on my personal expenditure, for wasn't I now a grown up fellow who was almost a graduate? I think that in the period of forty-five days I saw something like seventy-six cinemas! A record that I never even attempted to beat in my later life. It was crazy, of course, but I saw two of them on most days. I am sure it did no good to my already weak eyesight.

The holidays were soon over, seemingly before I even realised that I was on a holiday! The time came to leave, and I returned to B.H.U. as a senior student, and managed to get back my room No. 63 after being initially assigned a room in the rear wing. I had a room all to myself, and it was great to feel that one did not have to share a ten foot by eight foot room with anyone else. It was also very gratifying to see the new juniors glance apprehensively at me, for not only was I a senior, but I was also a big fellow physically.

The university routine took over, and things were totally different but not all that different, looked at in a different way — for there were the same classmates, the same messes, the

Life Besides the Ganges at Benares

same monotonous food, the same lecturers with but few changes, and so on. We now had the privilege of being lectured to by Dr. S.S. Joshi, the head of the chemistry department, as well as Principal of the Science College. He was a famous professor, credited with the discovery of a special effect named the 'Joshi Effect' after him. He was a very preoccupied person, completely immersed in his research work, and was credited with having left his wife behind at the cinema theatre on the few occasions that she was able to persuade him to take her to see one! Further, he would lock himself in his laboratory for several days, and the food left for him outside the door was left untouched! A typical research professor, it was said of him, albeit fondly.

The year went very well for me. The paper I submitted on Hinduism was accepted, and that cleared the way for me to appear for my final Bachelor of Science examination. I got my promotion in the U.O.T.C., and would have gone several steps higher in the ladder had I been longer at the B.H.U. I had an idea of going up for a Master's degree in geology, but was not keen to take a decision in this matter all by myself. My father made the mistake of leaving it all to me to decide. During the Dussera holidays which lasted a fortnight, I went to Dehra Dun to spend the time with my uncle Bhadran and aunt Gouri. They had a lovely home in the New Forest area, quite luxurious and secluded too. He was then the Director of Forest Education in India, and was a very important person in the field of forestry. The holidays passed swiftly, and soon I was on the platform of the Dehra Dun railway station waiting for my train to arrive, with Bhadran, my uncle, standing beside me manfully struggling to pretend that there were no tears streaming down his cheeks! He had a very soft heart but he unfortunately kept it well hidden under a stern and forbidding exterior — except on the few occasions that my father or one of us was with him.

Down Memory Lane

The last part of my stay in Benares passed very swiftly, and before one knew it the final examinations were upon us. The examination fever had already gripped us. There was a tremendous swapping of notes, and astrological and other consultations were freely available to those interested in them. The temple near the main gate was called the *Shankat Vimochan* — the temple where a person could be liberated from his troubles if he worshipped there! The temple did roaring business during examination times as almost every student on the campus went there to pray for success. The income of the priests was something worth speculating about, for it skyrocketed beyond their wildest hopes. All burnt the midnight oil, so to say, and milk was bought by the gallon and Ovaltine consumed in enormous quantities in a vain bid to overcome sleep. The question papers of the past years were studied assiduously to get a clue as to what the questions we were likely to be faced with could be. There was tremendous activity in all spheres, and this was something I had not noticed when I was a junior.

The examinations came, and left some in utter despair the very first day, for they knew that they had lost the match even before the game had begun! Others were more hopeful, and went on preparing for the next papers. The few who had prepared well seemed to fare well too, though there were the odd ones who had made the tragic mistake of preparing to answer only a few questions they expected, based on the study of the past years' question papers. There were gaps of several days between the various papers, thank heavens, and this gave us time to review each subject before entering the examination hall.

The practical examinations came last. I did very well in all the theory papers, but somehow bungled my chemistry practicals, and therefore I lost what should almost certainly have been top rank that year. My chemistry professor was going round and round watching my increasing despair. He glanced sympathetically at me, but of course could not offer me any help during the examination itself. I managed to pass the practical examination with some marks to spare, but it was a poor performance in a subject I had expected to top in. I was almost in tears, and rushed to the hostel when the ordeal was over, and there I realised what I had done wrong — but of course it was far too late to correct my errors. By my top level performance in geology and biology I managed to get 1st class, with a reasonable rank too.

There was then a scramble to get packed and head for home. There was such a rush to get things done in those last two or three days that friends were forgotten even before we left the B.H.U. campus. When we met each other at the railway station there was already a feeling of, "I have met that fellow somewhere — but where?" Strange, how soon friends can be forgotten! Soon I was on the train going to Bombay, for by then my father had relinquished his job in the Directorate General of Munitions Productions at Calcutta, and had been posted back to his parent railway, where he now occupied the position of District Controller of Stores, with his office in the Parel workshop compound. I reached Bombay and went to Thana where my father had been assigned quarters. Some weeks later, towards the end of July, I received the happy tidings of my having graduated with a 1st class.